ETHICS MOMENTS
IN GOVERNMENT
CASES AND CONTROVERSIES

American Society for Public Administration
Book Series on Public Administration & Public Policy

Editor-in-Chief
Evan M. Berman, Ph.D.
National Chengchi University, Taiwan
evanmberman@gmail.com

Mission: Throughout its history, ASPA has sought to be true to its founding principles of promoting scholarship and professionalism within the public service. The ASPA Book Series on Public Administration and Public Policy publishes books that increase national and international interest for public administration and which discuss practical or cutting edge topics in engaging ways of interest to practitioners, policy-makers, and those concerned with bringing scholarship to the practice of public administration.

Ethics Moments in Government: Cases and Controversies, Donald C. Menzel

Major League Winners: Using Sports and Cultural Centers as Tools for Economic Development, Mark S. Rosentraub

The Formula for Economic Growth on Main Street America, Gerald L. Gordon

The New Face of Government: How Public Managers Are Forging a New Approach to Governance, David E. McNabb

The Facilitative Leader in City Hall: Reexamining the Scope and Contributions, James H. Svara

American Society for Public Administration
Series in Public Administration and Public Policy

ETHICS MOMENTS IN GOVERNMENT
CASES AND CONTROVERSIES

DONALD C. MENZEL

CRC Press
Taylor & Francis Group
Boca Raton   London   New York

CRC Press is an imprint of the
Taylor & Francis Group, an **informa** business

CRC Press
Taylor & Francis Group
6000 Broken Sound Parkway NW, Suite 300
Boca Raton, FL 33487-2742

Library of Congress Cataloging-in-Publication Data

Menzel, Donald C.
   Ethics moments in government : cases and controversies / Donald C. Menzel.
      p. cm. -- (American Society for Public Administration book series on public
      administration & public policy)
   Includes bibliographical references and index.
   ISBN 978-1-4398-0690-6
   1. Public administration--Moral and ethical aspects--Case studies. 2. Civil service
ethics--Case studies. I. Title. II. Series.

JF1525.E8M47 2010
172--dc22   2009011867

Visit the Taylor & Francis Web site at
http://www.taylorandfrancis.com

and the CRC Press Web site at
http://www.crcpress.com

Dedication

Dedicated to

Bettie Jean, Juanita Laverne, and the memory of our mother and father

Contents

SECTION II: PRACTICING ETHICS—MANY FACES

Chapter 3

x ■ *Contents*

Chapter 5

Chapter 6

SECTION III: LESSONS LEARNED ALONG THE JOURNEY

Chapter 7

The Complete Ethical Manager

Foreword

Service, ethics, and trust are interrelated values that inform the nomenclature for public administration. These values constitute prime components of the social construct underpinning all government activity, including prescriptions for high standards of behavior. The "ideal" for public service ethics with a reciprocal link to the "public trust" is one of these prescriptions. The behavior of those who deliver public services is an important factor for citizens' trust, support, and participation in government. Ethical, effective, and equitable public services have been shown to inspire public trust. This trust facilitates the collaborative partnership that must exist between public servants and citizens to achieve good governance.

Citizens expect public servants to pursue the public interest. They also expect them to manage public resources for the common good. Failure to live up to these expectations affects public trust and support for public service. Moreover, the relationships between ethics, service, and trust are mutually reinforcing: ethical behavior engenders trust in government, which in turn engenders and strengthens support for public service.

Living up to the public trust, however, is much more than just an act of compliance. It also involves perceiving, preventing, avoiding, and resolving accusations of illegal or unethical behavior, including appearances of inappropriate behavior. That is, a system of public service ethics must prevail that empowers public servants with the prudence to not only do more than what is publicly required but also do less than what might be privately permissible.

Professional codes of ethics, ethics laws, ethics surveys, ethics seminars, and numerous other programs have been put forth to help achieve this type of behavior. Some focus on helping organizations develop ethical initiatives that are meaningful, obtainable, measurable, and sustainable. Others promote the alignment of actual behaviors, beliefs, and attitudes with stated organizational values to help achieve a culture of integrity and trust. Also prevalent are enforcement practices that rely on internal control systems and other instruments that create a preventive environment to thwart misconduct.

Research suggests that progress has been made. Managers are becoming more aware of what constitutes ethical and unethical behavior. More mechanisms have been put in place to prevent and discover fraud, waste and abuse. But, as this book illustrates, numerous ethical situations can exist that are not easily resolved or addressed by professional, legal, or institutionally based initiatives. Rather, it is up to the individual to sort through the situation at hand and make a decision that results in an ethical outcome. Easier said than done? Without question. Don Menzel has taken this challenge head on in this book. The reader is introduced to the essential elements of ethical reasoning and is able to strengthen his decision making. The cases and controversies, if carefully and thoughtfully considered, can enhance the skill and ability of both experienced and inexperienced administrators to resolve challenging ethical situations. Each case is accompanied by assessments from a practicing public manager and/or scholar to provide the reader with a benchmark to judge her own ethical reasoning. This book also introduces the reader to the brave new world of ethical competency. All cases are keyed to specific competencies that the author has distilled from the research literature on ethical decision making.

In short, Don Menzel has put together a book that is much more than a mere collection of cases. Indeed, it is unique in its composition and integration of practitioner assessments and contributions by members of the academic community. Moreover, the approach requires learning by immersion in cases that vary in complexity. Immersion learning requires the reader to be reflective and analytical.

Do public service ethics matter? Absolutely! They have significant implications for the idea and ideal of public service that enhances public trust and promotes higher standards and norms of behavior in other sectors of society. Efforts to make ethical behavior more practical and operationally relevant to decisions that face public servants every day is a very large step in this direction. The journey begins with this book.

Harvey L. White, Ph.D.
2007-08 President of the American Society for Public Administration
and
Director, Diversity and Public Service Initiative
Graduate School of Public and International Affairs
University of Pittsburgh

References

Galston, William A. and Elaine C. Kamarck. 2008. "Change You Can Believe In Needs A Government You Can Trust." ThirdWay Report (November).
Gershtenson, Joseph and Dennis L. Plane. 2006. "Trust in Government Across Levels and Institutions of Government." Paper presented at the annual meeting of the Midwest Political Science Association, Palmer House Hilton, Chicago, Illinois, (April).

Institute of Business Ethics. 2006. "Business Ethics Briefing: Ethical Conduct Within Business." Survey Findings 2005 (March).

Josephson, Michael S. 2005. Preserving the Public Trust: The Five Principles of Public Service Ethics. The Josephson Institute of Ethics and Unlimited Publishing

Menzel, Donald C. 2005. "Research on Ethics and Integrity in Governance: A Review and Assessment." Public Integrity, 7: 2 (March). 147–68.

Pelletier, Kathie L. and Michelle C. Bligh. 2006. "Rebounding from Corruption: Perceptions of Ethics Program Effectiveness in a Public Sector Organization." Journal of Business Ethics, 67: 4 (September). 359–374.

Udas Ken, William L. Fuerst and David B. Paradice. 1996. "An investigation of ethical perceptions of public sector MIS professionals." Journal of Business Ethics, 15: 7 (July). 721-734.

Preface

This book is about identifying, assessing, and resolving ethical issues and dilemmas that confront those who govern our cities, counties, states, and federal agencies in America. It is also about the quest to become an ethically competent public manager. This book is directed at professionals in public service careers, in government or elsewhere, as well as those who are newly seeking such careers.

This book and the CD offer a "one-stop" shop for practitioners, students, and those who teach ethics. Indeed, ethics education and training in both the private and public sectors have proliferated over the past decade, involving self-study, workshop training, and formal coursework at universities. All cases in the book are based on real situations; they are not hypothetical stories. In combination with practitioner and scholarly assessments and CD resource materials such as slide presentations and articles, these real-world cases are powerful learning tools. Most importantly, it is the author's belief that the combination will help students and well-intentioned public servants who might become ensnared in ethically difficult situations find their way forward in a manner that is effective and right.

In the pages and chapters that follow and the accompanying compact disc, the reader will discover how challenging it is to become ethically competent. The journey, however, is well worthwhile. Public managers and employees are critically located at the governance juncture in which, to use the cliché, "the rubber meets the road." Ethical lapses are the fodder of frequent media stories and often result in great harm to public trust and confidence in government. Practical guidance on reasoning through difficult decision-making situations is provided by case analyses and exercises designed to help the reader acquire ethical knowledge, skills, and abilities. As will be quickly discovered, there is no magic tonic to ingest that can make a difficult ethics moment disappear or a mysterious wand that can be waved to vanquish an unethical work environment. Nonetheless, one can learn how to deal with challenging ethics moments and change a disagreeable workplace culture.

This book has its case roots in a column "Ethics Moments" published monthly since February 1997 by the American Society for Public Administration in the *Public Administration Times*. Over these past dozen years, I have had the opportunity to identify, review, and assess numerous events and situations concerned

xix

with ethical and unethical issues in governance. These cases and controversies are, with one exception in which a city manager decides to seek gender reassignment, common occurrences. They offer valuable lessons and guidance on becoming an ethically competent government manager. The cases are relevant to all government settings, although there is a decided emphasis on local government challenges. This seems justified as far more people work at local governments, such as cities, counties, special districts, and school districts, than at higher levels of government. Nonetheless, even these cases are relevant to managers and employees as the situations that are described indeed occur at all levels of government.

Finally, it is my belief that strengthening one's ethical competency is very important from two perspectives—the individual and the organization. Ethically motivated members of a government are likely to foster a strong ethics culture that in turn builds and sustains public trust. And lest we forget, public trust in government is an essential ingredient for a vibrant democracy.

One-Stop Package for Training, Learning, and Teaching

This book and the CD are a one-stop shopping package that is well suited for practitioners, both as self-study and for workshop training sessions. It is also valuable for students in public affairs programs for whom ethics is essential. This book and its accompanying CD offer the reader "total immersion" in both real-world cases and the literature and scholarship on ethics and management in government.[1] The CD features a variety of resources that in combination with the book material provides the reader and instructor a full course menu to choose from to expand one's knowledge of public service ethics and probe the complexities of becoming an ethically competent government manager. End notes and references placed in the chapters identify relevant articles, slide presentations, codes of ethics and other resource materials that can be easily accessed. Indeed, this is one-stop training for ethics education and training.

Endnote

1. CD 4.37 "Research on Ethics" is a comprehensive discussion of the research literature.

Acknowledgments

This book has many contributors. In fact, nearly eighty public administration practitioners and scholars provided valuable comments and assessments of the cases and controversies. Their contributions set this book apart from others. It is a credit to their professionalism that so many stepped forward. Many are managers, supervisors, and line personnel who work in governments across America. They offer an especially valuable contribution from "ground zero" and the daily hum of the government workplace. Contributors bring a diverse perspective across the broad spectrum of cases and controversies. Although many are ethics scholars, not all are. But all join hands with practitioners to explore the complexities of ethical issues, and all are committed to strengthening ethical governance. However, the views of the contributors are just that, nothing more nothing less. No claim is made that their views or indeed the author's views are the final word. Resolving challenging ethics moments can take many paths. This, of course, is not to say that all paths lead to different outcomes—a relativistic notion of ethics. Nor is it to say that there is "one best path" for the "best" outcome. Rather, ethics issues are often shades of complexity and necessitate balanced approaches of reasoning and experience to resolve. Finally, it must be said that no contributor is responsible for any errors of commission or omission in this book, as these belong solely to the author.

Others who provided encouragement and made important suggestions in the preparation of this volume included Professors James S. Bowman at Florida State University, who offered helpful guidance early on; Terry L. Cooper at the University of Southern California; Melvin J. Dubnick at the University of New Hampshire; Carole L. Jurkiewicz at Louisiana State University (especially on framing reasoning questions); Manfred F. Meine at Troy University; Jeremy F. Plant at Penn State-Harrisburg; and Jonathan P. West at the University of Miami. Stuart C. Gilman at the United Nations Office on Drugs and Crime also made helpful comments. Jennifer Morrison, coordinator of the Batavia-Elgin-St. Charles, Illinois training consortium made helpful suggestions for improving the training workshops described on the compact disc and provided the author the opportunity to try out many cases in local government workshops on ethical decision making. A note of thanks as well is due to James E. Leidlein, City Manager, Harper Woods, Michigan, who shared ideas about the content and structure of a case-oriented text.

Special thanks go to Distinguished Professor Evan M. Berman at National Chengchi University, who, as the Editor-in-Chief, ASPA Book Series in Public Administration and Public Policy, made numerous valuable suggestions that improved the book.

Finally, a very warm note of thanks and appreciation to my partner and soul mate of more than fifty years, Kay Fortman Menzel, who lived with my order and disorder over the past two years while work proceeded on this volume. A discouraging word was never heard about the many hours that went into this project. I would also like to thank Sammy and Emmy who provided much needed "woof" time away from the computer.

Contributors

Stephen K. Aikens
Assistant Professor, Public
    Administration Program
Department of Government and
    International Affairs
University of South Florida
Tampa, Florida

Martin Black
(Former) City Manager
Venice, Florida

Stephen Bonczek
(Former) City Manager
Largo, Florida and Beaumont, Texas

Michael Bonfield
City Manager
St. Pete Beach, Florida

Chris Bosch
Fire Chief
Tracy, California

LaVonne Bower
MADD
Manasota, Florida

Pam Brangaccio
(Former) County Administrator
Bay County, Florida

Patrick Burke
Economic Development Manager
Moline, Illinois

Brian Bursiek
Assistant to the Village
    Manager
Schiller Park, Illinois

Gerald Caiden
Professor of Public
    Administration
School of Policy, Planning and
    Development
University of Southern
    California
Los Angeles, California

Robert C. Chope
Professor and Chair
Department of Counseling
San Francisco State University
San Francisco, California

Larry Cobb
Professor Emeritus, Public
    Administration
Slippery Rock University
Executive Director
Ethics Works
Slippery Rock, Pennsylvania

Steve Concepcion
Hillsborough County Management
    and Budget
Tampa, Florida

Terry L. Cooper
Professor and Director
Civic Engagement Initiative
School of Policy, Planning, and
    Development
University of Southern California
Los Angeles, California

Ed Daley
City Manager
Hopewell, Virginia
President (2007–2008)
International City-County
    Management Association

Randy Deicke
Deputy Fire Chief
Batavia, Illinois

Mary Delano
Center for Architecture & Building
    Science Research
New Jersey Institute of Technology
Newark, New Jersey

Jim Drumm
City Manager
High Springs, Florida

Melvin J. Dubnick
Professor and Director, Public
    Administration
University of New Hampshire
Durham, New Hampshire

Kevin Duggan
City Manager
Mountain View, California

Rod Erakovich
Assistant Professor of Public
    Administration and Management
School of Business Administration
Texas Wesleyan University
Fort Worth, Texas

Barbara Van Cott Fidler
Budget/Assistant District
    Attorney's Office
Dunedin, Florida

Pamela Gibson
Assistant Professor
Department of Urban Studies and
    Public Administration
Old Dominion University
Norfolk, Virginia

Stuart C. Gilman
Deputy Director, Stolen Asset
    Recovery Initiative
Senior Advisor, Governance, Security
    and Rule of Law Section
United Nations Office on Drugs and
    Crime
Geneva, Switzerland

Robin I. Gomez
City Auditor
Clearwater, Florida

Joanne Gram
Charitable Trust Analyst
Michigan Department of Attorney
    General
Lansing, Michigan

Bonnie Beth Greenball
Associate Director
Institute for Public Policy and
    Leadership
University of South Florida Sarasota-
    Manatee
Sarasota, Florida

Bruce Haddock
City Manager
Oldsmar, Florida

Sam Halter
ICMA Range Rider
(Former) City Administrator
Tampa, Florida

John Hamp
Lieutenant
Charlotte County Sheriff
Port Charlotte, Florida

Carl Harness
Assistant County Administrator
Hillsborough County
Tampa, Florida

Jody L. Harris
Director of Program Services
State Planning Office,
    Executive Department
State of Maine
Augusta, Maine

Ann Hess
Chief of Staff
Boston City Council
Boston, Massachusetts

Wally Hill
Deputy County Administrator
Hillsborough County
Tampa, Florida

Mary Jane Kuffner Hirt
Professor of Political Science
Indiana University of Pennsylvania
Indiana, Pennsylvania

William Horne
City Manager
Clearwater, Florida

Joanne E. Howard
Senior Consultant MCIC
    (Metro Chicago
    Information Center)
Chicago, Illinois

Roberta Ann Johnson
Professor of Politics
University of San Francisco
San Francisco, California

Jamil Jreisat
Professor of Public
    Administration
University of South
    Florida-Tampa
Tampa, Florida

Thad Juszczak
Director, Global Public Sector
Grant Thornton LLP
Washington, D.C.

Rebecca Keeler
Ph.D. Candidate
Florida Atlantic University
Boca Raton, Florida

Elizabeth Kellar
Deputy Executive Director
International City-County
    Management
    Association
Washington, D.C.

Paul Lachapelle
Assistant Professor, Extension
    Community
Development Specialist
Department of Political
    Science
Montana State University
Bozeman, Montana

Robert Lee
(Former) City Manager
Gulfport and Naples,
    Florida
Past President
Florida City and County
    Management
    Association

Jim Leidlein
City Manager
Harper Woods, Michigan

Kathy Livernois
Director of Human Resources
St. Charles, Illinois

Vince Long
Deputy County Administrator
Leon County
Tallahassee, Florida

Gilbert Machin
Operations Manager, Housing
    Choice Voucher Program
Hillsborough County
Tampa, Florida

Earl Mackey
(Former) Executive Director
National Conference of State
    Legislatures
Executive Director
Kentucky Legislative Ethics
    Commission
Lexington, Kentucky

Mary Mahoney
Management and Budget
    Department
Hillsborough County
Tampa, Florida

Henry Marcy
(Former) Deputy Commissioner for
    Administration and Finance
Division of Employment and Training
Commonwealth of Massachusetts
Boston, Massachusetts

Doug Matthews
Director, Public Communications
Clearwater, Florida

Fred Meine
Professor
Troy University
Troy, Alabama

Mark Monson
Deputy Director for Administration
Department of Health Professions
Richmond, Virginia

Karl Nollenberger
Assistant Professor
University of Wisconsin – Oshkosh
Former Lake County, Illinois,
    Administrator
Oshkosh, Wisconsin

Lauren Palmer
Assistant City Manager
City of Manhattan, Kansas

John Petter
Chief, Bureau of Compliance and
    Evaluation
Office of the Inspector General
Illinois Department of Human
    Services
Springfield, Illinois

James Pfiffner
Professor
School of Public Policy
George Mason University
Fairfax, Virginia

Jeremy F. Plant
Professor of Public Policy and
   Administration
Pennsylvania State
   University
Harrisburg, Pennsylvania

Randall Recklaus
Assistant City
   Administrator
Batavia, Illinois

Victoria Reinhardt
Commissioner
Ramsey County, Minnesota
St. Paul, Minnesota

Sandra J. Reinke
Associate Professor of Public
   Administration
Director, MPA Program
University of Central
   Florida
Orlando, Florida

Terrel L. Rhodes
Vice President
Office of Quality, Curriculum
   and Assessment
Association of American Colleges
   and Universities
Washington, D.C.

Bruce Rodman
U.S. Railroad Retirement Board
Chicago, Illinois

Philip Sallie
Member
American Society for Public
   Administration
Springfield, Illinois

Paul Sharon
ICMA Range Rider
Jacksonville, Florida
(Former) City Manager
Clarendon Hills, Illinois;
   South Haven, Michigan;
   Lombard, Illinois;
   North Andover and
   Ashland, Massachusetts;
   and Hudson,
   New Hampshire

James D. Slack
Professor
Department of Government
University of Alabama at
   Birmingham
Birmingham, Alabama

Sean Stegall
Assistant City Manager
Elgin, Illinois

Debra A. Taylor
Detective
Sarasota County Sheriff's Office
Sarasota, Florida

Karl Thoennes III
Judicial Circuit Administrator
Unified Judicial System
State of South Dakota
Sioux Falls, South Dakota

Steve Thompson
City Manager
Marco Island, Florida

Michael Vocino
Professor
University of Rhode Island
Kingston, Rhode Island

Susan Walker
Administrator
Neighborhood Services Department
Pinellas Park, Florida

Thomas Walkington
Strategic Management Coordinator,
   Research, Planning, and
   Development
Business Intelligence Program
Hennepin County
Minneapolis, Minnesota

Howard Whitton
The Ethicos Group, International
   Consulting Services
London, England

Regina Williams
City Manager
Norfolk, Virginia

Mylon Winn
Professor
School of Public Policy and Urban
   Affairs
Southern University
Baton Rouge, Louisiana

LaKeshia Wood
Student
University of Baltimore
Baltimore, Maryland

Mark Woodard
Assistant County Administrator
   and Chief of Staff
Pinellas County
St. Petersburg, Florida

Liangfu Wu
Director, Information Services
Downers Grove, Illinois

GETTING STARTED

Chapter 1

Understanding Ethics and Governance

> Few men have virtue to withstand the highest bidder.

George Washington

Ethics are involved in all manner of public activities, such as protecting us from criminals, ensuring that confidential information does not get in the wrong hands, keeping us safe from man-made and environmental hazards, and much more. Ethical behavior, which includes respect for citizens, the promotion of democratic values such as citizen participation in governance, and commitment to the rule of law, is of paramount importance. We expect those who occupy elected and appointed offices in our federal, state, and local governments to be ethical in carrying out their duties. In fact, Washington and state and local governments have gone to considerable length to ensure that the public's business is conducted properly. How? They have created ethics oversight commissions and adopted laws, ordinances, rules, and ethics codes to encourage ethical behavior.[1] Although these measures are useful and have a proper place, they are frequently insufficient. Following rules, regulations, and the law to stay out of trouble is important, but it is the moral minimum.

Rising above the Moral Minimum: The Four Failings

There are four obstacles that must be overcome by governments at all levels to ensure that the workforce can rise above the moral minimum. The first significant obstacle is *leadership myopia*—that is, failing to recognize the importance of ethics in getting the work of government done. Government does not exist to produce a product called "ethics."[2] Rather, government is expected to provide and produce valued public goods and services, such as justice, safety, security, transportation, clean air and water, parks and recreation, safe food and drugs, emergency services, and many, many more. Thus, it is not surprising that many government leaders do not place a high priority on ethics and typically recognize its importance only after there has been a serious ethical lapse. When put this way, ethics is the cornerstone of effective, efficient, democratic governance. "Ethics may be only instrumental, it may be only a means to an end, but it is a necessary means to an end," asserts Dennis Thompson.[3] The challenge is to ensure that one understands the importance of ethics in carrying out the work of government and then act on that understanding.

A second obstacle is *lack of top management awareness of misconduct*. As unimaginable as this may be, many high level officials do not know what is happening in their organizations. A national survey conducted by the Ethics Resources Center in 2007 reports that local government leaders are less likely than state or national government leaders to be aware of wrongdoing when it happens.[4] No government, of course, wants to encourage its workers to become vigilantes who take it upon themselves to police misconduct. Nonetheless, organizational leaders must find the ways and means to be informed of misconduct before a culture of ethical failure takes hold.

A third obstacle is the combined punch of *history and culture*. Organizational scholars are quick to point out the enormous influence of the past on the present. Governments with a checkered history in ethical governance are unlikely to be transformed overnight. Indeed, historical tentacles and norms can be deeply rooted in a culture that resists change and fosters benign neglect or, worse, permits outright unethical behavior. The phrase "this is how we do things around here" means just that—keep doing things the same way. The challenge is to find leaders who are able and willing to break with the culture of the past.

A fourth obstacle is *ethical illiteracy*. Leaders and followers who are unable "to grasp fully the intricacies of complex ethical issues and to see all of the consequences of one's actions" suffer from ethical illiteracy.[5] And it commonly surfaces when issues are seen from a fatally narrow and limited legal perspective. A large illiteracy blind spot can produce tunnel vision that severely damages a city or county's reputation as a fair and equitable provider of public goods and services. The challenge in overcoming this obstacle is to think and act outside the box of what the law requires. Sound ethical judgment calls for more than meeting the moral minimum of the law.

Many government managers understand that ethics and integrity are essential qualities that managers must embrace in order to be successful. When asked in a 2006 survey how much importance they would place on ethics and integrity to their organization, eight out of ten local government managers said "extremely important."[6] No other public service knowledge or skill (budgeting, program evaluation, public-private partnerships, and so forth) was ranked even closely to ethics and integrity. Successful managers understand that one's integrity is at the core of managing "without fear or favor."[7]

What Can Be Done?

But what can be done to encourage ethical behavior and prevent misconduct? Jurisdictions and their agencies typically adopt one of two approaches: a compliance approach or an integrity approach, with the former the far more dominant. A compliance approach depends heavily on rules and practices that, if followed, are designed to keep members of the organization out of trouble. Behavior deemed acceptable or unacceptable is defined for the employee usually in the form of rules or admonishments. Rules are typically placed in personnel manuals, codes of conduct, and new employee orientation sessions. Moreover, many governments require their employees to sign a statement that they have read and will abide by the acceptable behavior rules of the organization. Those who break the rules are presumed to do so out of ignorance or willful intention. The latter is viewed as more serious and can result in penalties ranging from a letter of reprimand to suspension with or without pay to getting fired. Those who commit misconduct out of ignorance are treated less harshly but are expected to reform themselves. Ignorance is not an excuse for misconduct as it is correctable.

Detection is the key to a successful compliance approach and can, if not implemented in a sensitive manner, foster an unhealthy "gotcha" culture. Figure 1.1 illustrates the key components of a compliance approach. As detection and punishment increase misconduct is expected to decrease.

A compliance approach is popular and widely adopted for several reasons. First, it is straightforward. Rules and penalties can be drafted and put into place with ease in most instances. However, implementing an effective detection system can be challenging as it can turn into a negative influence if it encourages a "tattle-tale" culture. Second, training and education can be developed that focuses on, yes, rules, detection, and penalties. Third, this approach often appears low cost once rules and guidelines are drafted. Monitoring compliance, however, is not necessarily cheap. Fourth, it presumes that with enough "dos" and "don'ts" most errant behavior can be deterred. In other words, the accent is on preventing unacceptable behavior.

An integrity approach, in contrast to a compliance approach, empowers the individual to make value judgments about right and wrong. It is value driven rather than rule driven. It presumes that there are not always, maybe even seldom, bright lines to help one choose the right thing to do. One must learn how to deal with ethical challenges.

What are the values that drive an integrity approach? One way to answer this question is to look empirically at what several communities actually do. Figure 1.2 lists the values of three communities in three different states, Indiana, Kansas, and

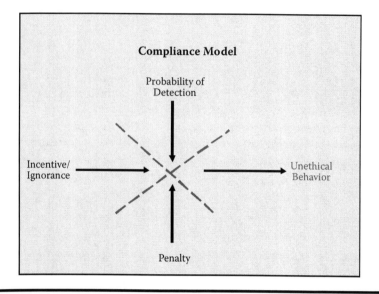

Figure 1.1 The compliance model assumes that unethical behavior can be prevented by penalties for wrongdoing and increasing the probability of detection.

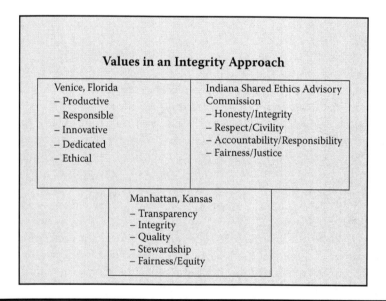

Figure 1.2 Values are the centerpiece of an integrity approach.

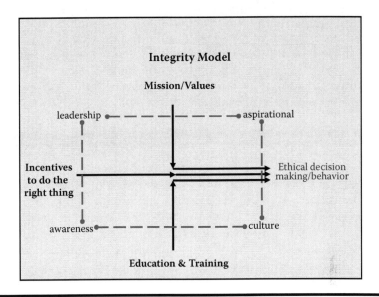

Figure 1.3   The essential components of the integrity model are awareness leadership, aspirational value, and culture.

Florida. These values do not exhaust the universe of values but they are reasonably inclusive.

Figure 1.3 provides a more detailed specification of the integrity model. As is evident from the four cornerstones—leadership, awareness, culture, and aspirations—the integrity model responds to the organization's mission and is bolstered with appropriate education and training to ensure that decisions are reached in an ethical manner and achieve ethical results. This model is comprehensive and reflects interdependency among the key elements. In this sense, it offers a systemic approach to building and sustaining a strong ethics culture.

The principal weakness, critics might contend, is a reliance on the reasoning ability and "goodness" of members of the organization. By contrast, the compliance approach emphasizes the dark side of human nature—that is, given the opportunity, people will opt for behavior that is questionable and perhaps crosses over to the unethical.

These approaches are not necessarily polar opposites. Rather, it is possible to blend the best of both in a "fusion" model. Carol W. Lewis and Stuart C. Gilman describe the fusion model as "a two-pronged, systematic approach that 'incorporates both compliance with formal standards and the promotion of individual ethical responsibility'."[8] One case (5.8) in Chapter 5, "Escape from an Ethics Swamp," provides a vivid and persuasive picture of the fusion model in action.

Ethics Defined

There are endless ethics moments throughout life, those occasions when we just don't know what to do in a "right" and "wrong" situation and sometimes, in a "right" and "right" situation. They occur in our private lives and our professional work. And, it is much easier to stumble into an ethics moment than it is to find a way out.

So why should I care? I'm an ethical person. Are you? Have you never told a lie? Bent the truth a tad? Doctored an expense voucher? Turned your head when you witnessed an unethical act by a friend or coworker? Enhanced a resume? Inflated a performance evaluation? Fudged on an exam? Made unpleasant remarks about someone because of their sexual orientation, race, religion, or ethnic creed? Treated another person disrespectfully? Overlooked unreported income on your IRS 1040 form? Chances are you have done some of these things. Does that make you a "bad" person? Not necessarily. But it may mean that your ethical compass is a bit ajar. As a human being, it is an unending challenge to keep your ethical compass pointed true north.

Humans err—sometimes with maliciousness in mind but most of the time we make misjudgments out of ignorance, intolerance, plain stupidity, or the inability to reason through a complicated ethical situation. The vast majority of government employees try to do the right thing most of the time. As Earl E. Devaney, Inspector General of the U.S. Department of the Interior, put it in a blistering report in 2008 that described the "culture of ethical failure" in a DOI agency: "I have gone on record to say that I believe that 99.9 percent of DOI employees are hard-working, ethical and well intentioned."[9] Still, a small number of unethical employees can wreak havoc in a government agency.[10]

If most of us are ethically well intended, what is the problem? It's not always easy to figure out what the right thing is, especially in complex organizations that have come to dominate modern governance. Rules and regulations, even laws, are helpful, but doing the right thing often means doing more than just following the rules.

The Founding Fathers understood human nature quite well and created a system of governance that checked ambition with ambition and power with power. "If men were angels, no government would be necessary," wrote James Madison in Federalist Papers No. 51. Of course, if men and women were angels, there would be no reason to concern ourselves with ethics. But ... humans roam the earth, not the heavens, so ethics are indispensable.

Ethics is a term invoked with considerable frequency in the professions, government, and the corporate world. But how might we define ethics? There are many definitions. Some define ethics as "morality in action"; others assert ethics involves "a consensus of moral principles." James Norden offers this definition: "Ethics are the internal rules that drive one to follow or not to follow external rules. Of course, this definition works best when morals are the external rules.

Simply being law-abiding begs the ethical question."[11] The definition used in this book is: "Ethics are values and principles that guide right and wrong behavior." The key elements of this definition are (1) values and principles, (2) behavior, and (3) right and wrong.

Values and Principles. A value can be an idea, object, practice, or almost anything else that we attach worth to. Of course, ethics do not encompass all values. Consider money or status as a value. Most of us attach worth to money and status but we don't call them values that are essential to a definition of ethics. A value that is translated into an ethic can be thrift (remember Benjamin Franklin), cleanliness (remember the startup of McDonald's), piety (remember the Puritan ethic), work (the Protestant ethic), justice, prudence, compassion, charity, courage, benevolence, and so on. A principle is a prescription for action. Consider the Golden Rule or treat people with dignity or tell the truth or treat others with fairness.

Values and principles are also defined by the professions—medicine, law, clergy, accounting, engineering, and others. Professional associations such as the International City/County Management Association (ICMA), the American Planning Association (APA), and the American Society for Public Administration (ASPA) set forth many values and principles that their members are expected to embrace. These values and principles can be classified broadly as public service values and principles. All call for their members to respect the law, promote the public interest, and serve with integrity. At the same time, more specific behaviors can be proscribed. The ICMA, for example, requires its city managers to serve a community for a minimum of two years unless there are persuasive mitigating circumstances. Service of shorter tenure is viewed as harmful to the community. Nor can city managers endorse products that might be used in his or her city government. Endorsements can lead to the reality or appearance of a conflict of interest that would erode public trust and confidence in the manager. Guidelines for Tenet 12 of the ICMA code states that:

> Members should not endorse commercial products or services by agreeing to use their photograph, endorsement, or quotation in paid or other commercial advertisements, whether or not for compensation.[12]

And politically, it is improper to support candidates for local elected offices, particularly in the manager's own governmental jurisdiction.

Behavior. Ethics is not a spectator sport; it is a contact sport, Carol Lewis (1991) so astutely notes. Ethics is about behavior and consequences. Thinking unethical thoughts is possible, but until those thoughts become translated into behavior, there are no consequences to define "right" or "wrong." Ethics shares with law the notion that it is behavior that matters foremost. Ethics is sometimes equated with morality, as the above definitions suggest. However, the act of thinking immoral thoughts can be defined as immoral itself. Consider the case of former President Jimmy Carter. As a presidential candidate in 1976, he was interviewed by Playboy magazine. "The reporter asked me if I had ever been guilty of adultery, and his next question was predictable. I replied truthfully. I've looked on a lot of women with lust. I've committed adultery in my heart many times."[13] To Jimmy Carter, lusting was an immoral act although it was not a behavioral act.

Ethics in Action

The vast majority of government employees and public officials in the United States are conscientious, dedicated, ethical persons who carry out their day-to-day work competently and with pride. Yet, as the cases and controversies in this book illustrate, there are many paths and pitfalls that can ensnare even the most ethically well-intentioned person. A kaleidoscope of rules, regulations, and laws certainly help individuals stay on an ethical path, but no matter how complex an organizational situation might be, it is up to the individual to exercise his moral agency. That is why ethical reasoning is so important. For without the ability to reason through a situation, one is largely left to the moral agency of the organization to determine "right" from "wrong." And, when taken to the dark side of organizational life, the individual's moral agency might be stripped away entirely. "What's good for the organization is good for me" might be the lament—a dangerous supposition for sure.

Progressive leaders and managers understand the dangers that lurk in the "shadow of organization" and have instituted practices that ensure an individual's moral agency is not sacrificed on the altar of organizational self-interest.[14] What are those practices? First and foremost is exemplary leadership. Those who pronounce that their supervisors and street-level workers must adhere to the highest ethical standards in the conduct of their work must themselves adhere to those same standards. Leaders must be exemplars in their personal and professional lives. Easier said than done? Certainly, but it is essential. Much the same can be said about peer leadership. Middle managers or even the cop on the beat must demonstrate day-in and day-out his commitment to ethical behavior. Failure to do so can result only in organizations without integrity.

Elected officeholders can also serve as exemplars. Consider the case of Mayor Steve Brown, Peachtree City, Georgia, population 31,580 residents. Brown ran successfully for office on a platform of bringing ethical government to his community, yet was soon embarrassingly sitting before the Peachtree City Ethics Board accused of violating the city's ethics code. What happened? He found himself in a situation in which he needed to get his daughter to summer camp and, at the same time, negotiate an agreement for a local option sales tax. His assistant volunteered to help and drove his daughter to camp—on city time! The city manager advised the mayor that he may have committed an ethics violation. Forty-five minutes later, Brown realized that the city manager could be correct, so, embarrassed by this ethical lapse, he took out his pen and filed an ethics complaint against himself.

After subsequent deliberation by the Ethics Board, it was determined that no formal reprimand was necessary but that Brown should reimburse the city for the assistant's time away from the office. Mayor Brown readily complied and reimbursed the city $8.94.[15]

Second, ethics training in cities and counties across America is becoming more common than uncommon. A recent study of all 554 U.S. cities with populations over 50,000 reported that there is a great deal of ethics training underway. Two of every three cities reported that they do training. New employees are the target of most training in six of ten cities while four of ten cities reported that managers are also trained. A smaller number of cities said that ethics training is mandatory.[16]

Management consultants and university faculty are often recruited to provide training workshops. In addition, professional associations such as ICMA and nonprofit organizations such as the Ethics Resource Center are frequently called on to conduct ethics workshops.[17] This training is generally much different from ethics training offered by state ethics commissions, which emphasizes laws, rules, and regulations. State training programs usually emphasize what the law says about (1) a conflict of interest, (2) what "having financial interests" means in a day-to-day, practical sense, (3) the meaning of personal honesty, (4) how to address ethics complaints, and (5) due process. Knowledge of ethics laws is necessary but, as noted before, is not sufficient. Normative ethics theories such as utilitarianism, principle or duty-based ethics, and virtue theory are unlikely to be touched upon in state ethics training sessions. The concept of ethical reasoning is likely to be quite foreign.

Governments that support ethics training workshops are much more likely to offer cases and experiences that enhance the participant's ethical reasoning knowledge and skills. Participants, usually in small groups, must grapple with decisions that involve identifying and evaluating ethical means to achieve ethical outcomes. The topic of transparency in government affairs is also typically included in ethics training workshops.[18]

Third, while government employees are usually subject to state ethic laws, many governments have chosen to adopt a higher standard that is expressed in their own code of ethics.[19] Elected and appointed public managers hold very positive attitudes toward codes of ethics. The conventional wisdom is that codes have a positive influence in governance, especially in deterring unethical acts by ethically motivated public servants. That is, unethical officials are likely to be unethical regardless of whether a code exists, but those who want to be ethical find a code helpful in guiding their behavior. Of course, the motivation for adopting a code is often a series of unethical behaviors or a scandal. The study noted earlier found that between 1992 and 2002 cities adopting a standard of conduct was up 27 percent, as was monitoring adherence to a code of ethics (up 26.5 percent) and requiring familiarity with the city's code of ethics (up 24.5 percent).[20]

Fourth, governments are increasingly conducting ethics audits, which can be described as an "appraisal activity, the purpose being to determine if changes need to be made in the climate, environment, codes, and the enforcement of ethics policies."[21] An ethics audit is not an accounting or financial management audit. Rather, it is a tool for benchmarking the strength of the organization's ethical culture and putting in place organizational initiatives to build an organization of integrity. One case (5.8) in this book, "Escape from an Ethics Swamp," provides a detailed example of how a city manager rebuilt an organization that had fallen into an unethical morass.

An ethics audit might also include an assessment of occupational risk or vulnerability. That is, some organizational work is inherently vulnerable to unethical abuse if not criminal wrongdoing. For example, occupational work that involves the handling and processing of financial matters, purchasing and contracting, conducting inspections, and enforcing rules and regulations are high risk, especially for workers whose ethical compass is amiss in the first place. A systematic assessment of the ethical risk factor of work is a necessary first step in putting into place appropriate accountability and transparency mechanisms. It is also a valuable step in identifying training priorities.

Fifth, recruiting and promoting employees based in part on their adherence to ethical standards is growing.[22] Personnel decisions—hiring, evaluating, promoting, firing—are essential features of all organizations. Stephen J. Bonczek, a former city manager with many years' experience in Michigan, Florida, Texas, and Pennsylvania, is a strong advocate of raising the ethical awareness of employees through hiring, evaluation, and promotion. He is equally adamant about installing an ethical consciousness in the organization through the use of codes, audits, committees, and weekly staff meetings. "It is advantageous," he claims, "to use weekly staff meetings to review all discussions and decisions for ethical implications. When a potential problem is identified, a staff member can be assigned to clarify the issue and develop a strategy for resolving it at the next meeting."[23]

Taken together–exemplary leadership, ethics training, codes, audits, and personnel selection processes that incorporate a standard of conduct—they represent a comprehensive approach toward strengthening the ethics culture in public governance.[24] This is not wishful thinking; this is happening across America today. Ethics is in action, although the enterprise remains a work-in-progress as the high-profile story of former Illinois Governor Rod Blagojevich so unflatteringly illustrates.[25]

Ethics Matters?

It may seem unnecessary in a book on ethics in government to conclude the first chapter with the contention that ethical behavior is important. However, the purpose of this book is not to transform an unethical person into an ethical person.[26] This is a task that no human can do. Rather, it is to help ethically well-intended government managers and employees avoid and, when the occasion calls for it, extricate themselves from a morally challenging situation. Another purpose of this book is to provide organizational leaders with a perspective on managing, not controlling, individuals who toil in the service of community and democratic governance.

So we might ask, "what happens when ethics is relegated to the sidelines?" The consequences for individuals and the organization can range from a loss of self-respect to heightened organizational tensions to embarrassment and, in a worse case, scandal that grinds the organization to the ground. One case (3.10) in the chapters that follow, for example, illustrates how a personal situation (a city manager who is charged with abusing his terminally ill wife) can cause one to overlook the potential embarrassment to himself and his employer when the unsubstantiated charges are first suppressed and then explode like a ticking time bomb on the front page of the local newspaper. Another case (4.9) involving high ranking county officials devolves into an ethical morass when everyone seems to "go along to get along."[27] The appearance of a "sweetheart deal" in this case along with the lack of due diligence eventually costs a highly regarded professional administrator and the long-serving county attorney their jobs. The political career of the elected official in this case is brought to an abrupt end as well. Meanwhile, the county commission is confronted with a public relations nightmare when a grand jury is convened to investigate. The work of the county government spirals downward as the leadership is adrift and the morale of dedicated employees sinks. In neither of these cases is anyone found guilty of breaking the law, but did they cross over an ethical line? Read the cases and decide for yourself.

Ethical awareness is the essential starting point for keeping yourself and your organization out of harm's way. The next step, which is often quite difficult, is to take action when a colleague or superior's behavior becomes ethically problematic. Moral muteness or turning one's head when an ethical violation happens is all too often the inaction that occurs. But it is not without price to the individual and the organization. Sometimes the failure to act corrupts the individual's integrity and the integrity of coworkers. And the resultant drift toward an amoral organizational culture endangers the organization's mission. The final chapter in this book returns to these concerns in an effort to profile the lessons learned from the cases and describes the journey to become an ethically competent public manager.

Endnotes

1. The CD has excellent overview articles of these efforts; see 4.12 Ethics "Management in Cities and Counties."
2. D.F. Thompson, "The Possibility of Administrative Ethics," *Public Administration Review* 45 (1985):555–561.
3. _____, "Paradoxes of Government Ethics," *Public Administration Review* 52 (May/June 1992): 255.

4. *National Government Ethics Survey* (Arlington, VA: Ethics Resource Center, 2008), 38.

5. T.I. White, "Data, Dollars and the Unintentional Subversion of Human Rights in the IT Industry" (Center for Business Ethics, Bentley College, Boston, MA, February 12, 2007), 7–8.

6. NASPAA/ICMA, http://naspaa.org/naspaa_surveys/main.asp (accessed December 10, 2008).

7. For an intriguing account of life in the trenches of local government management, see L.F. Harlow, *Without Fear or Favor: Odyssey of a City Manager* (Provo, UT: Brigham Young University Press, 1977).

8. C.W. Lewis and S.C. Gilman, *The Ethics Challenge in Public Service: A Problem Solving Guide*, 2nd ed. (San Francisco: Jossey-Bass, 2005), 18.

9. E.E. Devaney, Inspector General, "OIG Investigations of MMS Employees" (Washington, D.C.: U.S. Department of the Interior, Office of the Inspector General, September 9, 2008).

10. Controversy 6.19 "A Culture of Ethical Failure" is a chilling description of an unethical organization.

11. Posted on the ASPA Section on Ethics website, http://www.aspaonline.org/ethicscommunity/definitions.htm (accessed January 27, 2009).

12. http://icma.org/main/bc.asp?bcid=40&hsid=1&ssid1=2530&ssid2=2531 (accessed January 27, 2009).

13. http://speakingoffaith.publicradio.org/programs/jimmycarter/carter_playboy.shtm (accessed December 27, 2008).

14. R.B. Denhardt, *In the Shadow of Organization* (Lawrence: The Regents Press of Kansas, 1981).

15. S. Brown, "Managing Municipal Ethics," http://www.gmanet.com/event_detail/default.asp?eventid=6445&menuid=GeorgiaCitiesNewspaperID (accessed December 29, 2005).

16. J.P. West, and E.M. Berman, "Ethics Training in U.S. Cities: Content, Pedagogy, and Impact," *Public Integrity* 6 (Summer, 2004): 189–206.

17. Controversy 4.14 "San Diego on the Move" is an example of an ERC survey that helped the city strengthen its ethical culture.

18. Case 5.7 "Let the Sunshine In" illustrates the need for transparency.

19. See www.venicegov.com/ "City of Venice, Florida" for a code that requires a higher standard of conduct than does the State of Florida.

20. J.P. West and E.M. Berman, Ethic Training in U.S. Cities: Content, Pedagogy, and Impact." *Public Integrity* 6 (Summer, 2004): 189–206.

21. C. Wiley, "The ABC's of Business Ethics: Definitions, Philosophies and Implementation," *Industrial Management* 37: 1 (1995): 22–27.

22. Case 4.8 "Ethics and Performance Evaluations" illustrates how difficult it is to incorporate ethical standards in annual evaluations. See also CD 3.10 "Performance Evaluation for Managers."

23. S.J. Bonczek, "Creating an Ethical Work Environment: Enhancing Ethics Awareness in Local Government," in *The Ethics Edge*, ed. E.M. Berman, J.P. West and S.J. Bonczek, 72–79 (Washington, D.C.: International City/County Management Association, 1998).

24. D.C. Menzel, *Ethics Management for Public Administrators: Building Organizations of Integrity* (Armonk, NY: M.E. Sharpe, 2007). This book provides a detailed discussion of these important ethics management tools and strategies.
25. See http://americancityandcounty.com/admin/illinois_gets_bad_press_governor_arrest_1212/index.html.
26. CD 7.5 "Why Are People (Un)Ethical?" is a slide presentation that identifies ten reasons why people engage in unethical behavior.
27. See Case 4.5 "Going Along to Get Along?"

Chapter 2

Becoming Ethically Competent

Always do right—this will gratify some and astonish the rest.

Mark Twain

What knowledge, skills, and abilities does one need to be ethically competent? This is not an easy question to answer as there is considerable debate about the matter. James Heichelbech, an activist member in and officer of the Ethics Section of the American Society for Public Administration, puts it this way:

> Ethical competency is a grasp of some conception of legitimacy in governance, an awareness of one's commitments in relation to one's own interests and the interests of others, and most importantly an attitude of respect for the collective effort within an organization, reflected in participation within and promotion of a culture of justification. In other words, *my* view of ethical competency has nothing to do with codes of ethics, dilemmas, corruption or the appearance of impropriety.[1]

It is difficult to imagine that a government manager would be regarded as ethically competent if he had no knowledge of the profession's code of ethics, relevant ethics ordinances, or state ethics laws. Nor is it imaginable that one could become ethically competent without having the skills and ability to recognize an ethical issue and act appropriately to resolve it.[2]

The International City/County Management Association (ICMA) defines ethical competency in terms of integrity: personal, professional, and organizational.[3]

Integrity: Demonstrating fairness, honesty, and ethical and legal awareness in personal and professional relationships and activities (requires knowledge of business and personal ethics; ability to understand issues of ethics and integrity in specific situations). Practices that contribute to this core content area are:

■ Personal integrity. Demonstrating accountability for personal actions; conducting personal relationships and activities fairly and honestly.
■ Professional integrity. Conducting professional relationships and activities fairly, honestly, legally, and in conformance with the ICMA Code of Ethics (requires knowledge of administrative ethics and specifically the ICMA Code of Ethics).
■ Organizational integrity. Fostering ethical behavior throughout the organization through personal example, management practices, and training (requires knowledge of administrative ethics; ability to instill accountability into operations; and ability to communicate ethical standards and guidelines to others).

Another view of ethical competencies is offered by James S. Bowman and his colleagues.[4] They contend that ethically competent administrators must understand and practice moral reasoning (interpreted as ethical reasoning here), be able to sort through competing values, and engage in prudent decision making. More specifically, they note that four abilities are needed: (1) principled moral reasoning, (2) recognition of ethics-related conflicts, (3) refusal to do something unethical, and (4) application of ethical theory.

As might be surmised, becoming ethically competent is not a simple or straightforward task. Yet, it is doable, and if we accept the results of the ICMA survey noted in Chapter 3, it is imperative that men and women entering the profession of government management become ethically competent public servants. An ethically competent manager must have an awareness of and sensitivity to ethical concerns in her organizational environment and be able to differentiate between ethical and management issues when circumstances warrant a distinction.

DEFINITION OF ETHICAL COMPETENCY

For purposes of this book, an ethically competent government manager is (1) committed to high standards of personal and professional behavior, (2) has knowledge of relevant ethics codes and laws, (3) has the ability to engage in ethical reasoning when confronted with challenging situations, (4) is able to identify and act on public service ethics and values, and (5) promotes ethical practices and behavior in public agencies and organizations. (See Exhibit 2.1.)

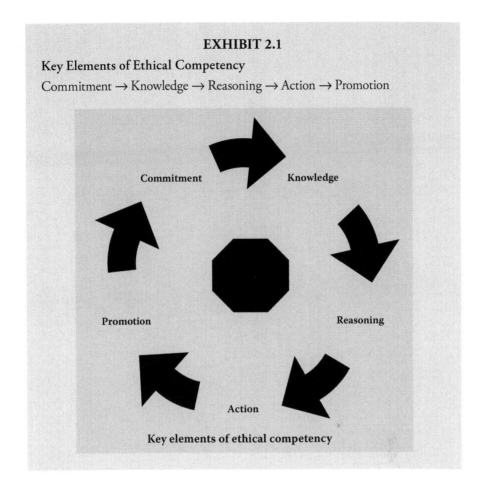

EXHIBIT 2.1

Key Elements of Ethical Competency

Commitment → Knowledge → Reasoning → Action → Promotion

Commitment

Knowledge

Promotion

Reasoning

Action

Key elements of ethical competency

The competencies in Exhibit 2.2 are drawn from the public service litera-ture and key principles in the Code of Ethics of the American Society for Public Administration.[5] They also reflect the central elements in the definition of ethical competency offered above. In this context, knowledge refers to an organized body of information; skills are the verbal, manual, or mental use of people, data, or things; and abilities are the power to perform a given act.[6]

High on the list of competencies is *"serve the public interest."* In short, serv-ing the public interest requires a government manager to place the public interest above his self-interests or the organization's self-interests. This is not an easy thing to do. As Kenneth Ashworth, an experienced public servant, puts it: "Working inside organizations, you will feel pressures to carry out orders you feel uneasy about, and, to get ahead, there will be temptations to compromise yourself and your principles or instincts."[7] This is not serving the public interest, is it? Of course defining the public interest from the vantage point of government management is not always a

EXHIBIT 2.2

Ethical Competencies*

- Be knowledgeable of ethical principles
- Be aware and informed of relevant professional codes of ethics
- Recognize and promote constitutional principles of equality, fairness, representativeness
- Recognize and support the public's right to know the public's business
- Respect the law
- Serve the public interest
- Engage in ethical reasoning
- Recognize and differentiate between ethical and management issues
- Respect and protect privileged information
- Embrace and promote ethical behavior and practices in the workplace
- Refuse to do something unethical
- Maintain truthfulness and honesty
- Guard against conflict of interest or its appearance
- Be responsible for one's behavior

*not prioritized

straightforward matter. Still, it is incumbent on the ethically competent manager to make every effort to carry out her duties in a manner that is consistent with the public interest. The ethically competent manager must draw on her knowledge of the public interest and possess the necessary skills and abilities to ensure that the public interest prevails.

Intertwined with serving the public interest is *"respect for the law."* The rule of law is critical to democratic governance, and it is expected that those sworn to uphold the law will do just that, although there can be a place for legitimate, principled dissent. Public managers may not be elected officials who are charged with the responsibility to enact laws that govern the land. However, they are vital actors in energizing the law. The ethically competent public manager understands his role in a democracy and must act in a manner that is lawful and respectful of his elected bosses.

Several competencies put the emphasis on skills and abilities. One is the skill and ability to recognize and differentiate between ethical and management issues. This is no trivial matter as it is often difficult to discern which is which and sometimes the two are undistinguishable. However, to mistake a management issue as an ethical issue or vice versa can result in mismanagement or improper intervention.[8] Consider the matter of solicitations in the workplace (see Case 6.2 "Workplace Solicitations."[9]

While this might be viewed as an unethical issue, it can also be viewed as a management issue. Consider fund raising efforts to support nonprofit organizations like United Way. How employees are solicited can make the difference in determining whether it is an ethical issue or a management issue. Should employees feel pressured to "go along to get along" there would most likely be considerable anxiety and ethical angst.

Another competency, *"embrace ethical practices and behavior in the workplace,"* also places an emphasis on skills and abilities. While most managers would find this meritorious, it is also the case that few managers actually do it. Why? Too often supervisors and top management fail to recognize the value in emphasizing ethical behavior until there is a serious issue or problem. There is a tendency to be reactive rather than proactive. Moreover, there is the possibility that higher level managers may be unaware of misconduct at work. A recent survey found that one of every three local government employees who observed misconduct did not report it.[10] If employees do not report ethical problems, organizational managers may not recognize problems until a crisis is at hand.

Becoming an ethically competent manager also means having the ability to engage in *"ethical reasoning"*, an approach to resolve issues and dilemmas that can be both taught and learned.

Ethical Reasoning: Becoming Aware

Public managers typically approach "doing the right thing" from a utilitarian perspective. That is, they try to make decisions that benefit the greatest number of residents (or employees when decisions apply only to the government workforce) while minimizing the potential harm. This "do no harm" approach is attractive because it is straightforward and, on many occasions, easy to understand. Still, there are times when these qualities are not sufficient. So what do practitioners do when faced with especially difficult ethics moments? Some apply a blend of normative philosophies—utilitarianism, principles, and virtues—in what James H. Svara calls the "ethics triangle."[11]

Others apply ethical reasoning, which incorporates some aspects of the classic normative approaches but also emphasizes a decision-making logic and process. Dennis Witmer has studied ethical decision making and contends that ethical judgment and behavior are conditioned by individual influences, such as age, experience, and employment tenure, and external influences, such as the prevailing reward/punishment structure, ethical work climates, organizational policies, and codes of conduct.[12] Central to his behavioral model of ethical reasoning is the individual's sensitivity to an ethical situation and the ability to exercise judgment in selecting a choice that results in ethical behavior. As Witmer puts it, "ethical decisions are a product (in part) of sensitivity and perception of the ethical issues and the reasoning used to arrive at some conclusion about what to do in the situation."

Terry L. Cooper places ethical reasoning at the center of choice intended to resolve an ethical problem. Cooper's model "does not assume that ethical decisions are, can, or should be purely rational and principled."[13] Rather, human feelings are an inseparable part of our ethical life, he asserts. Values and judgments are at the crucible of the decision-making process to resolve an ethical problem. The individual must learn how to draw upon one's moral imagination—acquire the ability to produce a movie in our minds with realistic characters, a believable script, and clear imagery—to project probable consequences of the ethical choices one makes in a given situation. Ethical reasoning emphasizes the dynamics and interplay between alternatives, values that might be derived from principles or virtues, and common-sense judgment to resolve a challenging ethics moment.

How then should we go about learning how to reason ethically and acquire other ethical competencies? One answer is to examine real-world cases and controversies—or what can be described as case learning.

Case Learning

How do cases help us learn about ethics and reason through a dilemma? How do we make sense of cases? What do cases offer that other learning approaches do not? First, cases are excellent for bringing abstract concepts down to earth. Trust, integrity, ethics, and the public interest, for example, are abstract concepts that must be grounded in reality; cases approximate reality. Second, cases bring context to bear on a situation that is crucial to an in-depth understanding of a difficult ethical situation. Most dilemmas are complex and challenging because they are embedded in a swirl of events, happenings, and circumstances.

Third, and perhaps most importantly, cases encourage learning by discovery, which is widely regarded as very effective in enabling the learner to retain information, concepts, and knowledge. Unlike lectures, which put the emphasis on the presenter's oral skills and the learner's listening skills, case learning emphasizes trial-and-error, self-analysis and assessment, and, in instances in which the learner is a member of a group, active learning. "The case method develops the readers' ability to reason by requiring that they perform analysis, engage in exploratory discussion, and find 'best possible' rather than right/wrong solutions."[14] Readers often generate solutions to problems they may never have experienced; it is thinking "outside the box."

Learning with cases means engagement with ideas and other learners. It emphasizes the ability to process contextual details and connect the dots. It is a combination of problem solving and, like a 10,000-piece jigsaw puzzle, putting the pieces together to form a large picture of the situation. Learners develop "a holistic understanding of the subject area."[15]

Cases lend themselves very well to learning how to engage in ethical reasoning. Moreover, the cases in this book as well as on-the-job situations can be effectively dealt with by learning how to address five ethical reasoning questions—see Exhibit 2.3. These five questions, if asked skillfully and thoughtfully, will help you reason through an ethics issue. The real-world cases in this book provide you with the opportunity to practice your reasoning skills. Most importantly, with practice and experience, when that ethics moment arrives—and it will—you will be much better prepared to deal with it.

In addition to focusing on these five questions, one can draw on the guidelines in Exhibit 2.4 to prepare for a case analysis.

EXHIBIT 2.3

Ethical Reasoning Questions

1. Is there an ethical issue? The answer to this question depends on one's ethical sensitivity and ability to size up a situation.
2. What is the ethical issue? An ethics issue can easily be mistaken for a management issue and sometimes the two overlap a great deal.
3. What might be done to resolve the situation? Once the issue is defined, a set of alternatives should be thought through in order to decide which alternative is the best course of action.
4. Does the preferred course of action satisfy the needs/preferences of the primary stakeholders, including yourself? This is where one's values enter into the decision.
5. Is the action itself ethical? An unethical means to an ethical end is no more justified than an ethical means to an unethical end.

EXHIBIT 2.4

Guidelines: Steps in Preparing for a Case Analysis

1. Go through the case as fast as possible, asking yourself, "What, broadly, is the case about and what types and amounts of information am I being given to analyze?" Often the problem or decision is laid out at the start and/or end of the case.
2. Read through the case very carefully, underlining key facts and making marginal notes. Data presented in tables or figures should be analyzed, a key maneuver some readers tend to avoid. For each exhibit ask yourself, "What is its point? What does it tell me?" Then ask yourself, "What are the issues facing the decision makers? Do the issues focus around a single point? Do they form a principal or main decision question?"
3. Go through the case again, fleshing out the issues that are important to the principal decision.

EXHIBIT 2.4 (Continued)

4. Develop a set of alternative solutions that will deal with the required decision and describe these solutions so you appreciate what they will involve.
5. Analyze each alternative in terms of the disciplinary criteria or issues important to the decision. Consider how it will deal with each of the issues you have identified.
6. Compare the alternatives to see which seems to best meet the criteria or deal with the issues.
7. Make a recommendation based on the comparison of the alternatives.
8. Prepare a statement, if appropriate, of what needs to be done to implement the recommendation.

Source: Adapted from K. Harling and J. Akridge, "Using the Case Method of Teaching," *Agribusiness* 4: 1 (1998): 1–14.

Other Learning Tools

There are other important learning tools in the pages that follow and on the CD that accompanies this book. First, every case has a practitioner and/or a scholarly assessment so that you will have a "yardstick" to measure your own assessment. In fact, nearly eighty practitioners and scholars have assessed or commented on the cases and controversies. Their assessments are just that; the

EXHIBIT 2.5

CD Resources for Chapters 1 and 2

Chapter 1—Understanding Ethics and Governance

■ Articles
   3.11 Public Management in the United States
   4.10 Ethical Decision Making in Local Government
   4.11 I Didn't Do Anything Unethical
   4.12 Ethics Management in Cities and Counties
   4.13 Ethical Environment of Local Government Managers
   4.14 Strengthening Ethics in Local Government
   4.15 Why Council Manager Governments Fail
   4.17 Service Challenges and Governance Issues Confronting American Counties

4.18   Federal-State Ethics Management
4.33   Public Administration History
■ Computer presentations
7.4   Ethics in Government: Fact, Fiction, Fantasy?
7.6   Ethical Illiteracy in Local Governance
7.13   Public Service Ethics and Professionalism
7.14   Challenges to Ethical Governance in the 21st Century
7.16   Leading with Integrity
7.19   In Pursuit of Ethical Governance
■ Codes of Ethics
6.1   American Society for Public Administration
6.2   ICMA Code of Ethics
6.3   Government Finance Officers Association
6.4   American Institute of Certified Planners

Chapter 2—Becoming Ethically Competent
■ Articles
1.2   Teaching and Learning Ethical Reasoning with Cases
4.17   President Obama's Executive Order
4.34   Research on Ethics
4.37   Public Service, Ethics, Democracy
■ Computer presentations
7.3   Withholding Information
7.8   Teaching with Cases
7.5   Why Are People (Un)Ethical?
7.9   Building Public Organizations of Integrity
7.12   Moral Development and Reasoning
7.14   Challenges to Ethical Governance in the Twenty-First Century
7.16   Leading with Integrity
7.19   In Pursuit of Ethical Governance

correctness of the assessments is a matter of judgment. Second, all cases and controversies are cross-indexed to enable the learner to focus easily and quickly on key issues and topics. Third, each chapter has an Ethical Competency Matrix that links cases and controversies directly to the competencies listed in Exhibit 2.2.

The primary learning approach is a combination of total immersion in the cases and controversies and the give-and-take of self-assessment or group assessment when engaging the material with others. How will a "total immersion" approach, which is used widely in language acquisition, assist you in becoming ethically competent? The direct answer is that total immersion envelops you in a "natural" learning process. That is, just as people learn how to speak a language by listening to the meaning that others attach to sounds, learning ethics means listening to the "sounds" in the cases and the assessments of practitioners, scholars, and peers. No single case necessarily produces "sounds" that can be attached to each element. However, the cases span a range of topics and situations about which public managers need *knowledge* such as understanding (1) the motivation that leads to (un)ethical behavior, (2) the context in which individuals choose the right or wrong course of action, (3) the manner in which a troubling situation is resolved for better or worse, (4) why ethical leadership among peers and subordinates is crucial, (5) why rules and laws, however plentiful, are not sufficient to produce ethical behavior, and (6) how professional associations contribute to building organizations of integrity.

By wrestling intellectually and thoughtfully with the many situations that cause problems, some quite serious, readers build up *commitment* to ethics and doing it rightly. Knowledge and commitment go hand-in-hand with developing *reasoning skills* to assess alternative choices and values that produce ethical behavior. All cases are decision driven. That is, the reader is faced with deciding what to do about an ethically difficult situation. Some cases place an emphasis on the need to take *action* when an ethics breach is observed among peers or top management. Moral muteness or turning one's head are choices but are not always the best thing to do. Confronting a coworker or an organizational superior who is engaging in questionable ethical behavior is very difficult and can have serious repercussions (see Case 5.4 "What's a Whistle-Blower to Do?"). Finally, becoming ethically competent means that one must *promote* public service values and appropriate behavior in public organizations.[16] The cases in this book illustrate how this is done through exemplary leadership, codes of ethics, benchmarking an organization's culture, and the development of ethics standards for inclusion in hiring decisions, promotions, and annual evaluations.

At times, total immersion in ethics cases and controversies may feel like "messy" learning. But messy learning is part and parcel of making sense out of the many complex dimensions of ethical and not so ethical behavior. However, if you probe, explore, and analyze the cases and controversies with diligence and serious intent, you will surely have taken a significant step toward becoming an ethically competent government manager. To repeat, the key ingredients in ethical competency are Commitment → Knowledge → Reasoning → Action → Promotion.

Organization of Cases and Training Materials

Chapter 1 provided an overview of ethics and governance. Four obstacles were identified that government leaders must overcome to encourage ethical behavior and discourage unethical behavior. Chapter 1 also described the two primary approaches—compliance and integrity—that governments typically take to promote ethical behavior and noted that both have shortcomings. However, when combined in a "fusion" model, the two approaches can have a powerful and positive influence. Chapter 2 shifted the focus to the challenge of becoming an ethically competent government manager. The chapter defined what ethical competency means, discussed the case method of learning, and described how other tools and the resources on the accompanying compact disc can be drawn on to learn how to become an ethically competent government manager.

Now Part II, with four chapters, takes the reader on a journey through thirty-nine cases and thirty-seven controversies that together form the substance of the book. Chapter 3 "Professionalism and Ethics" introduces a variety of cases and controversies that confront professionals in government. Several cases in Chapter 3 deal with the stress and strain that occur when one's duty and sense of morality clash or when obeying the law collides with one's conscience. (See Case 3.8 "When Duty and Morality Clash" and Case 3.9 "Follow the Law or Your Conscience?")

Chapter 4 "Encouraging Ethical Behavior" presents nine cases and seven controversies involving successful and unsuccessful efforts by government managers to foster ethical behavior. Laws, rules, and regulation are often used to combat unethical behavior but frequently fall short of producing ethical behavior. Ethical leadership and management are necessary additions to laws and rules to produce ethical governance.[17]

This chapter is followed by nine cases in Chapter 5 that explore "Building Organizations of Integrity." Integrity in governance is the bedrock of a healthy democracy. Government employees are the front-line providers of vital public services which, if compromised by unethical acts, undermine democratic governance. It is imperative that organizations of integrity be built and maintained in jurisdictions and agencies. Some cases in Chapter 5 require the reader to distinguish between ethical problems and management problems (see 5.1 "What Would You Do if You Were the Sheriff?" and 5.9 "City of Progress I"). Other cases present situations in which one must decide how to do the "right" thing when organizational pressures encourage one to do the "wrong" thing (see 5.4 "What's a Whistle-Blower to Do?" and 5.5 "When the Chief Asks You to Lie"). This chapter also highlights a case in which the city manager must rebuild an organization that has experienced ethical failure (see 5.8 "Escape from an Ethics Swamp").

Chapter 6 "Ethics in the Workplace" contains ten cases and seven controversies dealing with challenging situations. There are more than 87,000 local governments in the United States, fifty states, and one national government with thousands of employees. Good governance demands a workforce housed in organizations with cultures that emphasize honesty and integrity in carrying out the peoples' business. The last case in each of Chapters 3 through 6 is accompanied by the five ethical reasoning questions presented earlier in this chapter. The reader is challenged to apply these questions to other cases as well.

The concluding chapter, Chapter 7 "The Complete Ethical Manager," draws together the "sounds" and assessments of many practitioners, scholars, and others. The purpose is twofold: (1) to identify important lessons gained on the journey to becoming an ethically competent manager, and (2) to describe the journey with particular attention focused on the competencies needed to reach a destination that always beckons but seems just beyond one's grasp.

All cases and controversies have discussion questions that, either on your own or in a small group discussion setting, provide a start point for further exploration. The cases in each chapter are ordered by their complexity starting with those that are "low" and moving to those that are "moderate" and then "high." The appendix contains matrices for each chapter that cross-list the cases with the ethical competencies in Exhibit 2.2. The matrix cells enable the reader to identify specific cases with specific competencies. The matrix in Appendix 1 lists the cases and competencies in Chapter 3. For example, the competency *"respect the law"* is highlighted in two cases in Chapter 3: 3.8 "When Duty and Morality Clash" and 3.9 "Follow the Law or Your Conscience?" Other appendices cross-list competencies and cases in each subsequent chapter. Each competency, of course, is not necessarily reflected in a case in each chapter, but all competencies are covered in some manner by the complete set of cases.

The matrices also make it easy for the reader to identify cases that span one or more competencies. For example, Case 4.9 "Mired in an Ethics Swamp" touches on nine of the fourteen competencies, whereas Case 3.7 "A Purely Private Matter?" deals with only one competency— *"recognize and differentiate between ethical and management issues."*

One-Stop Package for Training, Learning, and Teaching

As mentioned earlier, this book and the CD are a one-stop shopping package that is well suited for classroom use and workshop training sessions. In combination, they offer the reader "total immersion" in both real-world cases and the literature and scholarship on ethics and management in government.[18] The CD features a variety of resources that in combination with the book material provides the reader and instructor a full course menu to choose from to expand one's knowledge of public service ethics and probe the complexities of becoming an ethically competent government manager. End notes and references placed in the chapters identify relevant articles, slide presentations, codes of ethics, and other resource materials that can be easily accessed.

Description of CD Resources

Codes of Ethics

Six codes of ethics are on the CD that the reader can examine and explore to discover similarities and differences among professions and public organizations.

They include codes from the American Society for Public Administration; the International City/County Management Association; the Government Finance Officers Association Standards; the American Institute of Certified Planners; and the County of Hillsborough, Florida.

Workplace Policies

Cities, counties, states, and federal agencies have put in place many policies to encourage proper behavior in the workplace and discourage improper behavior. These include matters like what can and cannot be placed on bulletin boards, Internet use, emailing messages, and acceptable solicitation practices. Specific workplace policies are shown for Hillsborough County in Florida.

Slide Presentations

The CD includes 19 PowerPoint presentation slide shows that focus on ethical behavior in government.

Government Articles and Papers

Articles and papers on the CD cover a range of ethics related and government topics, such as research on ethics, the ethical environment of governments, strengthening and managing ethics in government, and Internet acceptable use policies. Some articles include reprints of prior, peer-reviewed work by the author.

Workshops

Two workshops are described on the CD. One is "Ethical Decision Making" and the other is "Leading with Integrity." Computer presentations for each workshop are included and can be adapted for most training situations. These workshops were conducted in 2008 for seven municipalities, four in northwest Indiana and three in suburban Chicago. Approximately 400 persons participated in these workshops with a mix of front-line workers and management personnel, including fire and police chiefs as well as top ranking city administrators. The logistics and startup instructions for the workshops are detailed (see 3.1 "Workshop Guidelines").

Tests and Scales for Use in Workshops and the Classroom

Two exercises—the Ethics Rating Scale (see 3.7 Rating Scale.doc) and the Local Government Ethics Test (see 3.8 Ethics test.doc)—are used to foster ethics sensitivity and awareness. The Ethics Rating Scale exercise is complemented by the Local Government Ethics Test. This exercise lists eleven short scenarios and asks the respondents to choose a response. The scores are not reported or recorded. Rather, participants are invited to offer comments and questions about the scenarios.

Online Ethics Resources

Links to universities, governments, and international associations that promote ethical governance are provided. One article (4.36 "International Ethics Organizations") describes a dozen organizations that are engaged in combating corruption and/or unethical governance.

Instructor's Guide

This guide examines the strategies and approaches used to teach ethics with cases in the classroom and online.

Syllabi for Online and In-Class Instruction

The CD contains a collection of syllabi for online and classroom teaching of ethics courses in public administration. Two syllabi are especially designed to illustrate how the cases and controversies in this book can be incorporated in a graduate level public administration ethics course.

Endnotes

1. J. Heichelbech, Email correspondence, September 19, 2008.
2. See H. Whitton, "Developing the Ethical Competency of Public Officials: A Capacity-Building Approach." In R.W. Cox III. Ed. Ethics and Integrity in Public Administration. Armonk NY: M. E. Sharpe, 2009, 236–256 for an excellent discussion of ethical competency.
3. icma.org/main/bc.asp?bcid = 120&hsid = 11&ssid1 = 2495 (accessed December 27, 2008).
4. J.S. Bowman, J.P. West, E.M. Berman, and M. Van Wart, *The Professional Edge: Competencies in Public Service* (Armonk, NY: M.E. Sharpe, 2004).
5. CD 6.1 "American Society for Public Administration Code of Ethics" is here.
6. www.cdc.gov/hrmo/ksahowto.htm (accessed December 10, 2008).
7. K. Ashworth, *Caught Between the Dog and the Fireplug or How to Survive Public Service* (Washington, D.C.: Georgetown University Press, 2001), 162.
8. Case 3.7 "A Purely Private Matter" and Case 4.2 "What Should a City Manager Do when an Employee Behaves Badly toward a Neighbor?" challenge the reader to sort through management issues that might look like ethics issues.
9. See also CD 5.2 "Hillsborough County, Florida, Solicitation Policy."
10. *National Government Ethics Survey* (Arlington, VA: Ethics Resource Center, 2008), 32–33.
11. J.H. Svara, *The Ethics Primer for Public Administrators in Government and Nonprofit Organizations* (Sudbury, MA: Jones and Bartlett Publishers, 2007).

12. D.P. Witmer, "Developing a Behavioral Model for Ethical Decision Making in Organizations: Conceptual and Empirical Research," in *Ethics in Public Management*, ed. H.G. Frederickson and R.K. Ghere (Armonk, NY: M.E. Sharpe, 2005), 49–69.

13. T.L. Cooper, *The Responsible Administrator*, 5th ed. (San Francisco: Jossey-Bass, 2006), 29.

14. K. Harling and J. Akridge, "Using the Case Method of Teaching," *Agribusiness* 4: 1 (1998): 1–14.

15. Ibid., p. 2.

16. CD 7.13 "Public Service Ethics and Professionalism" is a slide presentation that focuses on public service values.

17. CD 6.6 "Code of Personal Responsibility, Executive Office of the Governor of Florida" illustrate the limitations of law.

18. CD 4.34 "Research on Ethics" is a comprehensive discussion of the research literature.

PRACTICING ETHICS—MANY FACES

Chapter 3

Professionalism and Ethics

> If you're walking down the right path and you're willing to keep walking, eventually you'll make progress.

President Barack Obama

Medicine, clergy, and law are the classic professions. Contemporary practitioners—doctors, ministers, lawyers—must complete lengthy education and training programs to acquire the knowledge and expertise to enter into a life-long practice. With knowledge not possessed by an ordinary person, the professional also has the ability to inflict harm on others, although that is certainly not the intention. This is where ethics becomes an inseparable part of being a professional. The admonishment "do no harm" requires one to be competent (knowledgeable and skillful) and aware of his ethical responsibilities to his client. Stated differently, it is not sufficient to claim to be a professional based entirely on possessing expertise. One must also possess ethical principles to guide the application of expertise.

The twentieth century witnessed the phenomenal growth of occupations that laid claim to being professional. Accountants, financial specialists, pharmacists, nurses, engineers, teachers, military officers, planners, architects, pilots, physical therapists, librarians, and social workers have claimed the mantle of professional. Those working in occupational trades such as plumbing, hair styling, electrical wiring, computer programming, and a host of other specialized occupations (baseball, basketball, football, hockey) have also claimed professional status.

Public administrators as well have laid claim to expertise and ethics in carrying out their duties. Among the oldest established administrative professions is city management. In the United States and Canada, the advent of the council-manager plan at the beginning of the twentieth century gave rise to the search for persons who could manage a city. By 1914, more than thirty local governments had joined together to form the International City Managers Association. A decade later the association adopted the first public service code of ethics for local government administrators. Today, public administrators possess expertise in many specialized fields, such as budgeting and finance, personnel and human resources, information technology, computer engineering, management systems, public works, police, and fire services. Each specialty has a professional education requirement and an association that provides its members with ethical guidance.

The cases and controversies in Chapter 3 suggest just how challenging it is to be an ethical public administrator even though a code of ethics defines the practice. The concluding case (3.10 "Withholding Information: When Is it Ethical or Unethical?"), for example, involves a candidate for a highly sought after city manager job who decided to withhold information that might embarrass the city. As the case unfolds, the candidate is put through a difficult public vetting that nearly costs him the job. In yet another case (3.9 "Follow the Law or Your Conscience?"), a county clerk confronts the choice of following the law or her conscience in dealing with same sex marriages. Finding an ethical balance in this case is no easy task, and some would say that there is no balance. Other cases raise issues of trust, loyalty, conflict of interests, and serving the public interest.

The cases in Chapter 3 are cross-listed in a matrix with the ethical competencies in Appendix 1. The matrix cells enable the reader to identify specific cases with specific competencies. For example, the competency "respect the law" is highlighted in two cases—3.8 "When Duty and Morality Clash" and 3.9 "Follow the Law or Your Conscience?"

3.1 Public Managers as Private Consultants

Controversies: 4.10, 5.2, 6.19
Key Words: consultant, expertise, county, business
Case Complexity → Low
CD: 4.11 I Didn't Do Anything Unethical . . .
CD: 6.3 Government Finance Officers' Code of Ethics

Assume you are a county administrator whose annual salary is more than $160,000 and you have come up through the ranks having served the county for 15 years as head of the Data Processing Department. Assume also that as head of data processing you acquired considerable computer and information management expertise which other local governments in your region would like to tap.

Discussion Questions

1. Would you make your expertise available pro bono to other local governments?
2. Would you work with and through professional associations to help local governments in the region?
3. Would you form a consulting firm with your wife to market your expertise? If you did, would this be a conflict of interest? Why or why not?

Case Assessment

Posted on the ETHTALK listserv by ASPA member Tom Babcock:

> I am not sure it matters if the public employee is high ranking or in the trenches doing the day-to-day work that is the backbone of all public organizations. The only difference is one of visibility; and level of visibility should not guide ethical considerations. I would pose the question in a slightly different manner. Is it ethical for a public employee to market the job knowledge and skills he has acquired while on a public payroll? If the answer is yes, then by extension, we must all be chattel of the first public agency for which we work. For certainly, unless I am brain dead when hired, I have learned something at each place I have worked. Like many progressive public employers, my current one even encourages me to go to school, workshops, and seminars, and pays for all or part of these. I don't know how I would leave that gained knowledge behind if I were to move on to another position or another government (or private) organization. The human brain is not like a computer hard drive that can be selectively purged of information. Unfortunately, it also cannot be zipped for more compact storage and efficient retrieval.
>
> Many of us move from agency to agency, state to local government, local to national government, and each of us is a value-added knowledge product which should become more valuable over time. Is it unethical to market this skill and knowledge base to another agency? And if that is not unethical, then why does marketing ourselves to the business world via revolving door employment make it somehow unethical?

Mark Monson, Deputy Director for Administration, Department of Health Professions, State of Virginia:

> To me, the crux of the matter lies in the difference between what is allowable versus what is moral. Here I'm using as the definition of

moral the sense of noble, defined by *Webster's* as "moral eminence and freedom from anything petty, mean, or dubious in conduct or character." Under the laws of Illinois, providing consulting services to other local governments appears to be allowable, in the sense of something that can be done. There is no indication in the article that there are formal, legal restrictions against doing so.

However, there's an old adage that just because a person can do a thing doesn't mean that he or she should do a thing. In this case, providing consulting services for a fee in an area in which I am already employed does not meet the noble test —in my mind it is clearly "dubious in conduct or character." My selection would, therefore, be both to pro bono where I can and through professional associations where appropriate.

My choice to place public service first is simply a reflection of my personal priorities. If we want our profession to be considered as noble as we say it is, it is incumbent upon us to act accordingly.

Posted on the ETHTALK listserv by Thad Juszczak, Director, Global Public Sector Grant Thornton LLP:

The issue here is appearances. There is an ethical problem for the consultant, his wife, and the agency. The consultant should not have bid on any contract at his wife's agency. His wife should have notified the agency that a company of which she was an officer was bidding on an agency contract. To preclude any appearance of impropriety, the agency should not award the contract to anyone whose spouse is in the management of the agency or whose spouse is an officer of the corporation winning the contract. Appearances are just as real as facts.

Author's Note: This scenario is based on a real case in which the county administrator of DuPage County, Illinois, and his wife formed a computer consulting firm in 1994 and did more than $100,000 in government business. When asked about whether or not this was a conflict of interest, the county administrator replied "no." His consulting firm has never done work for DuPage County which would certainly be a conflict of interest. Rather, his consulting work was done with other local governments and done on his own time—vacation days, nights, and weekends. On the legal side, this case was deemed to not be a violation of Illinois ethics laws. The consultant conducted the training. Case based on a story reported in the *Chicago Tribune*, 12/29/99, p. D1

3.2 When the Findings Don't Jive!

Controversies: 3.19, 6.19
Key Words: county agency, study, contract, truthfulness, transparency
Case Complexity → Low
CD: 4.42 Violating Public Trust
CD: 6.1 American Society for Public Administration Code of Ethics

Assume you are the director of the county's foster care agency and are a strong advocate for preventive services such as counseling and parenting skill education as an alternative to the placement of neglected children in foster homes. Believing that a reputable study of the cost-effectiveness of preventive services would bolster your position, your agency enters into a contract with a university school of social work to conduct a series of evaluation studies. The first study involves a controlled experimental evaluation of county sponsored preventive services. To your dismay, the findings show no evidence that preventive service is a cost effective alternative to placing children in foster care homes. Before making the findings public, the researchers provide an interim report to you for your comments.

Discussion Questions

Dismayed with the findings, what should you do?

1. Consider canceling the contract with the researchers?
2. Prepare a public relations strategy to counter the effects of the study's results when released?
3. Have the training office prepare a list of deficiencies in the researchers' study?
4. Is this situation merely a matter of honest differences of policy opinion or is it a matter of policy ethics?
5. From the standpoint of promoting the public interest, what would you do?

Case Assessment

Bonnie Beth Greenball, Associate Director, Institute for Public Policy and Leadership, University of South Florida Sarasota-Manatee:

> Faced with findings from a university's school of social work, which did not meet my expectations, I would take several steps before making the findings public. First, I would use this as an opportunity to take stock of the preventive services the agency and others like it provide, spend

time with those who conducted the research, and work to understand what might be done to improve the preventive care we provide. The university's evaluations would likely be helpful for the agency to use in streamlining and refining its mission and strategies.

Once I had thoroughly reviewed the findings and determined whether they could be helpful to me in improving the agency's functioning, I would be in a good position to determine whether the findings themselves were indeed valid. If based on my education and experience, following my thorough analysis of the findings, I did not feel that they were legitimate, I would dig deeper (presuming I had already done basic due diligence research before contracting with the team) into the backgrounds of the research team members to ensure that no one in the team had a personal conflict of interest or bias that would potentially result in invalid findings. If I discover any such problem with the researchers or the institution, I would cancel the contract.

If, however, I determine that the findings are legitimate, I would begin to put in place certain changes to reposition the agency to better meet the needs of its client base. Once I felt confident that I had adequately addressed the weaknesses in the preventive care strategy that may have resulted in the research team's findings, I would release them to the public in a carefully crafted press release. Although I would hold fast to my belief of the significance of preventive care and would advise that the agency continue to advocate for a preventive care strategy, I would emphasize that the agency plans to utilize these findings to improve its standard of care. I may even choose to hold a press conference to place the findings in context and to explain to the public how the agency intends to respond to them. Throughout the press conference and in any statements made to the public or the press, I would emphasize that the most important function of the agency is to serve the best interests of the children, and that we will utilize all of our resources, including these findings, to achieve that aim.

Thomas Walkington, DPA, Strategic Management Coordinator, Research, Planning, and Development, Business Intelligence Program, Hennepin County, Minnesota:

I would stay the course. Since this is the "first" in a series of evaluation studies, I would move forward with the agreed upon contract. I would also do a review of the study that includes key stakeholders of the organization and pose a series of questions related to the results of the study: What are the current practices? How are they interpreted? What was the unit of analysis for the study? In other words, I would want to understand the methodology of the study. Was it appropriate to this situation? If so, and the findings are valid, what are the gaps identified in the study relative to the practices in place? What can be done differently?

Note that this is the first in a series of studies and that the results of this study will be considered in light of findings in future studies, at which time appropriate action will be taken to address the findings of the study in total.

3.3 Hi-Tech Entrepreneurialism at Its Best or Worst?

Controversies: 3.11, 4.15, 6.12
Key Words: urban planners, county, conflict of interest, consultant
Case Complexity → Low
CD: 6.2 International City/County Management Association Code of Ethics
CD: 6.4 American Institute of Certified Planners Code of Ethics

Jan and Bill are ambitious, energetic urban planners employed by a county planning agency in a growing metropolitan region. Their work on several city comprehensive plans brings them much praise, including several positive stories published in the local newspaper. One day Jan says to Bill, "Why don't we try to make some money as planning consultants? We can advertise ourselves on the World Wide Web with a web site. The costs would be minimal, and as long as we don't contract with clients doing business with our agency, there shouldn't be any ethical or legal issues to contend with."

Bill gives Jan's suggestion a few days of thought, and a week later they have a web site in place. On the web page, Jan and Bill are presented as J&B Associates, Urban Planners. Services that their firm can provide include, among other things, market analysis, community planning, business site selection, and geographic information systems.

Although the web page does not identify Bill and Jan's current employer by name, it does note that they have local government experience as planners I and II. Moreover, the page contains their firm's e-mail address and telephone number.

Two weeks later Bill, while working on county time, receives a telephone call inquiring about his services as a consultant. You overhear the call.

Discussion Questions

1. What should you do?
2. Should you report the matter to your supervisor?

3. Should you approach Bill and Jan and inform them that they are dangerously close to being unethical?
4. Should you accuse them of being unethical?

Case Assessment

Lauren Palmer, Assistant City Manager, City of Manhattan, Kansas:

> Many local governments have policies that require employees to seek supervisory approval before obtaining outside employment. Nearly all restrict or limit the use of organization resources (phone, computer, employee time, etc.) for personal matters. Because I overheard Bill's phone call, I would approach him and politely suggest that if he has not already talked with his supervisor, he may want to make him or her aware of the new business endeavor. I would also be clear that failing to both disclose the situation to management and limit his personal phone calls puts me in an awkward position of having to be the tattle-tale. Bill and Jan should be given an opportunity to correct any policy violations before the matter is reported up the chain of command. However, as a public servant, my obligation is first to the public. If Bill refuses to voluntarily comply with policy, I would report my observations to a supervisor.
>
> A more challenging situation is one in which no policy violation has been committed. The scenario does not indicate that the county has any policies or ordinances that would specifically prohibit Bill and Jan's activities as described. An ethical dilemma is created when no clear policy or legal answer is present. Ethics guide us in life's gray areas. Ethics are highly personal and are influenced by a variety of factors including faith, family, and life experiences. Based on my personal code, I feel that Bill and Jan are acting unethically. Even if they are careful not to contract with county clients or use county resources, the appearance of impropriety still exists. Visitors to their web site may presume that Bill and Jan are operating their private business at taxpayer expense. This appearance alone would dissuade me from engaging in a similar private endeavor, but my personal ethical code does not govern the actions of others.
>
> In any event, I would discuss the matter with Bill as a colleague, rather than as an enforcer: "Bill, have you thought about any ethical issues in your new consulting business with Jan? I'm curious to know how you're balancing your public and private workloads." Before talking with Bill, I would consult the American Planning Association (APA) for advice. Many professional organizations have ethics codes to guide the conduct of their members. Seeking input from peers in the profession gives me credibility in discussing the situation with Bill. Sometimes the greatest outcome in an ethical dilemma can be

the dialogue toward finding a solution. Even if Bill, Jan, and I never see eye-to-eye, if I confront them, it may encourage them to take extra precautions in how they run their business.

Sean Stegall, Assistant City Manager, City of Elgin, Illinois:

My comments assume that I am a peer to the planners and not in a supervisory position.

My initial move would be to speak privately to both parties to let them know that I was aware of the recent establishment of J&B enterprises. I would begin by congratulating them on being in a position to undertake such an endeavor and then query them on how they came to the determination that their enterprise was not going to negatively impact the county. Essentially, I would seek to discover whom they sought for advice (i.e. county legal department, American Planning Association, supervisor, etc.). This dialogue will force them to reexamine the steps they took (or didn't take) in arriving at their decision.

During the course of our conversation I would also offer my opinion on the matter. It is important to note that I would refrain from stating my opinion at the open of our conversation and I would try to avoid having it appear that I am judging their actions as being unethical. I would convey to them that even if their actions are technically legal, consistent with the American Planner's Association's ethical guidelines, and have been approved by their supervisor, they should remain concerned about the appearance of such an arrangement. Furthermore, it is inevitable that they will be sending a "mixed message" to their potential clients who may find it nearly impossible to distinguish their private and public roles. It is also probable that some clients may seek to take advantage of the situation by hiring them for non-county projects when their true intent is to gain ownership and influence over them when it comes to other projects which may require county approval.

3.4 Zeroing-Out a Grant

Controversies: 3.11, 3.19, 6.19
Key Words: state grant, contracting, misuse of money, public interest
Case Complexity → Low
CD: 4.42 Violating Public Trust
CD: 6.3 Government Finance Officers Code of Ethics

Your agency has received a state grant. At the end of the fiscal year you face a decision whether to return unspent portions of the grant to a state that is in dire need, to spend the money on nonessentials, or to encourage employees doing valuable work on other projects to list their unfunded work under the budget for this grant, thereby zeroing-out the grant. You know that if all of the money is not spent, next year's grant will be reduced by a substantial amount. What should you do?

Discussion Questions

1. Is this an ethical matter?
2. A management matter? Both? Neither?

Case Assessment

Joanne Gram, Charitable Trust Analyst, Michigan Department of Attorney General:

> An ethical manager will resist overstepping programmatic and financial boundaries to maintain future funding levels. The situation presented is particularly common in the first year of program funding. Initial proposals often lack a historical perspective to fully anticipate outcomes. A program manager imagining ways to cover noncompliance with grant requirements has an ethical dilemma. Justification based on perceived good purposes is a serious step toward breaking down the integrity of the grant process. That breakdown will result in a diminished ability to measure performance, inaccurate reporting, and potentially depriving other worthy programs of state funds. An ethical program manager contemplating unspent funds will honestly seek assistance from the grant administrator.
>
> Grant administrators are specifically charged with ethical, auditable behavior. They have experience assisting program managers who must sort through acceptable and unacceptable methods to zero-out grants. For example, near the end of a fiscal year a manager may be able to project certain deliverables needed in the coming year. The grant administrator may allow ordering those items from current funds for the future use. In some cases, the grant administrator may determine funds must be returned to the state. Even if funds are returned, future proposals will gain a historical basis for committing future resources. By working with the grant administrator, a program manager supports programmatic and financial grant elements in an open and ethical manner. Thus, the integrity of the process and the manager will be preserved.

Gilbert Machin, Operations Manager, Housing Choice Voucher Program, Hillsborough County, Florida:

> Unused funds are often an indicator of agency capacity. Many agencies in their grant applications promise the world and only delivery an island. Unfunded work products associated with the funded service should always be presented to the funding source (the state in this case) for consideration and generally are approved. Agencies may consider necessary purchases for the upcoming year and purchase products in bulk, providing they have the necessary storage space. This action will free up funds from the next year's budget, even if it is reduced, and will enable the agency to purchase needed items at this year's discounted bulk rate. However, purchasing non-essentials from public funds just for the purpose of retaining current funding levels in the upcoming year should not be practiced, unless and only if prior approval is received from the state. Failing to participate in assisting the state in dire need can only reap near-term benefits and could affect your ability to be considered when additional funds become available for distribution to responsible service agencies.

3.5 When Is a Deal a Deal?

Controversies: 3.11
Key Words: contract, promise, verbal agreement, legal, city manager
Case Complexity → Moderate
CD: 3.8 Ethics Test and 3.81 Ethics Test Answers
CD: 6.2 International City/County Management Association Code of Ethics

You are the city manager of a suburban community of 20,000 residents and have been the manager for ten years. You receive a salary of $109,000 but believe you can do better in a larger (38,000 residents) neighboring community whose city manager with a salary of $117,000 has just retired. You apply for the job and receive an offer of $125,000. You verbally agree to take the job. In the meantime, your current employer decides to counter-offer, promising to increase your salary to $156,000 over the next three years. Although you have agreed to accept the larger city's offer, no contract has been approved or signed.

Discussion Questions

1. Should you back out of the offer and accept the counter-offer?
2. Would you violate your profession's ethics if you renege on the verbal agreement?
3. What is the right thing to do?

Case Assessment

Henry Marcy, (former) Deputy Commissioner for Administration and Finance of the Division of Employment and Training, State of Massachusetts:

> Yes, there is a deal, but there are a number of issues at play here. Is the verbal acceptance of the offer a contract? I believe that the verbal acceptance does constitute a contract. However, my argument is not from a legal perspective; it's from the ethical context. In other words, the manager who has verbally accepted the neighboring community's offer has entered into an ethical contract or relationship. One can argue that the neighboring community's hiring manager should follow up the verbal offer with an offer letter and require the manager's signature on the offer letter. (Indeed, this letter may be in the mail.) Yet, the notion of a formal offer letter following a verbal offer suggests that the neighboring community can renege on the verbal offer. Would the manager feel that the verbal offer, in that case, was not a contract? No. At the least, the manager would consider the verbal offer to be an ethical contract and expect the neighboring community to honor that ethical contract.
>
> Furthermore, if either the manager or the neighboring community reneges on the ethical contract, that manager or that community government may become open to ridicule, damage to reputation, censure, etc., both in the short term and, potentially, in the long term. The city manager world, at least in Massachusetts, is a very small world. Everyone knows everyone else. The damage could be considerable, even resulting in the manager or the community government being characterized as unemployable or unworthy as an employer, respectively, by the Municipal Management Association (as it is called in Massachusetts).
>
> If the manager in this case seriously considers reneging on the verbal offer, he or she should first, outside of the strictly ethical context, carefully analyze the two offers. It is easy to jump to the conclusion that the promised stay-where-you-are increase to $156,000 in three years is more money than the offer of $125,000. Yet, that may not be the case. At the very least, I would want to know what the $125,000 had the potential of

becoming in three years. More to the point is the question of whether the difference in the money is worth the risk of alienating others (especially the neighboring community). Even more critical, despite the emphasis on money as the decision-making factor, is the careful assessment of all the factors (e.g., the ability to continue to contribute meaningfully to the current community versus the ability to contribute meaningfully in the neighboring community, the particular challenges in the respective communities, the opportunity to learn new things from new people versus continuing to develop staff in the current community, etc.) that ought to go into a change in employment decision.

Finally, if the manager reneges on his acceptance of the offer, is he required (ethically) to recompense the employer for damages incurred by the employer? Such damages might include the cost of communications (letters, e-mails, etc.) sent by the neighboring community employer to the other (unsuccessful) candidates telling them that the position has been filled, the cost of a new hiring process if one should be necessary, the cost of the additional time lost (prior to the filling of the position) that might transpire, etc. I believe that he should offer to do so.

William Horne, City Manager, Clearwater, Florida:

> I could not in good conscious back away from a verbal commitment I made to the larger neighboring community. I intentionally explored a city manager position that paid me more money than my current salary and was fortunate to get an offer from a nearby community. Although the counter-offer is considerably higher than what the larger city offered me, I feel an obligation to act consistent with my original intentions. My word is my bond. The right thing for me to do is take the $125,000 offer and move to the neighboring community. I would violate the spirit and intent of my profession's code of ethics if I reject the larger city's offer.

3.6 Politics and Professionalism

Controversies: 3.14, 4.10, 5.15, 6.11
Key Words: city manager, politics, elected office, conflict of interest
Case Complexity → Moderate
CD: 4.13 Ethical Environment of Local Government Managers
CD: 4.33 Public Administration History
CD: 4.15 Why Council-Manager Governments Fail

You are an assistant to a city manager in a small, no-growth suburban community. You live approximately twenty miles from the community in which you work and have been involved politically in your home city for about five years. Your home city has a population of 15,000 and is growing rapidly. Several years ago while serving as the treasurer of your home city, the city council refused to take action on your request to hire a full-time finance officer, instead ceding responsibility to the city manager and department heads for financial responsibility. Moreover, the council refused to take action on new investment strategies intended to make the most of short term excess cash flows and responsibly reinvest them for a small yield. When the council ultimately hired a finance director, they hired someone who had never held a responsible position in a finance department in either the public or private sector.

You were told by the council that if you felt you could do a better job making decisions for the future of the community you should run for city council. Hmmm! This was a difficult decision because you recognized that you would have to resign from your professional city management association. This you did by not renewing your membership and sending a letter to this effect to the association. You were elected in November and are currently serving a four year term on city council. You are also continuing your day job as assistant to the city manager in the neighboring community.

You were elected during a sweeping change in the council. Only one of three members was reelected, and many citizens you spoke with cited the need for change and responsibility in public institutions as the reason for ousting incumbents on council. Essentially, you ran to protect the integrity of your home community and the city management profession that, in your estimation, was being tarnished by irresponsible actions.

Discussion Questions

1. Do you feel that administrative public service and political public service are mutually exclusive as your professional city management association feels? (You know for a certainty—three lawyers reviewed the circumstance of your roles prior to running—that you have not violated any laws.)
2. Is there a conflict of interest?

Case Assessment

Barbara Van Cott Fidler, Budget/ADA Office, City of Dunedin, Florida:

> In my opinion administrative public service and political public service are mutually exclusive. The mission of the political public servant is to

set policy based on input from the community, business, and higher levels of government. The mission of the administrative public servant is to find the solution that will benefit the community as a whole. This is done through research and analysis. The administrative public servant hires staff members who have the education and experience to provide the expertise needed to implement the policy set by the political public servant.

The case study reveals a conflict of interest for the individual. The person in question is employed by one city as a staff person (assistant to the city manager) and holds an elective office in his or her community twenty miles away. One would feel divided loyalties to each community. Decisions made as city commissioner in one community may impact the other community. One example would be a business considering relocation to the rapidly growing community from the home community. Another example is competition for grant funding, state aid, or the availability of limited resources. To be a volunteer on a board or committee for one's community is one thing, to be on the governing board of that community is another. Sharing best practices from one community to another would be beneficial. Being a politician in one community and a public servant in another would be harmful to both communities.

Earl Mackey, (former) Executive Director of the National Conference of State Legislatures and Executive Director of the Kentucky Legislative Ethics Commission:

It seems to me that the first issue that arises is one of full disclosure in both sectors of your professional activities. You are employed full time as an assistant city manager in city one. You owe your employer full disclosure of your professional activities in city two. This will allow your employer to decide if your professional activities in city two are incompatible with your responsibilities. The same public disclosure should have been made to voters in your election campaign. This becomes even more important in that the two communities are in close proximity to each other. An employer that hires a full time employee should have the opportunity to decide if other paid employment is consistent with the position. This is the case regardless of legal opinions related to conflict of interests. Full disclosure serves the best interests of all parties concerned. In dealing with ethical issues, it is often wise to go beyond narrow legal definitions of conflicts and to consider whether an appearance of conflict will be raised by particular activities.

3.7 A Purely Private Matter?

Controversies: 5.17, 6.18
Key Words: county, finance, extortion, hearsay
Case Complexity → Moderate
CD: 4.37 Public Service, Ethics, Democracy

As county finance director, you are contacted by a bank official who is also a social acquaintance. The banker indicates that he is calling "off the record" to ask about Fred, one of your assistant directors whose work you regard as exemplary. Your friend's concern is about an elderly depositor who has written more than 150 checks of over $1,000 each to Fred's wife—totaling over $500,000—within a four-year period. He further relates to you that in contacting this customer, the banker could only ascertain that this gentleman (in his 90s) lives next door to Fred—the conversation was otherwise confused and incoherent. Concerned about your privacy obligations to your employee, you reveal little to your friend other than that Fred is an assistant director in your agency.

After much thought, you decide to tell Fred about the banker's inquiry. In response, Fred explains how his wife has "cared for" this neighbor (who has no living relatives) by accompanying him to numerous physician appointments, ordering him clothes from catalogs, and hiring someone to paint his house. Growing increasingly indignant, Fred emphasizes the neighbor's frequent desires to "do something special" for him and his wife. Finally, Fred explodes, "You may be my boss, but this discussion is completely off-base. How we deal with our neighbors is a purely private matter. This is an invasion of my privacy!" He then walks out.

Discussion Questions

1. Did you err in discussing the matter with Fred in the first place?
2. Is this a "purely private matter" outside your purview?
3. If "no" to either, how do you proceed from here?

Case Assessment

Mark Woodard, Assistant County Administrator and Chief of Staff, Pinellas County, Florida:

> Divining the difference between an employee's activities within and outside of the workplace can be a challenge for many managers. In the final analysis, managers should focus on an employee's adherence

to the rules and policies of the organization and job performance. To do otherwise can create confusion, ill-will, and ultimately impact the morale and productivity of the employee and possibly the entire workgroup.

In this case, the employee's (Fred) performance is exemplary, but information provided by a third party (the banker) called into question the activities of Fred's spouse as it relates to the finances of an elderly neighbor. The potential ethical cloud created by this activity outside of the workplace leads the manager to discuss the matter with Fred.

The manager erred in discussing this matter with Fred as the information provided by the banker fell outside of the scope of the subordinate's employment. The banker is the party with the fiduciary responsibility to protect his customer, the elderly neighbor, not the manager. The ethical obligation falls with him. Further, the banker may have breached his responsibility to maintain the confidentiality of his client by sharing this information with the manager.

Certainly, the manager has an obligation to contact the banker and suggest that the appropriate local or state agency (Department of Elder Affairs) be contacted. He should have taken this position during his initial conversation with the banker. The banker previously reported that the neighbor was "confused and incoherent"; therefore, it is important to determine his competency. This determination is best made by the state, which may appoint a guardian to ensure that the elderly neighbor's best interests are represented. The manager should also bring closure to this issue with Fred by apologizing for raising his outside activities in the workplace.

Mark Monson, Deputy Director for Administration, Department of Health Professions, State of Virginia:

> I think the county finance director was way off base talking to Fred about the phone call from the banker. The fact that Fred is an exemplary employee should, at the least, give him the benefit of the doubt. There is absolutely no reason to think that there is any illegal activity, certainly none that involves his work. The banker has every right to be concerned, but he has his own avenues of investigation. The suspicion on the part of the banker amounts to nothing more than anecdotal information. For all we know, Fred and his wife could have been investing the money on behalf of the old man in conjunction with other family members. The boss jumped to a conclusion based on nothing more than hearsay from someone who is only a social acquaintance. Unless the boss has some direct evidence of his own to indicate that what Fred and his wife are doing adversely impacts his job—and the fact that

his performance is exemplary indicates that it isn't—Fred's boss should have stayed out of it.

3.8 When Duty and Morality Clash

Controversies: 4.12, 5.13
Key Words: duty, morality, law
Case Complexity → Moderate
CD: 6.1 American Society for Public Administration Code of Ethics

Can you ever imagine a moment when you might quit your job because you object to a direct order from your supervisor to lower a flag in honor of a fallen leader? It does happen, although not frequently.

Imagine that you are the head of the county's convention and visitors bureau (CVB). You have worked your way up through the ranks to become the head of the CVB after a distinguished twenty-nine year county career and have a strong sense of ownership in the bureau. You have been largely responsible for building it into a successful agency. As it happens, an aging former, now retired but long serving chairman of the Board of County Commissioners dies (let's call him Mr. Smith). The current chair orders the building supervisors of all county facilities to lower the county flag to half-mast out of respect for the passing of the chairman. You object! Why? The former chair in your opinion was a model of "negativity, hate, and prejudice"—a racist. You do not believe it would be appropriate to honor Mr. Smith by lowering the flag.

Your boss disagrees and you receive a string of e-mail messages informing you that you could either lower the flag or retire effective immediately. You are fifty-one years old and earn $65,235.

Discussion Questions

1. Do you lower the flag?
2. Do you plead with your boss to be allowed to keep your job?
3. Do you resign?

Assessment

Martin Black, (former) City Manager, Venice, Florida:

> You've prided yourself on a strong sense of what is morally right and ethically appropriate; honoring someone whose actions carry community

conflict-laden values like hate and prejudice would turn back the clock. You've put in your time so take a firm stance, but do it professionally. Let your boss know that you've got deeper concerns about honoring a past official whose actions and core values may reignite community dissension and isn't the type of display you believe the county should encourage nor one that would be supported by important members of a community that is broadly diverse and engaged. Most importantly let the chair know privately that this is a core value issue for you and that you have concerns for the community's reaction and perspective.

Since there's no clear violation of local, state, or federal law involved in refusing to lower the flag, and given that the chair has provided you with a written ultimatum in a series of progressively stronger e-mails, it's time for you to "walk the talk." First, make it clear why you refuse to lower the flag, document your reasons, and provide the opportunity for a graceful retreat by the current chair. Make sure that the chair understands that you are prepared to sever the relationship you invested your career in and they must likewise be prepared for the wrongful termination case. Prepare your exit memorandum announcing your decision to the chair and the remainder of the board to submit a forced resignation subject to the terms of a severance agreement that allows you to retain your integrity and core values. Know that, in any event, you won't recover nor trust the judgment of the chair going forward, so it's better to leave the CVB position, keeping true to your twenty-nine years of integrity in service to the community. You've gained the experience that will allow you to find another opportunity, you'll sleep better at night, and your actions might become a catalyst to reinforce change for the right reasons.

Melvin J. Dubnick, Professor and Director, Public Administration, University of New Hampshire:

Perhaps the most difficult cases of ethical dilemmas seem trivial to those who view it from the outside, and some might see this as a "no-brainer"—why put your career and economic well-being at risk over a matter that seems so inconsequential in the larger scheme of things. But there are instances when personal feelings and beliefs exercise a powerful influence over our reactions and choices, and in this case the CVB head (let's call her Ms. Jones) has very strong feelings about the deceased Mr. Smith.

There are all sorts of factors to consider here, including whether the negative view Jones has of Smith is widely shared and whether Smith's behavior in recent years had been more positive. (On the national political scene, we have examples of major figures such as George Wallace and Strom Thurman who advocated segregationist policies earlier in their careers but who changed their public stands by the 1980s.)

Jones has to make an economic calculation about how to deal with the situation, but let's assume she puts financial and career considerations aside. What seems to be driving her is a sense of indignation about efforts to honor Smith, but it would be foolhardy for Jones to ignore other emotions such as the value one assigns to being a responsible employee and the professional obligation of a public servant to implement the will of elective officials. Like it or not, there is a nonfinancial cost in terms of one's reputation to pay for taking the kind of stand Jones is considering. She really has to consider what reputational price she is willing to pay for her actions.

There might be ways to shape the situation in a way that can somewhat ameliorate the dilemma. Jones might suggest that lowering the flag to half-staff in all county facilities should be reserved as an honor for those who gave their lives in the line of duty, and that Smith's service be memorialized in a more limited way—for example, perhaps a picture of the deceased can be placed in the lobby of the county courthouse, surrounded by black crepe for a week or so. In presenting this option, Jones can mention to the county supervisor that this is a politically wise option given the memories and issues that might arise if too much is made of Smith's role in county government. This approach can still work even if, as the case narrative suggests, Jones has already made her strong opinions known and received the harsh e-mail response. A meeting with the county board chair can be arranged in which Jones admits that her reaction was driven by some very strong feelings about Smith's record, and that while she regrets being so confrontational about the order, she is probably not alone in her opinions and feelings about Smith. The conversation can lead to a suggestion that it would be in the board chair's (political) interest to reconsider the flag order and instead think more in terms of the "lobby" option.

Indignation is a powerful and useful force in public service ethics—but there are times when one has to take a more considered approach before letting one's emotions put a career (and reputation) at risk.

Stuart C. Gilman, Deputy Director, Stolen Asset Recovery Initiative and Senior Advisor, Governance, Security and Rule of Law Section, United Nations Office on Drugs and Crime:

This case revisits the classic issue of exit, voice, or loyalty. Unfortunately, this is more common for civil servants than one would think. I believe the answer to this question has to be weighed in a series of steps. First, the head of the CVB should validate his opinion of Mr. Smith with colleagues or members of the community. Is this an isolated position or is it widely held in the community? After all, lowering the flag, which is usually governed by rules, is to honor a person's public service. If this is primarily her opinion, she needs to weigh whether this is a moral position, or a personal position. Taking this example, would we still agree if she decided that because Smith supported abortion, violating her beliefs, would she have the same right? I am not suggesting that even if she is alone in her beliefs that she not act, but rather that she has an opportunity to hear how others perceive this issue.

Second, if this is a shared ethical perception, the question is, "Was the approach to the commissioner clear and open?" It appears that all communications are via e-mail, which is a notorious means for creating misunderstandings. Has she talked to the commissioner? If not, she should try to engage to explain her strong ethical objection to respecting Mr. Smith (although it sounds like the atmosphere is fairly poisoned at this point). It should be noted that in addition to the personal ethical issue, the head of the CVB has a professional obligation to explain the impact of such an honor on visitors coming into the community. It is important to note both an ethical and professional issue in such a display.

In a real case that I am familiar with, the civil servant printed the order for the (equivalent) supervisor's signature. He told his supervisor that he would be ill tomorrow and his deputy could be given it tomorrow. Instead of being fired, he was thanked by the supervisor (once he cooled down) because he realized how important the issue was to his subordinate. Sometimes there is good news!

Exhausting these two steps, she is confronted now with exit, voice, or loyalty.

She can just raise the flag. Nonetheless, we don't know what her personal situation is. For example, she could be a single mother with three children, one a special needs child. One of the children could be in college and she could have a sick mother. I am not being cute. At 51 she could be confronted with a multitude of challenges—that's why there are usually protections for civil servants. It is rare to have a supervisor capable of ordering someone to retire. Obviously, if there is no appeal possible or protections in place, she can try to get a peer of the commissioner to intercede. Negotiation can often lead to a reasonable compromise.

Give voice: She can call in the media, explain her objection and the threats that have been made against her. She can use any civil service rules available to her and seriously consider getting legal advice should this result in an administrative action against her for insubordination.

She can retire, either quietly or with voice. I would argue retiring quietly, without voice, means that the head of CVB was not as serious about the issue as she thought. If this is only personal, she is not taking into account her responsibility to the citizens in the community. Retirement with voice is the only ethical position if this is her choice.

Voice can take many forms, including organizing an open forum on racism, a news conference, or a public letter to the commissioner's superior. Someone with this many years of public service will be taken seriously.

Author's Note: This case is based on a real case that occurred in July 2008 when L.F. Eason III, the head of the North Carolina Standards Laboratory (a unit of the state Department of Agriculture), ordered his staff to not lower the flag in honor of the passing of former U.S. Senator Jesse Helms. Mr. Eason "told his staff that he did not think it was appropriate to honor Helms because of his 'doctrine of negativity, hate, and prejudice' and his opposition to civil rights bills and the federal Martin Luther King, Jr., holiday." Mr. Eason chose to retire. Would you have done the same thing? Why or why not?

The *News & Observer*, July 9, 2008. http://www.newsobserver.com/politics/politicians/helms/story/1135443.html (accessed August 12, 2008)

3.9 Follow the Law or Your Conscience?

Controversies: 3.12, 3.20
Key Words: civil servants, law, same sex marriage, California, religion
Case Complexity → High
CD: 4.31 Citizen-Client-Customer
CD: 6.2 International City/County Management Association Code of Ethics

Suppose you are a county clerk who works in an office that has responsibility for processing same sex marriage licenses in California. (The California Supreme Court ruled that the state's law barring gays from marriage was unconstitutional.) You feel strongly from a religious perspective that same sex marriages are immoral. Do you have an obligation as a civil servant to issue the licenses? Or, does this violate your conscience to the point that you refuse to do it?

Discussion Questions

1. Do civil servants have the right based on religion to pass judgment on the "correctness" of the law?
2. Should clerks who refuse to issue licenses to gays lose their jobs?
3. If you were the head of the county clerk's office and employees tell you they don't want to follow the law, what would you do?

Commentary

Karl Thoennes III, Judicial Circuit Administrator, Unified Judicial System, State of South Dakota:

> The same sex ceremony issue is just the latest variation of a public service situation that's been around for years. I don't see why it's any different, really, than prison employees in death penalty states who oppose capital punishment. They're generally not compelled to participate in executions. Court employees and even some judges have sometimes objected to handling abortion bypass cases (those petitions where minors are seeking the court's permission to skip parental notification), although I know accommodation has varied around the country in those situations. My previous position with the courts in Minnesota included performing civil wedding ceremonies. I had a similar struggle with wedding requests where the couples wanted to include "Wiccan" practices. Luckily there were lots of other civil ceremony officiates around, so my declining to perform those few ceremonies really made no practical difference to the public. Similarly, death penalty states simply assign other prison employees to executions. Likewise, the military allows conscientious objectors to choose alternative forms of service. I'm pretty sure there will be no shortage of religious and civil officials in California willing to perform those ceremonies, so I don't see why we shouldn't make some accommodation for religious or moral objections on this issue, when it makes little or no practical difference in the delivery of public services.
>
> I know, there's the old slippery slope issue, do we let public servants pick and choose their duties and tasks based on subjective religious claims, etc. If they have moral or religious objections to some of the job tasks, then they shouldn't have taken the job or the oath office in the first place, etc. On the other hand, no public employee that I know of is required to perform every single duty he is necessarily authorized to perform. We routinely divide labor to some degree in even the smallest rural local governments. I also wonder if those who are so deeply offended and shocked at public employees who want to decline performing same sex ceremonies also think all prison staff should be compelled to participate

in executions or conscientious military objectors should be compelled into combat because, after all, it's a public duty under the law.

Finally, if we do want to draw hard lines about public duty, imagine how recruitment bulletins for public jobs would read if we really wanted to be frank with applicants. "Ardent Catholics, pro-lifers, Baptists, Christian fundamentalists, pacifists, and all others who oppose [abortion, capital punishment, dispensing abortion-triggering medication, same sex marriage, choose your hot button issue depending on the job...] and who cannot set aside their most deeply held moral or religious beliefs for the sake of a public job need not apply."

Posted on the ETHTALK listserv (anonymous)

I'm extremely religious, and I'm a public servant. My obligation is to my faith first, then to the public ... Therefore, George Washington's prayer for the U.S.A. is a predominant display in my office (you can't help but see it even before you enter). The more subtle Ecclesiastes is also a dominant "decoration." I've had this discussion with colleagues before because a majority opposes these ... outward displays. If there is something that directly interferes with my obligation to my faith and my service to the public, then I really do need to have someone else do it, or just don't and offer options.

I would have to side on religion in this case, if the carrying out of the public duty destroys a person's ability to reconcile what they do with what they are. We can never predict what rules, laws, or court cases will come about in a person's work history. So, the assumption is that the clerks were working under one set of predicated understanding of their duties. When that changed, I think they should have the ability to bow out. There are ... local governments that refuse to provide a day off on MLK. Call it racist, call it religion, call it rebellion. It's their prerogative. Thus ... my inclination is to trust the civil servants. Provide that prerogative. You may be surprised how many (after some time) are able to reconcile and get the job done anyway. Further, we are talking about the "ends," not the means. If, at the end of the day, the duty gets accomplished, then let it go (regardless of who does and does not do it).

And, we don't necessarily "back" anybody (despite the first statement I made in the last paragraph), we back the ability of government to still carry out its duty.

John Petter, ASPA member and Doctor of Public Administration, Springfield, Illinois:

It's amusing to me that the surface issues change (Jim Crow laws, abortion, capital punishment, interracial marriage, morning after pill, ...)

but the fundamental challenge for all individual public administrators to balance differing ideas of what is appropriate behavior remains.

The ASPA Code of Ethics rightly reflects varying principles of what is ethical (e.g., public, personal, legal), providing material for some excellent classroom discussions. But it doesn't fully recognize these ideas of responsibility sometimes give opposing guidance, nor does it provide much direction in how to balance those ideas when they conflict.

Conflicting types of responsibility cannot be resolved easily or universally. A public servant in the Third Reich may be forgiven for not foreseeing the unthinkable, yet he or she must be held responsible even though acting as a good law-abiding and subordinate public servant. I have elsewhere suggested eight types of responsibility: moral, professional, hierarchical, leadership, fiscal, legal, consumer, and public. Teaching differing types of responsibility without also teaching they sometimes conflict should be considered public administration malpractice.

The practical result is that we must make exceptions when there are conflicts; for example, allowing for matters of conscience (moral responsibility) despite an organization's bureaucratic routine (hierarchical responsibility), allowing for meeting clinical needs (professional responsibility) despite budget limitations (fiscal responsibility), allowing for providing service to a needy individual (consumer responsibility) who doesn't quite meet the statute's requirements (legal responsibility).

At the same time, we must not overemphasize any of them; for example, allowing for service provision to needy individuals with disregard for any statutory requirements, allowing for building large clinical systems without recognition of the financial costs involved, allowing for lightly-held "feelings" to overrule departmental policies.

To always emphasize the need to follow bureaucratic routines or case/statutory law to avoid the feared chaos that may result, or to always emphasize the need for moral or professional morality to avoid the neutering of personality and religion, are illogical and unreasonable. It would also prevent the discussion that is necessary to help each of us public servants perform our duties and to evaluate the performance of others, when called to do so.

Michael Vocino, Professor, University of Rhode Island:

In California it is now illegal to deny gay Americans their civil rights, including marriage rights. Because a person religiously may believe something different than what the courts have decided makes not one wit of difference ... it's still illegal to have more than one wife even if you believe it is a commandment of God, as the fundamentalist Mormons in Texas have discovered … believe what you will but follow the law … not to do so if you are a county clerk in California is illegal and un-American.

If, as a public manager or public servant, that is not possible for you as a believer, then you must choose between what is required of your work as a public manager dedicated to equal rights under the law, or you should find work more in line with your religious beliefs or moral code and happily lead a life that does not interfere with your particular moral code.

Terry L. Cooper, Director, Civic Engagement Initiative, School of Policy, Planning, and Development, University of Southern California:

If one cannot carry out the routine duties of one's office, resignation is clearly required, but public managers who are so rigid as to refuse to address unusual situations that may occur from time to time will have a difficult time functioning effectively in the complexity of American society. I really thought we had gotten beyond the kind of dichotomous thinking I see in some of the comments in this exchange. Ethics has to do with going beyond the law, or carrying out the spirit of the law, or dealing with situations that are not clearly covered by law. From an ethicist's perspective, law is generally viewed as the moral minimum that we can agree to broadly, and sufficiently to impose on all. I believe we must respect and uphold that moral minimum, but the reason ethics emerged as centrally important in the mid-1970s was the growing recognition of the necessary exercise of discretion by public administrators. If our responsibility is only to do what is legally prescribed, then in many instances we will either be unable to act or unable to address the particularity of diverse situations.

3.10 Withholding Information: When Is it Ethical or Unethical?

Controversies: 3.12, 3.13, 4.10, 6.17
Key Words: deception, truthfulness, code of ethics, recruitment, city manager
Case Complexity → High
CD: 4.12 Ethics Management in Cities and Counties
CD: 7.3 Withholding Information (PP)
This case includes ethical reasoning questions.

You are a candidate for a very competitive, high profile city manager job. During the search process conducted by a reputable consulting search firm you are asked, "If we conducted a thorough background check on you, would we find anything in your background which might embarrass a future employer?" You pause for a moment as your mind flashes back to an allegation that was made about you when you were a city manager of a small community. It was alleged by two staff members of the community hospital where your wife was terminally ill that you slapped and verbally abused her. The police investigated the allegation as did the Department of Children and Family Services (DCF). During the investigation you assert that the staff members misinterpreted a situation in which your wife was choking and you were helping her. Your wife states to the investigators that you did not abuse her. Neither the police nor the DCF investigations report that there is any physical evidence (e.g., redness on the face) that you had slapped her. Nonetheless, the investigative report is sent to the state attorney to determine whether or not to press charges. The state attorney declines to pursue the matter due to a lack of evidence. Thus, the allegation is unsubstantiated.

Decision 1: How should you reply to the question asked by the search firm? Should you or should you not disclose the incident?

Let's assume that you reason that the incident was entirely personal and was found to be unsubstantiated. Therefore, you decide to respond, "There is nothing in my background that would embarrass a future employer."

You receive an invitation to interview.

During the interview, you stress your honesty and high ethical standards.

Decision 2: Do you or do you not disclose the incident to the city's HR staff and the city commissioners? Once more you decide to not disclose information about the incident for the same reason you did not disclose it to the search firm.

The interview goes very well. City commissioners are impressed and decide to offer you a $170,000 job contract. The local newspaper reports the story with the headline: "Ethics and Experience Bring Jones to the Fore."

On the day the contract is to be voted on, city commissioners receive information that you were accused of slapping and verbally abusing your wife in the hospital where she was terminally ill. The commission decides to call an emergency meeting to discuss the situation. You are invited to appear before the commission and answer their questions.

Decision 3: Do you accept the commission's invitation?

You decide "yes" as the air needs to be cleared and you need the full trust and confidence of your new bosses. During the questioning, you assert, "I haven't lied. I have not told an untruth." One commissioner asks, "Why didn't you tell us about this allegation?"

Decision 4: What do you say?

1. I forgot.
2. I didn't think anyone would find out.
3. You didn't ask me.

4. It was merely an unsubstantiated allegation as my wife and I had a very loving relationship right up to the moment of her death.
5. Withholding information is acceptable under these very personal circumstances.
6. I thought the allegation, although untrue, would place my candidacy in jeopardy if it became public.

Outcome

The commission decides to postpone approving your contract for two weeks while they seek more background information about you. Meanwhile, you have withdrawn as a city manager finalist for several other positions and are now worried about ending up without any job.

You muse, "Am I being treated fairly by the city commission? The media? I know I haven't done anything wrong. Why am I being subjected to such scrutiny?"

Investigation Results

A three-member committee, which included Commissioner Kent, the director of HR, and a representative of the police department, was formed and traveled to the community where you had served as the city manager for four years.

After visiting the community and meeting with former and current town council members, the town manager who was assistant town manager under you, the president of the Chamber of Commerce, a police sergeant, and the town attorney, the committee reported that "we have no concerns about his honesty or integrity." Commissioner Kent summed up his thoughts to the city commission by stating, "You exercised poor judgment as a candidate who sold himself on honesty, integrity, and character, but that is not a sufficient reason to not offer a contract. Poor judgment is not an unethical act."

The city commission voted 4-1 to approve your $170,000 a year contract. "Congratulations," said Commissioner Ann, "we want you here as soon as possible." Meanwhile, commissioners decide to withhold the final payment to the head hunter until the city attorney determines whether or not they could penalize the firm for not conducting a thorough background investigation.

Discussion Questions

1. Is there a difference between poor judgment and committing an unethical act?
2. How will you go about convincing the one city commissioner who voted against hiring you to change his mind about you?
3. Should you accept a job as city manager without the full support of the governing board? Why or why not?

Ethical Reasoning Questions

1. Is there an ethical issue facing the candidate? Did he display ethical sensitivity in answering the search firm's question: "Is there anything in your background that might embarrass a future employer?"
2. What is the ethical issue?
3. What might be done to resolve the situation?
4. Does the preferred course of action satisfy the needs/preferences of the primary stakeholders?
5. Is the preferred course of action ethical?

Case Assessment

Jim Leidlein, City Manager, Harper Woods, Michigan:

> He should have disclosed this to the recruiter. He should have been prepared for the question about the background check (a common question used by recruiters and hiring managers … I use it myself). He should have admitted to it when asked and have written documentation showing that the accusation was groundless. He certainly could have downplayed its significance but, nonetheless, has to own up to it.
>
> In our business, it is essential to be up front. Most importantly, it is the morally and ethically correct thing to do. As well, he should have been aware that somebody likely would have dug it up, which they did. Police unions and fire unions are notorious for doing their own background checks on new or prospective city managers by calling their counterparts in the city that the manager is coming from. It has happened to me. (Fortunately, they did not find anything!) And, of course, there is our new friend Google.
>
> Recruiters and, I hope, city councils understand that city managers are exposed to public scrutiny and accusations made are not always as they appear. He could have used this as part of his approach.
>
> Several years ago, a council member of mine, who was not a supporter, spread wild and vicious rumors about me all over town. It involved a drunk driving accident in which I was supposedly driving after leaving a topless bar at two in the morning with one of the dancers in the back seat. Absolutely, totally false … How he came up with this is beyond me as absolutely none of it ever happened. I handled it and, fortunately, it never made the local paper. But, it could have, and I would feel obligated to admit the publicity to future potential employers or recruiters.

Ed Daley, City Manager, Hopewell, Virginia and former President, International City-County Management Association:

> This is an easy one from my perspective. The applicant has an obligation to reveal and explain the accusations before they hear about it from someone else—and they will hear about it from someone else. But think about where he would be if it came out later or from another source—we always say that ethics and integrity separate us from the politicians!
>
> An applicant should always "over disclose" when there is any doubt. This is clearly a failure and "I didn't think it mattered" doesn't cut the mustard. If the applicant had been hired and then the governing body learned of this, there would always be a question of what else is the manager hiding. The only thing worse would be if the news media reported it as a surprise to the governing body.

Mary Jane Kuffner Hirt, Professor of Political Science, Indiana University of Pennsylvania:

> I would ask the search firm how they were going to handle the information I had shared. If the search firm discloses the information, and an interview is scheduled, there should be some expectation that the incident and its resolution were accepted by the governing body. If the search firm does not disclose the information, then I think the candidate should be ready to provide the information ... Here, the key is what the search firm does with the information. Ultimately, the governing body will be responsible for answering questions should the person be hired.

Rebecca Keeler, J.D. and ASPA Member:

> In my view, particularly given the high profile of the position, this history should have been disclosed at the interview. The incident was one that had potential for a criminal charge and actually triggered an investigation—facts that render it relevant in my mind. Disclosure would go far to build trust and reveal the applicant's integrity. And, it would defuse later malicious revelations—thereby protecting the public's trust in the official and his office. For the reasons just stated, I would refer to guideline no. 4 in Patrick Dobel's book *Public Integrity* (1999, 184), "Keep the circle of scrutiny to the lowest possible number." The interview or meetings with individual members of the city commission would provide an opportunity for controlled disclosure—which

might have mitigated the impact of the news from an outside source just before voting on the contract.

The second step in the hiring process (the interview) raises the question about withholding the information in the initial inquiry if it really was relevant (as I just argued). This is a classic dilemma in the job search context and is important to discuss. In discussing this kind of dilemma while training local government employees, trainees/employees often came to the conclusion that the interview is the more appropriate forum for the revelation because it is more protective of the individual's privacy. Though there was a strong contingent that would likely consider the information totally private, so not subject to disclosure at all. But, my trainees were most often front-line supervisors, not executives. They generally agreed that the relevancy standards change depending on the position sought.

Author's Note: This is a hypothetical case based on a real case reported in the *Sarasota Herald-Tribune* June 2, 5, 13 & 19, 2007.

Controversies

3.11 Deception: The Good, the Bad, and the Ugly

Cases: 3.3, 3.4., 3.5, 4.9, 5.4, 5.9, 5.10, 6.2

When is deception good? When is it bad? In sports and war we expect deception—at least within certain bounds. In these arenas, we applaud deceptive acts that succeed. In private life we also engage in considerable deception—most of which is probably not so good. Consider infidelity. The deception that takes place when one spouse cheats on the other is endless until that moment when it all comes crashing down.

Perhaps the most interesting story about deception reported in a long time is a fellow, an engineer, who would search the Internet for hotels near where he was traveling for business. Once he found one to his liking, he would search for a prominent business nearby. Here's the hook—once he identified a nearby business he called the hotel and asked if they had a special rate for that company. He invariably got the discounted rate. The hotel clerk rarely asked him to provide evidence that he was a legitimate employee of the nearby business.

Discussion Questions

1. Did our engineer friend do something illegal?
2. Did he do something unethical?
3. Was he simply being clever and entrepreneurial? After all, don't hotels gouge businessmen every day by charging high rates?

Commentary by Author

Deception is a tricky business and can have hurtful consequences. Do you imagine that one who engages in deception like that reported here is an honest person nonetheless? Or, is this behavior likely to be indicative of how our engineer friend goes about the rest of his professional and personal life?

Do you remember the opening ceremony at the 2008 Beijing Olympics when an adorable nine year old child, Lin Miaoke, in a beautiful red dress sang "Ode to the Motherland?" It was a breathtaking event to watch. Alas, it was not what it appeared to be. The voice heard by the viewers actually belongs to another little girl, Yang Peiyi, whose singing talent was eclipsed by the Chinese Communist Party's bosses' overwhelming desire to put in front of a worldwide audience a beautiful little girl. It turns out that Yang Peiyi had imperfect teeth. The deception in this situation was heartbreaking for both children. Of course, everyone was deceived, including the Chinese people. This act of deception, said Cheng Li, a fellow at the Brookings Institution, was hurtful to the Chinese public.

The Chinese debacle is a glaring example of the bad and the ugly when deception is resorted to by governments—local or national.

Author's Note: Information based on *New York Times*, August 10 & 14, 2008.

3.12 Truth Telling: What Is It?

Cases: 3.9, 3.10, 5.5, 5.9, 6.3

Most of us subscribe to the view that telling the truth is better than not telling the truth about a situation. But are there occasions or circumstances under which we can tell the truth but withhold information? Take, for instance, the resume. Job seeking candidates often view a resume as a "best foot" forward document emphasizing one's personality, experience, and educational achievements. Conventional wisdom has it that a resume can be "fluffed." Right? Wrong?

Discussion Questions

1. Is it okay to omit certain job related information if you feel it is not relevant for the position you are applying for?
2. Suppose you are applying for a top management position in a municipality. Would it be okay to omit information about a previous management position you held with a private sector firm, especially if you had a falling out with the CEO?
3. Or, suppose you are a college professor who teaches graduate courses in public administration and who supplements her salary with a respectable income from consulting with public agencies. And, suppose you are seeking employment with another college—should you withhold information about your consulting work? Is this relevant?
4. Is the practice of "selective disclosure" truth telling?

Commentary by Author

Resume inflation or fluffing can be a tricky, if not hazardous, exercise. Consider the case of the interim city manager of Eagle Pass, Texas, population 22,413, a border community located 131 miles west of San Antonio.

The interim city manager for six months very much wanted the permanent job. In an impassioned address to city council he extolled his accomplishments as interim city manager and dismissed critics who charged that he had lied repeatedly on his impressive resume. Council members praised his speech and set a special meeting when it would consider hiring him for the $85,000 a year job.

Elated, he looked forward to the hiring decision. Alas, it was not to be. His claim that he had worked as an assistant city manager in a nearby community and as an aide to a former U.S. Congressman turned out to be false. So too did his claim that he had earned three degrees from a major state university. His "degrees" were from an online diploma mill that sells degrees based on "work/life experience."

When the hiring decision moment arrived, the council ended its 45 minute closed door session by announcing to a standing room only crowd that they had voted unanimously to fire him. The worse was yet to come for the interim city manager—he was arrested by the county sheriff on charges of fraudulently seeking a government job. He was released on a $5,000 bail and if convicted of a misdemeanor charge could get six months jail time and a $2,000 fine.

Author's Note: Story based on a real case. Sources: http://www.mysanantonio.com (accessed January 16, 2008) & http://www.swtexaslive.com/node/5925 (accessed January 30, 2008)

3.13 Honesty and Ethical Standards

Cases: 3.10, 5.1

The *USA Today*/Gallup Poll (2007) on honesty and ethical standards of people in different occupations found that nurses, grade school teachers, pharmacists, military officers, medical doctors, clergy, policemen, and judges are considered the most honest by the American public. At the bottom of the "I am honest" pile are lobbyists, car salesmen, advertising practitioners, and slightly higher up, business executives.

Public officeholders don't do too well either. Local officeholders and lawyers are ranked above business executives while state officeholders and congressmen are ranked lower yet.

Discussion Questions

1. Do rankings of honesty by occupation or government office have positive or negative consequences?
2. Why are local government officials perceived as more honest than state officials or members of Congress?
3. Why do most people view their Congressional representative as "honest" and "trustworthy" but believe that the U.S. Congress is not?

Commentary by Author

While elected public officials are typically viewed as having lower ethical standards than those in professional fields, there is no shortage of people who want to become elected to a government position—local, state, or federal. Thus it would seem that the status accorded to government by the public has little consequence. At the same time, the public's trust and confidence in government's ability to solve pressing public problems is deemed important.

The Katrina debacle has left many people with the feeling that no matter how well intentioned public officials might be in helping people in crisis situations, there is too much political sleaze in the system to make government reliable and dependable when catastrophic events occur. Do you agree or disagree?

Information drawn from http://www.gallup.com/poll/103123/Lobbyists-Debut-Bottom-Honesty-Ethics-List.aspx (accessed November 30, 2008).

3.14 Politics and Managerial Ethics

Cases: 3.6, 4.3

There has been a long-standing belief that public managers, especially those protected by civil service laws and ordinances, should not engage in political activities nor voice their views on important public policy issues of the day. Professional public managers, so the conventional wisdom goes, cannot and should not entangle themselves in electioneering or other sundry political and public policy matters that are expected of ordinary citizens. The Hatch Act of 1939, for example, although now liberalized, placed severe restrictions on the political voice and activities of federal employees.

At the local level, the political activities of city managers has long been a source of some confusion and contention. The International City/County Management Association Code of Ethics states that members should "refrain from all political activities which undermine public confidence in professional administrators." Above all, the ICMA code admonishes managers to not participate in the election of members of their employing legislative body and shall not run for elected office. Managers running for office while holding appointed administrative positions? Yes, it happens. One manager defended his recent decision to run for political office while simultaneously serving as an assistant city manager by claiming that it was not a violation of the code because he was not running for the city council in the city he served.

The ICMA Executive Board has revised the guidelines for political activity by declaring that "members shall not participate in political activities to support the candidacy of individuals running for any city, county, special district, school, state or federal offices. Specifically, they shall not endorse candidates, make financial contributions, sign or circulate petitions, or participate in fund-raising activities for individuals seeking or holding elected office." The ICMA revisions, however, encourage members to exercise their "right and responsibility to vote and to voice their opinion on public issues."

Information drawn from *Cincinnati Star*, ICMA Daily Newspaper, September 18, 2000.

Discussion Questions

1. What does it mean "to voice their opinion on public issues"?
2. Suppose a citizens' movement is launched to change the structure of a local government from a council-manager form to a strong mayor form. Should the city or county administrator voice her opinion?

3. If so, in what manner and forum?
4. Letter to the editor?
5. Speaking before citizen groups?

Commentary by Author

Voicing one's opinion on public issues as a sitting city or county manager can be fraught with difficulties. Are not high ranking administrators in local governments thought to be politically neutral? What if one voices his opinion and loses? Is not voicing one's opinion mixing professional expertise with politics? Administrators who voice their opinion are likely to find themselves in a political minefield, either partisan or nonpartisan.

3.15 Wanted—Loyalists with Professional Credentials

Cases: 4.5, 4.8, 5.4, 6.9

There has been much commentary about the changing nature of professionals in the public service with the demise of the "neutrally competent" administrator and the rise of the "responsively competent" professional. From city hall to the state house to the White House, elected public officials want qualified professionals managing the business of government, but they also want politically, if not ideologically, loyal professionals.

This demand is finding new expressions in some cities and counties. In Cook County, Illinois, for example, County Board President John Stroger put it rather plainly: "I think that present day government leaders are looking for people who are professionally qualified to do the job, but they also want some of the old time loyalty." Cook County may be on the cutting edge of this movement as 100 of 115 members of President Stroger's 8th Ward Regular Democratic Organization have appeared on county, city, or state payrolls in the past five years. Family members have also found their way on to the public payroll. President Stroger's niece, who holds a master's degree in business, was appointed to a $101,662 post as the Deputy Director of Finance in the Cook County Finance Department. She was the only applicant for the job.

When asked about why so many political and family members were appointed to well paying public jobs, President Stroger asserted that it is because they are qualified. "If I brought anybody in and they didn't have the qualifications ... I would be cheating myself as the president of the County Board and the constituents."

President Stroger contends since he became president in 1994 that he has stream-lined Cook County government and made it run more like a business.

Discussion Questions

1. Is it possible to mix old time loyalty and expertise? Or is this just "pie in the sky" wishful thinking?
2. Is there such a thing as a "responsively competent" professional?

Commentary by Author

The hallmark of professionalism in government has been and remains to a very large extent expertise unfettered by politics. Public administration as a profession has its origins in the separation of politics and administration. Are we indeed experiencing a reversal of this history? It would certainly seem so in many respects. How much of a reversal? It is difficult to say with a high degree of confidence, but the unending appointments of politically responsive but professionally incompetent officials in the George W. Bush Administration does not auger well for the future of national governance. One only has to recall the name of Michael Brown, FEMA director during the Katrina disaster of 2005, to appreciate the limitations of loyalty.

Information drawn from the *Chicago Tribune*, October 3, 1999.

3.16 Taking a Bonus

Cases: 4.1

You have been working for the city for twenty-four years and have been the city manager for the past eighteen years. The city has experienced substantial population growth over the past twenty-five years, growing from just under 19,000 in 1980 to nearly 57,000 in 2007. The current median age is 44.7 years and median household income is $38,632. Your performance as a city manager is highly regarded by the city council and the community.

Your current salary is $116,646. You have put $3,200 in next year's budget for a 2.5-percentage increase in your salary, the same percentage as other city employees will receive.

Alas, the economy is sagging with growing pressure to cut taxes.

Discussion Questions

1. Should you accept the pay raise?
2. If you decide you should not accept the raise as a recurring expenditure, should you accept a bonus equal to the raise of $3,200? Why or why not?
3. Is there a significant difference between accepting a salary increase that is recurring and a bonus?

Information drawn from a real case see http://www.news-journalonline .com/NewsJournalOnline/News/Neighbors/South/evlNS01080308.htm

Commentary by Author

In difficult financial times, organizational leaders often view a recurring expenditure as a serious problem. Thus, accepting a bonus can be a feasible alternative. In this case, the city manager explained that "right now, the re-occurring cost is something I am trying to avoid. Until we get this economy sort of calmed down, I'm not trying to put more money in the budget." Consequently, he told city council not to give him the money that was earmarked for his raise. In last year's budget, he did accept a one-time payment instead of an increase to his annual salary. He didn't say to council this time around whether he would or would not accept a bonus. What do you think he will do?

3.17 Sticks and Stones …

Cases: 4.4

Do you recall the childhood saying that "sticks and stones may break my bones, but words will never hurt me"? Surely you do. It is often used as a defense against unwanted name calling and taunting. But words, of course, can be hurtful. Consider Ken Livingstone, the former Mayor of London, who uttered a few words in February 2005 that landed him a thirty-day suspension from office. Mayor Livingstone, in response to sharp questioning by *The Evening Standard* reporter, asked him what he did before he worked for the newspaper. "Were you a German war criminal?" the reporter, whose name is Oliver Finegold, replied, "No, I'm Jewish. I wasn't a German war criminal." The Mayor retorted, "Well you might be, but actually you are just like a concentration camp guard. You're just doing it 'cause you're paid to, aren't you?"

Three days later, the Board of Deputies of British Jews filed a complaint with the Standards Board of England setting in motion an investigation of whether the mayor had breached the code of conduct of the Greater London Authority. The Standards Board was formally established in 2001 by the Local Government Act of 2000. The Standards Board's main task is to ensure that standards of ethical conduct are maintained across local government authorities and to deal with complaints of misconduct against individual members.

After a year-long investigation that cost British taxpayers more than $83,000, the findings were handed over to the independent, nonelected Adjudication Panel for England that ruled the mayor had broken the Local Government Code of Conduct. The chairman of the panel said that the mayor "does seem to have failed, from the outset of this case, to have appreciated that his conduct was unacceptable, was a breach of the code and did damage to the reputation of his office" (*New York Times*, February 25, 2006). The mayor's four-week suspension was to begin on March 1, 2006, but was postponed pending an appeal for judicial review of the panel's decision. The High Court of Justice heard the appeal and overturned the suspension.

Discussion Questions

1. Are "words" sufficient to call into question an elected official's ethics?
2. Should a nonelected body have the authority to remove an elected official who has not committed a crime but may have behaved in a manner that "brought disrepute to his or her office"?
3. Are the ethics of local elected officials in Great Britain different than their counterparts in the United States?

Commentary

LaKeshia Wood, ASPA member and University of Baltimore student:

> Are the ethics of local elected officials in Great Britain different than their counterparts in the United States? My answer is no indeed.
>
> I am a graduate student studying for my master's degree in public administration, and I have been hearing story lines constantly on certain elected officials who have disregarded the concept of ethical behavior by portraying rude and disrespectful behavior against groups of people, and yes, these people get hurt. Recently certain minorities have come to the media and expressed this hurt.
>
> My concern is how can an elected official be of the public interest acting as a public servant and act so unethical. It should not be tolerated at all, and I am elated to see that the local government in London took measures immediately on the misconduct of the mayor, unlike some U.S. jurisdictions where officials are repeatedly acting unethically.

Information drawn from http://news.bbc.co.uk/1/hi/england/london/
5410872.stm (accessed November 30, 2008).

3.18 Where Corruption Lives

Cases: 4.9

Illinois has been accused of being among the most corrupt states in the country. Responding to the "pay to play" scandal unleashed by the investigation into Governor Rod R. Blagojevich's attempt to sell the appointment of Barack Obama's Senate seat, Chicago FBI Chief Robert Grant said, "If it isn't the most corrupt state in the United States, it's certainly one hell of a competitor." Six Illinois governors have been charged with crimes during their administration or afterwards, with three—Democrat Otto Kerner, Jr. (1961–1968), Democrat Daniel Walker (1973–1977), and Republican George Ryan (1999–2003)—serving prison time. In the case of George Ryan, a web of corruption was spun in the 1990s when public officials from the bottom to the top in the Secretary of State's (SOS) office mixed money, politics, and the issuance of drivers licenses to wannabe truck drivers. And, on the dark side, nine persons lost their lives in accidents with truckers holding illegally issued drivers licenses. The laundry list of the fifty-one persons indicted and forty-four convictions was shocking.

Since 1972, seventy-nine elected officials have been convicted of wrongdoing, earning the state the nickname of "the land of greased palms." Among the seventy-nine are fifteen state legislators, two congressmen, one mayor, twenty-seven aldermen, nineteen Cook County judges, and seven other Cook County officials. Then there is the case of Secretary of State Paul Powell (1965–1970) who was an undefeated politician for forty-two years. Three months after his death in 1970 while still in office, it was discovered that he left an estate worth more than $2 million—$800,000 of it in bills packed in shoe boxes in the closet of his hotel suite in Springfield.

Not everyone agrees that Illinois is the "land of greased palms." The Illinois City/County Management Association released this statement: "The problem with such broad statements is that it creates the impression that public officials at all levels of government throughout the state are using their positions for personal gain. In response to the corruption, greed, and graft that plagued U.S. government in the early 1900s, reformers developed the council-manager structure of government and professional local government management. Thanks to these reforms, today, there are literally hundreds of cities, counties, and villages across

Illinois that have hired professional managers who are committed to ethical, transparent, and responsive local government."

Discussion Questions

1. Are elected officials more corrupt than appointed public officials? Why or why not?
2. Should we hold appointed administrators, such as city managers, to a higher standard of behavior than elected officials? Why or why not?
3. How does corrupt behavior resemble or differ from unethical behavior?

Commentary by Author

Broad brushing elected officials or high-ranking appointed officials in Illinois or elsewhere as corrupt is a sad reality and undermines the good work done day in and day out by many dedicated city, county, and state employees. The Illinois City/County Management Association concludes its letter with this statement: "Not every elected and appointed official in the State of Illinois is corrupt. Many are quietly striving day by day to improve the lives of the millions of citizens of Illinois and to serve the people of our state with honesty and integrity." It is so.

http://www.msnbc.msn.com/id/28141995/
Source: Chicago Tribune, May 22, 2002
    www.enewspf.com/index.php?option=com_content&task=view&id=5421
&Itemid=88889651&ed=118 (accessed January 12, 2009).

3.19 Falsifying Documents for the Greater Good?

Cases: 3.2, 3.4, 5.4, 5.6

Ethics is such a personal predicament. Sometimes, the theories, the situations, the "I would NEVER do that," may not really be real compared to life. One might believe that violating "ethics" for the greater good may not be a violation at all, except for the person violating it. One's theories on ethics may not be the correct ones at all. The cultural diversity of it does not make it cut and dry. Every situation violates some person's ethics, so, whose do we choose? And at what point do we as administrators determine that our ethics are above that of another employee's? There are obvious ones that, generally speaking, we say never to do—knowingly falsifying documents, for one.

Discussion Questions

1. Is knowingly falsifying documents for the greater good an abstract, throw away argument? Or, is it real?
2. Is it possible to imagine a situation in which doing that particular thing would be more ethical than not doing it? Is it possible that falsifying a document could lead to a greater good?
3. Do you think it is ever ethical to falsify a document?

Commentary by Anonymous

I was working for the Department of Defense in the contracting department in a Middle Eastern country. Over $250,000 worth of equipment ordered by U.S. Air Force agencies was held up in customs on the other side of the country port. The politics of the time were such that the United States did not want to rock the boat.

As contracting officer, I thought I'd figure out how to get the equipment released. One requirement had to do with a release document from a high United States official that was notarized. The document was time sensitive. One of the finance offices fell through on their end, and to there was a delay by one day. Of course, the document would now be null and void, and guess what? The official was no longer available.

I had no authority to do this, but I called the legal office on the West end and told him to redo the whole document, whatever you have to do and change that date for the next day. He asked me a bunch of questions; he was an attorney after all. So, I instructed him on how to cut, paste, and copy, and redo the official seal. In essence, we falsified the document.

I felt I had no choice. This process of negotiations to even get to the point of getting the equipment out of customs was over several months. Lining up and coordinating all of these agencies took a very long time, and I wasn't about to blow it on a stupid piece of legally required document.

You may ask all the what-ifs. But there are only two of us who know that the document was falsified—myself and the attorney. I received an award for my work in getting the equipment released. I did not pay for those goods, the taxpayers of the United States did. And if it were my money, I'd have done the same. If I had not been able to secure the release of the equipment, it was going to go into the Middle Eastern country's local market. They were not going to return it to the vendor.

3.20 Resolving Right versus Right Dilemmas

Cases: 3.9, 41, 4.3, 6.10

An ethical dilemma is typically cast as a "right" versus "wrong" situation. Yet there are occasions, perhaps more than we realize, when the choice is choosing one "right" over another "right." These situations can be equally troubling. Consider the choice that Lt. Col. Oliver North had to make about "telling the truth" about the Iran-Contra arms-for-sale deal in the 1980s. In his mind, if he told the truth, lives would be lost in Nicaragua because the Contra rebels would be unable to defend themselves. He decided that the right thing to do was to protect lives rather than to tell the truth.

Although perhaps less dramatic, local government officials can find themselves in a "right" versus "right" dilemma. Consider the case of the city manager in a community of 25,000 residents. To save money and avoid layoffs, the council unanimously voted to cross-train police officers to serve as fire fighters to supplement the fire department. Alas, the fire fighters union adamantly opposed the measure and with support of the state fire fighter's union filed recall petitions against four of the seven council members with the promise to "get the other three" when they come up for reelection. The union also vowed to support candidates who would get rid of the city manager.

The city manager felt strongly that these measures, if successful, would cripple the city economically and force laying off police officers at a time the city was experiencing a significant increase in crime. He believed he had a commitment to promote the public interest and began to consider his options:

1. He could do nothing and thereby maintain his commitment to political neutrality—a right thing to do.
2. He could quietly support and assist the council members who are the target of the recall initiative because he believes that the public interest would be better served if they stayed in office—another right thing to do.
3. He could speak out about the issues and thereby educate the public about the merits of balancing public safety needs with fiscal realities.
4. He could resign and speak his mind.

Discussion Questions

1. What should he do?
2. How should he sort through this dilemma? Should he invoke a principle, make a decision based on a virtue, treat the matter as a duty?
3. Should he seek the counsel of his best friend? Spouse? Professional code of ethics?

Commentary by Author

Once the city manager crosses the line to support, covertly or overtly, council members targeted for a recall he has moved into the political arena with eyes wide open. There will be no turning back. His future is now in the hands of opponents and proponents of the recall. If he ends up on the winning side, his reputation as a professional is in jeopardy in his community as well as in other communities where he might become a candidate for another city management job. If he ends up on the loosing side, his career as a city manager may be permanently ended. This is a "lose-lose" proposition from the manager's perspective. Perhaps the best thing to do is to stay politically neutral. Does this mean that he has compromised himself by not promoting the public interest? Possibly, but given the vagaries of what constitutes the public interest and the unknowns of the future, does he have any other choice?

Chapter 4

Encouraging Ethical Behavior

It takes many good deeds to build a good reputation, and only one bad one to lose it.

Benjamin Franklin

Why do "good" people who want to be ethical sometimes find themselves in an unethical situation? Could it be that they don't know what the bright lines are that define (un)ethical behavior? Perhaps there are no bright lines, or they are fuzzy at best. So, the important question becomes, what can be done to encourage ethical behavior and discourage unethical behavior? These challenging questions are likely to be asked for many years to come. Does this mean that there are no answers? No. It means that our understanding of (un)ethical behavior is incomplete at best and very inadequate at worst. Still, there is no shortage of efforts to encourage behavior that is deemed acceptable and ethical. One significant way for managers to encourage ethical behavior is to serve as a role model. Kenneth Ashworth (2001, 166) advises that while there is some risk in "attracting attention to yourself or appearing stuffy, you should not be reluctant to see yourself as a model of ethical behavior."

The cases and controversies in Chapter 4 illustrate in part why good people can find themselves in an ethical quandary and why many tools and practices (codes, standards, rules, performance evaluations, and just common sense) intended to encourage ethical behavior are not always successful in doing so.

The concluding case in this chapter is an excellent example of how public officials in a progressive county are all too often unaware of the ethical dimensions of an issue until they are mired in an ethics swamp. One could say that they suffered from ethical illiteracy. Another case presents a city manager with the challenge of advocating against a statewide referendum that would cut taxes and necessitate a reduction in city services. Does advocacy go beyond the pale of acceptable professional behavior? Other cases deal with religious expression in the workplace, the behavior of a city employee who finds himself in a nasty quarrel with a neighbor, going along to get along with the boss who wants to put the best face on a difficult situation, a decision by a city manager to accept or reject a pay raise that exceeds the raise of city employees, strengthening the ethics culture of the organization by adding an ethics component to employees' annual evaluations, and the development and implementation of a policy to ban married employees in the sheriff's office from engaging in extramarital affairs. Could the sheriff be accused of trying to manage the morality of employees? Do police officers have a right to privacy in how they conduct their private lives?

The cases in Chapter 4 are cross-listed in a matrix with the ethical competencies in Appendix 2. The matrix cells enable the reader to identify specific cases with specific competencies. For example, the competency *"be aware and informed of relevant professional codes of ethics"* is highlighted in two cases: 4.3 "Information or Advocacy—Is There a Difference?" and 4.9 "Mired in an Ethics Swamp."

4.1 Should You or Shouldn't You Accept a Pay Raise?

Controversies: 3.16, 3.20
Key Words: equity, fairness, city manager
Case Complexity → Low
CD: 4.32 Leading with Integrity

You are the city manager of a bustling, growing city of 128,000 that is ranked 27th in *Money Magazine's* 2006 list of 100 Best Places to Live. In fact, your community is the highest ranked in your state. The crime rate is low, with a city index indicating that your city is the 23rd safest in the United States. The city's credit rating is a healthy AAA, which enables funds for capital projects to be borrowed at the lowest possible interest rate. The city is working towards becoming one of the few cities in the nation to be recognized as a Community Wildlife Habitat by the National Wildlife Federation (NWF).

You have been the city manager for more than ten years and draw a base salary of $197,000. You also receive a $7,000 vehicle allowance and a cell phone with all business calls paid.

City commissioners have very positive views of your leadership, business smarts, and professionalism. In recognition of your performance, the city commission wants to give you a 10-percent raise in your base salary. City employees during the same time period were limited to a maximum of a 7-percent increase.

Discussion Questions

1. Do you take the 10-percent raise?
2. Do you refuse to accept the 10-percent raise, saying that "I appreciate the recommendation, but I am unwilling to accept any more than what our employees can receive."
3. Is there an ethical issue?

Case Assessment

Wally Hill, Deputy County Administrator, Hillsborough County, Florida:

> Under these circumstances, I believe the proper course of action would be to accept no more than a 7-percent salary increase, unless doing so would violate any existing governing board policy or employment contract the city manager may have. That judgment is based both on ethical issues as well as pragmatic management principles.
>
> The city manager's ethical obligations that are relevant to this situation would be to: (1) act in a nondiscriminatory manner in all personnel transactions, emphasizing fairness and equity; (2) provide unbiased and responsive advice to the governing board on policy matters; (3) support and execute all legal policies of the governing board; and (4) honor any personal commitments made to the governing board through an employment contract.
>
> Accepting no more than that offered for other employees supports the ethical obligation to act in a nondiscriminatory manner that emphasizes fairness and equity. It could inject a degree of self-interest bias in recommendations to the governing board on compensation, as the city manager would benefit from the increases recommended for other employees. However, not to advise the governing board on important matters of compensation, in order to avoid that potential bias, would fail to be responsive to their need for professional guidance. Ethical issues number (3) and number (4) cannot be assessed with the given information, as it is not clear whether the proposed increase is based on existing city policies or an employment contract with the city manager.

Apart from ethical concerns, it makes sense from a management perspective for the city manager to decline a salary raise that exceeds that possible for other employees. Doing so would demonstrate the city manager's concern for fairness and equity, show a willingness to be regarded as a team member, and inspire greater loyalty from the other employees. Those perceptions would facilitate cooperative actions to achieve organizational goals and strategies. If the city manager were to accept a greater raise, it could promote an image of the city manager as aloof, insensitive, and self-serving. Who would want to follow the lead of such a person?

Stephen Bonczek, (former) City Manager of Largo, Florida, and Beaumont, Texas:

> The question is a good one that probably doesn't affect too many managers as councils are sensitive to the public's reaction to manager compensation—*It's too high*! I would accept the raise if it had substantial support on council. In times of financial stress where there are budget cutbacks and layoffs, I have accepted no raise while union and other employees did receive wage increases. It was more of a leadership rather than ethical issue.
>
> The manager, as a contractual employee working for a political body that can remove the manager on a whim, is not comparable to what most public employees experience. In general, CEO's compensation and benefits exceed other employees by a substantial amount in order to attract and retain talented individuals dedicated to public service. Most employees understand the challenges of a local government manager and have no desire to work under the difficult conditions every day facing the possibility of being fired for no or any reason.
>
> While you could make this an ethical decision based on the fairness of receiving a larger raise on a larger salary base, I don't see it as a conflict of values or right versus wrong. Accepting the raise is not inherently wrong or right, but a judgment based on many factors. What good will be achieved by accepting only a 7-percent raise? Will this have a dramatic influence on the council's and the public's perception of your integrity? Will your credibility be enhanced by accepting less? Will anyone care or remember a year from now? If everything in the community is good as you describe it, this may be one of the few opportunities to be offered a reward for high performance and the ability to accept it with limited negative reaction.

Steve Thompson, City Manager, Marco Island, Florida:

> Clearly there is good work and success taking place, and although there are no ethical issues involved, the success is success of the team's

effort and this should be reflected in public comments on the issue of compensation. At the same time, the city council is willing to publicly compliment and support the manager, and any comments should recognize the leadership of the council and avoid placing the council in the difficult position of appearing out of touch or being corrected by the manager for their generous support.

Clearly, accepting the 7-percent increase is appropriate and in keeping with the maximum increase for other team members who contributed to the city's success. This also supports the team effort and sends the message that we are truly dependent on each other and "in this together."

So, the remaining question is how to graciously and publicly accept the compliment from the city council, without putting the council in a difficult position with the public. We don't know the financial situation of the manager or the salaries in comparable jurisdictions, but the manager has options:

1. Simply accept the 7-percent increase and meet privately with each member of the council to express thanks before giving a public comment thanking the council for their support, accepting the 7 percent as equal to the highest raise for members of the team and acknowledging the compliment and their leadership. The comment in this instance should reflect that the higher salary rate increase was high praise indeed, and that the manager's hope is that future years will be equally successful.
2. The manager could also deflect the compensation into another path—if retirement is a concern, this could go into an annuity or as a contribution to the manager's retirement plan. The manager often has a different retirement plan than other employees, and this may be an acceptable alternative to an outright salary increase.
3. Or, use this as an opportunity to suggest a multi-year incentive plan—if the manager stays with the organization for three to five years and maintains a good or better evaluation for each year, the manager receives the funding as a salary "bump" recognizing longevity and performance.

Under any conditions the team should be recognized, and the hard work and leadership of the council acknowledged so that future kind words and support are encouraged.

Author's Note: Based on a real case reported in the *Sun-Sentinel,* September 21, 2006.

4.2 What Should a City Manager Do When an Employee Behaves Badly toward a Neighbor?

Controversies: 5.17, 6.12
Key Words: city planner, off-duty behavior, harassment
Case Complexity → Low
CD: 6.2 International City/County Management Association Code of Ethics
CD: 6.4 American Institute of Certified Planners

Gary is your city planner, and he's very good at his job. Recently, though, Gary has been in the local news, not because of his work but because of his off-duty behavior. It seems that Gary is having a conflict with his neighbor over a fence. Last year Gary and Thom had an argument over trimming a tree that sits on their property line. Thom, in reprisal for having lost the argument, erected a six-foot fence between the properties (the maximum allowable in the city). In return, Gary painted the side of his house that faces Thom's property an awful shade of orange. Thom sued Gary for disturbing the peace and Gary countersued for harassment.

Legally Gary did nothing wrong, but his behavior is an embarrassment to the city.

Discussion Questions

1. Is there an ethical issue here?
2. Do you, as city manager, have any responsibility to supervise Gary's off-duty behavior, even when legal, when it has the potential to reflect poorly on the image of the city workforce?
3. What would you do if you were the city manager?

Case Assessment

Brian Bursiek, Assistant to the Village Manager, Schiller Park, Illinois:

> While I don't believe you can be responsible for the behavior of all your employees off duty, I believe you should probably speak to him about his conduct and tactfully suggest to him that it doesn't make him look good to do things like he's done thus far. I would tell him that while you aren't officially reprimanding him or disciplining him, that you hope he will give what you said some thought. If it goes much further you may have grounds to officially warn him. Another possibility is

whether he has an employment contract with provisions in it that may address this type of behavior.

Pat Burke, Economic Development Manager, City of Moline, Illinois:

Gary has brought unwelcome attention to the city although he has done nothing wrong legally. I would ask Gary if he would take the first step to de-escalate the situation. I would suggest that Gary paint his house the original color. Painting the one side of his house orange was done to spite his neighbor. It was a childish decision that reflected poorly on Gary's judgment. Hopefully, the neighbor would reciprocate by dropping the lawsuit. I would not go any further than this. Gary does have a right to a personal life. So far, nothing has affected Gary's job performance. Until I notice a problem with Gary's work that appears to be related to the dispute with his neighbor, I would only offer advice even if unsolicited.

4.3 Information or Advocacy—Is There a Difference?

Controversies: 3.14, 3.20
Key Words: city manager, taxes, revenues, advocacy
Case Complexity → Moderate
CD: 4.16 Cities-Counties Ethics Issues

As the city manager of a small community (population of 4,300) facing the prospects of a $124,000 shortfall in property tax revenues if the voters statewide approve the tax referendum Save Our Homes cap of 3-percent assessment increases, you are distressed about what the impact will be on the quality of life for residents. You know that it will be necessary to cut services severely, which will surely lower the quality of life in Lake Alfred. You muse, "What can I do about this?" "Should I mount an information drive to alert residents of the situation?" "Should I be a public advocate urging voters to vote 'no' on the referendum?"

You consider the following options:

1. Call for a town hall meeting and forcefully present the case against the referendum.
2. Put pro/con information about the referendum in the residents' utility bills.

3. Post flyers around town at such places as city hall and the utilities department drawing attention to the service cuts.
4. Write a letter to the editor of the local newspaper.

Discussion Questions

1. If you decide to write a letter to the editor, what should you say?
   a. Vote "no" on Amendment 10?
   b. Describe the cuts in services that will follow?
2. As an appointed city official, is it your job to advocate against the amendment?
3. What would you do if your city council voted to oppose the amendment? Voted to support the amendment?
4. Do city managers have the duty to voice what they believe is in the best interests of the community even if the council disagrees? Agrees?
5. Is there a bright line between providing information and advocating a policy preference, even if you feel it is the right thing to do?

Case Assessment

Douglas E. Matthews, Director, Public Communications, Clearwater, Florida:

> Ultimately, our role as public managers is to serve the will of the community as articulated through our elected officials. There are many times when our professional judgment and opinion may run contrary to the direction given by the elected body or, as in this case, the state and the voters. It's important to remember that our code of ethics specifically prohibits us from personally engaging in political activity of any kind. With that said, this isn't a case where there is a "bright line" to guide you. Generally, the tipping point between information and advocacy happens the moment that you tell the community to "vote yes" or "vote no." That's the key difference between you and your elected bosses. They are free to advocate as they wish. You are not.
>
> That being said, you have a civic responsibility to share specific information about the impacts of any decisions that may be made. In fact, that's your primary role as manager. The best and most effective thing you can do is share your realistic analysis of the potential impacts and where the requisite cuts are most likely to be made should the amendment pass. Given this information, the community can decide whether those reductions in services are acceptable or not, then vote accordingly. Your best approach is to outline potential service reductions in a public discussion with the elected body before putting any information out to the community. Remember that they were elected to represent the wishes

of the community, and they should be part of the process of setting budget priorities before they are outlined to the paper or any other group.

Your best message is that "passage will have very real impacts locally for a marginal savings on local tax bills, but we will go about making the necessary reductions openly and professionally should the community choose to pass the amendment." Let your elected body take a stronger stand if they choose to, armed with the information you've provided on the potential impacts. But before you put pen to paper, and you write a letter to the paper, be absolutely sure that you have the support of your elected officials in doing so. Otherwise, you run the very real risk of "getting ahead" of your bosses, which has led to the demise of many a public manager.

Pam Brangaccio, (former) County Administrator, Bay County, Florida:

The most important point in this example is the position of the City Council of Lake Alfred, that is, the "majority" political position, on the referendum, that *should* guide the local actions of the city manager. If the city council has stated a public position against the referendum, then by all means, the city manager should put together a communication plan for the media and public, expanding the impact of the reductions on the quality of life in Lake Alfred. This communication plan should also have the approval of the city council and their involvement would also be a welcome part of the plan. The mayor or an individual city commissioner could accompany the manager to the local editorial board, and also write articles to the paper and the citizens. The manager should present the facts, that is, no threats, just the facts on the service reductions in parks, libraries, fire, police, street maintenance, etc., which will greatly impact the residents of the town.

The only stoppage that I would see, in a public information campaign ... we have had legal counsel advise us in the past that we can include "vote" and the facts on information from the city or county, but that we cannot say "vote no" or "vote yes." But, there are cities that have used the "vote yes" or "vote no, so" again, the manager should follow the advice of the local city attorney on the wording of any city publications. We have also worked with citizen PACs in the past by providing information on local government sales tax ballot questions, and they can say vote yes, or no. Also, remember there are now 2008 restrictions imposed by the state on local governments, which should be followed.

If the city council in Lake Alfred does not take a stance on the tax reductions, then the manager will need to limit his involvement to his association efforts, that is, Florida City/County Management Association or Florida League of Cities, in which the information is given to the state associations for Lake Alfred to be included in their materials. The city manager could also prepare the information for the council as part of the budget process, which makes it public for media coverage, but will not be able to be involved in a local campaign which does not have the approval of his council, against the amendments.

This position is very clear in the ICMA Code of Ethics, which states that the manager should not be politically involved, *unless* it's a local referendum issue and the town has authorized his involvement. For me, we have taken our campaign against the tax reductions to *all* groups within the community, with board approval, from editorial boards, public forums, government websites, to Tallahassee, voter mailings, newspaper ads, meeting with unions and employees, payroll inserts, local colleges, working with formal PACs, state associations, and local municipal leagues, as well as TV and press conferences.

Randall Recklaus, Assistant City Administrator, Batavia, Illinois:

The city manager of Lake Alfred in question does have a difficult choice regarding the balance between advocacy and providing information. The CAO position is generally charged with making sure decision makers are basing their decisions on the best information possible. In many circumstances, that information comes in the form of a staff recommendation, and in others it may be a more balanced analysis of facts. However, in this case, the city manager is not working with his or her own city council on a city issue, but the electorate-at-large on a state-wide issue. That distinction is an important one, despite the dramatic impact the referendum may have on Lake Alfred.

A key question in the city manager's analysis ought to be: has my city council taken a position on this issue? The manager must remember that he or she serves the council first. If the council has taken a formal position formally opposing the referendum, then the question is one of how best to communicate the council's opposition and contribute to the public discourse on behalf of the elected office holders. In that case, having an open house with an informational presentation on the city's reasoning for opposing the measure, informational flyers on the impacts, and even a carefully worded letter to the editor may be warranted and/or appropriate.

However, if the city council did not take a formal vote on the issue or is clearly not in consensus on the issue, the city manager must be much more cautious with his or her approach. In this case, the manager may still want to lend information to the discussion, but must be careful not to advocate voting one way or another, or portray a "city position" on the issue when it doesn't exist. Under this scenario, well-worded informational (nonadvocacy) flyers and utility billing inserts may be considered as nonconfrontational ways to communicate the impacts. Even these methods should only be utilized if the city council and mayor have been made aware of the staff's intent, and they have no objection.

Lastly, if the city council actively supports the measure, the city manager most likely should not actively or passively oppose the measure with any correspondence or information that is not explicitly approved by the city council. It is the city council's right to take a position on an issue, even if the manager believes that position will be detrimental to the community. The city manager serves at the pleasure of the city council. If the manager cannot in good conscience even passively support the city council's position, he should communicate his feelings to the group, and if necessary, resign.

Elizabeth Kellar, Deputy Executive Director, International City-County Management Association:

One of the most important principles in the ICMA Code of Ethics is the respect that a city manager has for the democratic process. Tenet 1 emphasizes the manager's dedication to democratic local government by responsible elected officials. For that reason, the city manager's first obligation is to represent the city council's official position. If the city council has taken a position to oppose this ballot measure, then the city manager is on strong ground to advocate that official position. ICMA members may assist the governing body by making presentations, particularly to explain the financial implications of a referendum. If the city council is supportive of an activist role, it can be appropriate for the city manager to write a letter to the editor or to organize a town hall meeting to explain the city's position.

If the city council has taken no position on the referendum but the city manager wants to be an advocate to persuade voters to vote "no," ICMA would advise him or her to (1) work through a state municipal league or other state-wide organization to help educate voters; (2) conduct any personal advocacy on his or her own time and without using any city resources; and (3) take care not to pressure city employees to get involved. City managers may make financial contributions to issues they wish to support and may advise advocacy organizations on strategies that may be effective. If the city council has no position on the referendum, the city manager should not write a letter to the editor or call a town hall meeting. Using the city manager's position or title to advocate would not be appropriate as the community could reasonably believe the city manager is representing official city positions.

Should the city council take a position in favor of the referendum and the city manager strongly opposes it, the city manager still has an obligation to represent the city council's official position, if requested. He or she is still free to make financial contributions or work with a state-wide organization to oppose a referendum. However, such activism comes with this caveat: the city manager may lose the confidence of the governing body should his or her support be highly visible. In such circumstances, the city manager could face termination or might feel it necessary to leave employment with the city because of fundamental disagreements with council direction.

Author's Note: Based on story "Lake Alfred Manager Works Against Higher Property Tax Exemption" at http://www.theledger.com/article/20080109/ NEWS/801090359/1244/last14days (accessed January 10, 2008).

4.4 Religious Expression in the Workplace

Controversies: 3.17, 5.14
Key Words: equity, religion, Muslim, state government, First Amendment rights
Case Complexity → Moderate
CD: 4.31 Citizen-Client-Customer

You are the chief of the County Division of Vehicular Licensing, with 1,250 employees located at three offices. The director of the District 2 office approaches you about a thorny problem—what to do about providing employees who are Muslims a suitable time of the day to worship. The problem began on October 30 when the state shifted from Central Daylight Savings Time to Central Standard Time. As it turns out, the "fall back" of the clock pulled the Muslim sunset prayer back into the work hours.

A group of Muslim coworkers requested that the District 2 office allow them to conduct their sunset prayer at 5:00 p.m. The office closes at 6:00 p.m. The group said that they would be willing to work from 6:00 p.m. to 7:00 p.m. to make up for the time lost.

The director is unsure what other districts have done and does not know if state or county laws require public agencies to accommodate employees' religious beliefs.

It is, of course, clear to all that public agencies cannot promote religious beliefs and practices, but this is not quite the same thing.

As the division chief, you inform the director that other district offices have not faced this issue before. Moreover, state law is reasonably clear—employers (public and private) must accommodate employees' religious beliefs as long as the requests are reasonable and do not create a hardship for the agency.

Discussion Questions

1. Is the request by the workers reasonable?
2. Would shifting the sunset prayer hour to 5:00 p.m. create a hardship for the District Office of Vehicular Licensing? (Remember that the primary work of the District Office is to issue licenses to the public on a first come, first served basis.)
3. Would agreeing to the request be viewed as favoritism toward one group of employees? If so, would this create morale problems?
4. What recommendation would you, as division chief, make to the district director?

Case Assessment

John Hamp, Lieutenant at the Charlotte County Sheriff's Office, Florida:

> This case involves at least two primary issues: accommodating the employees with their religious prayer and continuing service to the public. District 2 poses the issue that certain Muslim coworkers want an hour for sunset prayer, which is at 5:00 p.m. The district office closes at 6:00 p.m. State law requires employers to accommodate employees religious beliefs as long as it does not create a hardship for the agency.
>
> As the chief of the State Division of Vehicular Licensing, I would first gather information on exactly how many employees would be affected by the religious prayer in District 2. I would also find out how many employees would want the same opportunity in the other five districts so as to keep policy consistent and uniform. If there are a limited number of employees per district requesting the one hour of prayer to the point where the particular district would not feel a hardship, then policy would be set that these employees may use the one hour prayer at 5:00 p.m. and return to work at 6:00 p.m. and work until 7:00 p.m. I would get a report from the district directors to determine if this one hour shift in work will hinder production and/or service.

Issues to consider: What is the job function the employee holds at the district? If the employee serves the public, then the employee working from 6:00 to 7:00 p.m. would be a waste as the agency would be closed. Can the district office still serve the public adequately with the loss of the employees involved for the one hour? And if the employees involved make up the hour between 6:00 and 7:00 p.m., would they be doing constructive work or just staying the extra hour?

Each district would have to determine the maximum amount of staffing it could afford to have leave for one hour for the prayer. If the number of employees exceeds this maximum number, then those with seniority will be given the opportunity for the prayer and those at the cutoff point will have to wait for an opening or may be given the option of transferring to another district if there is an opening. I believe this method will accommodate as many employees as possible and still maintain business practices of serving the public, though there is the understanding of the possibility of not making everybody happy.

James D. Slack, Professor, Department of Government, University of Alabama at Birmingham:

The first right in the First Amendment pertains to religion—a reflection of both the centrality of religion in the American community and the Founders' concern for protecting this value. The case study deals with the Free Exercise Clause, which states that "Congress shall make no law … prohibiting the free exercise [of religion]." The U.S. Supreme Court "incorporated" the Fourteenth Amendment into the Free Exercise Clause in *Cantwell v. Connecticut* in 1940 and, thereby, its protection extends to actions taken by state and local governments. Further, Title VII of the Civil Rights Act requires the same kind of accommodation for religious expression as it does for nonreligious expression. The legal issue centers on this: the employee does not have to incur more than *de minimis* cost, but those costs must be real and not speculative. The ethical issue centers on what is fair for Muslims in comparison to what is fair for non-Muslims.

It is important to understand that each religion is unique and can affect the workplace differently. For instance, the Sabbath is on different days for Muslims, Jews, and Christians. Most public workplaces are structured to accommodate the Christian Sabbath (Sunday), but not necessarily the Sabbaths of Islam (Friday) or Judaism (Saturday). The same is with prayer. While Christians and Jews can pray at their own discretion, practicing Muslims are required to pray five times a day. Hence, the director of District 2 will soon be faced with more issues about work day prayers—not just the required "sunset" prayer but also the required "noon" prayer and "mid-afternoon" prayer. Further, the director will have to consider providing an acceptable space for these workplace prayers. Unlike in the Christian and Jewish faiths, more structure is required with Muslim prayers: (1) rather than simply folding one's hands and closing one's eyes, a Muslim must kneel and lean forward so that his or her head is touching the ground; (2) the Muslim must pray in the direction of the *Kaaba*—a sanctuary built by Abraham and Ishmael, located in the *Haram* mosque in Mecca, Saudi Arabia; and (3) women and men must pray in separate spaces. All this is to suggest that the ethical resolution will be much more complicated than simply the issue of flex-time at the end of the day.

I would encourage the director to do the following: (1) He or she should learn more about Islam by talking to the Muslim employees about all aspects of worship that could potentially require workplace accommodation. (2) He or she should then contact an Imam—a prayer leader—at a local mosque to affirm the positions taken by the employees. The Imam should reflect the Islamic sect represented by the Muslim employees in the Division of Vehicular Licensing, so several Imams may have to be contacted. (3) The director should then examine the kinds of accommodations possible and weigh those against the real costs that extend beyond *de minimis* status. Must prayers last a full sixty minutes? (The answer is "no.") Are two (one for men and one for women) spaces available? Answers might be found in an office that could be used temporarily or even an open area in a somewhat unused hallway)? Can the noon, mid-afternoon, and sunset prayer times be staggered slightly to accommodate practicing Muslims while maintain effective workplace services? (The answer usually is "yes.") How will providing such accommodations disrupt the workplace? (Discussion and explanation will be needed with all employees, and a memo of understanding/expectations must be sent to all employees once an accommodation is determined.)

4.5 Going Along to Get Along?

Controversies: 3.15, 6.16, 6.18
Key Words: city, health code, abuse of power
Case Complexity → Moderate
CD: 6.1 American Society for Public Administration Code of Ethics
CD: 6.2 International City/County Management Association Code of Ethics

You have been newly hired as the director of the city's bureau of restaurant inspection services. One of your first acts is to conduct a few site visits as a way of learning firsthand about your job. To your surprise and dismay, you find that many inspectors are ignoring serious health code violations.

You decide to discuss your findings with your boss, Sally, who is the head of the city's health department. Sally, who has recently proposed a substantial budget increase to a receptive city manager and city council, suggests to you that there might be some negative fall out to the department if the problems in the restaurant bureau become public—as they might if an inspector under investigation decides to argue publicly that department brass knew about the situation. Sally advises you to handle the situation with appropriate discretion and regard for the interests of the organizational team.

Discussion Questions

1. Should you go along to get along with your boss, Sally?
2. Should you be a good team player and postpone corrective action so as not to upset the financial applecart?
3. Or should you launch an investigation and take appropriate disciplinary and site corrective actions to protect the public interest?
4. Has Sally put you in an unfair, perhaps compromising position? For instance, if the problem becomes public and you postpone corrective action, have you been set up by Sally for a fall?

Case Assessment

Susan Walker, Administrator, Neighborhood Services Department, City of Pinellas Park, Florida:

> As a newly hired director, you have a unique opportunity—and very appropriate method—to handle this situation without placing blame, launching an investigation, or otherwise "damaging" the department's or Sally's organizational interests. You should develop a bureau procedure for restaurant inspections, including all the necessary forms, inspector check sheets, supervisory sign-offs, examples/photos of acceptable versus unacceptable conditions, violation processes, etc., prepared in the interests of the public health, safety, and welfare—that's your job to do. Review the procedure with Sally and get her buy-in. Then have a bureau staff meeting—ask Sally to be there as department head and to show her support for you and the bureau staff. At the meeting, discuss your goals for the bureau and towards the end, review the new procedure and encourage discussion from your experts, the inspectors. Let your inspectors know

that you will tweak the procedure as needed, and to do that you need to learn and appreciate their job ... so you will be spending a day or two with each of them in the field. Discuss any concern items with each inspector one-on-one. Update the procedure as necessary. Take any corrective actions that result from the procedure not being followed.

Jamil Jreisat, Professor of Public Administration, University of South Florida-Tampa:

In this case, the adage of *going along to get along* is a poor choice to follow by the health inspector. Sally's "suggestion" that revealing the mistakes, involving serious health code violations, might have "negative fall out" is disingenuous and outright unethical. It is tantamount to a cover up. Getting along is fine, being a team player is preferable and commendable, but these values and norms are not the purpose, and cannot be a substitute, for the mission of the organization or the reason for hiring the inspector.

The basic value for the inspector is to serve taxpayers and to implement the rules and regulations of the organization with competence and integrity. Compliance with Sally's suggestion, in this situation, does not serve the organization or the citizens nor show the inspector as a responsible person.

The inspector need not be obstinate or denouncing of Sally's suggestion. The first task for the inspector is to have a discussion with Sally to communicate with her sensibly about three facets to this dilemma: First, the inspector, too, is concerned about the fall out and the potential of undermining Sally's concerns for the organization and the team. Second, the inspector, however, believes that the risk is greater to the organization's integrity by not revealing the information and taking corrective measures. Third, the inspector would like to work with Sally on the method of handling the matter without violation of the inspector's sense of responsibility and with high regard to the organization's mission and citizens' mandate to the organization.

The inspector needs to alert Sally to the consequences of not being transparent and not ensuring accountability. The inspector needs to convince Sally that sooner or later the matter will be revealed and will then incur far more harm than otherwise. Actually, the inspector should suggest that handling the matter expeditiously and effectively will improve the image of the health bureau and increase trust by the city manager, the council members, and citizens at large. The inspector should convey affirmatively and clearly his understanding of the need for positive support and team playing in the department, but that, at the same time, he believes that correcting errors and admitting mistakes are signs of strength and organizational integrity. Final, the inspector needs to communicate without pomposity that he is a professional person with a deep sense of commitment to principles of good management, including transparency, accountability, building trust, and always putting the interest of the public ahead of all other considerations.

4.6 Moral Management: Fact or Fantasy?

Controversies: 6.11
Key Words: county, morality, policy
Case Complexity → Moderate
CD: 4.12 Ethics Management in Cities and Counties
CD: 4.32 Leading with Integrity

Imagine that you are the top elected official of a county constitutional office, such as the sheriff or clerk or property appraiser. As part of your campaign to get elected, you promise that you will demand that employees of the organization behave properly and not behave in a manner that jeopardizes the credibility and integrity of the office. A week after you take office, you learn that several married employees are engaging in intimate behavior which offends your sense of morality and is causing disruption in the agency.

What do you do?

Discussion Questions

1. Do you turn your head and hope the situation disappears?
2. Do you call the employees to your office and teach them a lesson in moral behavior?
3. Do you consider revising the agency's written standard of conduct to prohibit married employees from dating or entering into intimate relationships with other employees, single or married?

After much discussion with your top staff, you decide to issue an order prohibiting married personnel from engaging in adulterous affairs. The order reads as follows:

"Agency personnel, whether married or single, shall not develop an association with another member whom they know or should have known is married to another person. Married members also shall not develop an association with agency members who are single. Excluded from this are members who are separated and residing apart from their spouse, or those who have legally filed for divorce. For the purpose of this policy, 'association' means, residing with, dating, or entering into any intimate relationship with."

How to enforce this policy is the $64,000 question.

4. Suppose you were called by the sheriff to advise him on how to enforce the policy. What would you say to him?

Results

Two married employees (not to each other) entered into an intimate relationship. As fate would have it, the husband (let's call him Matt) of the woman (let's call her Heather) who was in the forbidden relationship came home around noon to find his wife's lover (let's call him Joe) napping in bed while Heather was in the shower! The incident was the breaking point for Matt. He ran downstairs and grabbed a video camera to record the proof. With this evidence, along with pictures, e-mails, and hotel receipts, he filed a complaint with the sheriff's department. After evaluating the evidence, the sheriff concluded in letters sent to Joe and Heather that "You engaged in an intimate relationship with a member of the agency whom you knew was married."

Joe received a three-day suspension and Heather received a written reprimand. The moral of this story—enforcement is in the eye of the beholder!

Discussion Questions

1. Is this a management issue or an ethics issue? Both? Neither?
2. Is moral management fact or fantasy?
3. Should one's religious beliefs influence the situation?

Assessment

Karl Thoennes III, Judicial Circuit Administrator, Unified Judicial System, State of South Dakota:

> I love the sheriff's delicate use of the phrase "develop an association with ..." I think we can manage morals on some behaviors—outside employment at the strip club, Internet porn—but I do think trying to manage adultery at the office is a fantasy.

Bonnie Beth Greenball, Associate Director, Institute for Public Policy and Leadership, University of South Florida Sarasota-Manatee:

> As the top elected official in a county constitutional office, I have obligations both to uphold the constitution and to ensure that the office is a productive work environment. Faced with employees engaging in inappropriate intimate behavior, I would take several steps before making a major change such as the personnel rule proposed in the second portion of this case study. First, I would like to know whether these actions were taking place in the workplace and/or during normal business hours. If married employees are engaging in intimate behavior outside of the workplace and/or normal business hours, I would not become involved in this at all. I am not in the business of regulating the morality of my employees; rather I believe that what they do on their own time is their own business. I believe that there is a certain "zone of privacy" that all citizens can expect under the U.S. Constitution and that government agencies should not create rules or regulations which might prohibit certain private activities.
>
> However, if either of the parties involved was in a superior/subordinate relationship with the other, and the relationship became financial as well as romantic, then I would seek to enforce the county's conflicts of interest policy, provided that it had a clause prohibiting financial relationships between superiors and subordinates. In all likelihood, I would transfer the subordinate to another portion of my office, if at all possible, so that he or she would not be a direct report to the other.
>
> If, on the other hand, these amorous activities are taking place at work or during business hours, I would likely take action. Engaging in sexual activity in the workplace is completely inappropriate for several reasons. It is disruptive to the office, and more importantly, all employees are expected to work in the best interests of the citizens and not be distracted by amorous activities at work. In contrast, if these activities take place off site during a lunch hour or break and do not interfere with the employees' work product, then I would, as stated above, stay out of this matter.
>
> I would not revise the agency's written standard of conduct to regulate morality because I believe the employees have a right to engage in private activities on their own time, provided those activities do not conflict with their work. It is my view that we ought to give public employees respect and autonomy to make their own decisions about their personal lives.
>
> However, if, as proposed in the hypothetical case, an order prohibiting married personnel from engaging in adulterous affairs was on

the books, and I had overwhelming evidence to support a claim that Heather, a married woman, and Joe were indeed involved in such an affair, I would have to advise the appropriate enforcement agency that there was sufficient evidence (once I reviewed it) to make a finding of probable cause of a violation of the personnel rules. I would certainly not want to set a precedent of permitting activities that are in violation of the personnel code; however, I would personally have trouble with this case in that I do not agree with the validity of the rule. I may suggest that the two be reassigned to avoid disruptions in the workplace and then work to remove the rule from the personnel code, which I find overly invasive.

Author's Note: Based on a case published in the *St. Petersburg Times*, December 28-29, 2007. Policy statement is actual wording contained in the Pinellas County (Florida) Sheriff's Office, General Order 3-1, section 3.4.

4.7 Appearances Matter—Investing in Real Estate

Controversies: 4.10, 5.17
Key Words: appearances, conflict of interest, county
Case Complexity → moderate
CD: 4.12 Ethics Management in Cities and Counties
CD: 6.2 International City/County Management Association Code of Ethics

You have been the county administrator for fifteen years in a rapidly growing county and have a stellar reputation for getting things done. One day your daughter, a local TV news celebrity, calls you and says, "Dad, can you loan me $120,000 to help my husband invest in a condo in the county? We will repay you with interest." Innocent enough? So it seems.

Alas, the plot thickens—it turns out that your daughter's husband has been indicted on twelve federal fraud charges involving two land deals, and it appears that your money may have been involved in three different real estate investments that would benefit from the extension of a county road. You claim to have no knowledge of money laundering or any other misdeed.

As the situation evolves, the county commission decides to order an independent investigation into your account of the investments to determine whether you are covering something up and may even have lied. The investigation finds that you are not invested in the property that your son-in-law owned. Moreover, the investigation concludes that you did not lie or tell any untruths.

The county commission is relieved but somewhat dismayed. One commissioner says to you in public, "Did you lie? No. Did you engage in activities that brought about the appearance of indiscretion? I know you did. You're guilty of that. Actions that reflect poorly on your representation of county government? I find you guilty of that." Another claims the "board is whitewashing the county manager's involvement." Still another asserts, "I have determined you have not violated your contract to the point you should be terminated and beg you to not invest in land in the county again. There should be an ethics requirement added to your employment contract."

A fourth commissioner adds, "Is it a sad and pathetic day when we have to amend the county manager's contract to include a requirement that he be ethical?" The board voted unanimously to have the county administrator and the county attorney draft ethics guidelines to include a policy about land investments for county workers.

Discussion Questions

1. What should the guidelines include? Your task as the county administrator is to draft guidelines. How would you begin?
2. Would you consult survey professional associations such as the International City/County Management Association? The American Society for Public Administration? The American Planning Association?
3. Should you have made the loan to your daughter? Why or why not?
4. Is the appearance of a conflict of interest sufficient reason to not make the loan?

Case Assessment

Carl Harness, Assistant County Administrator, Hillsborough County, Florida:

> Yes, appearances do matter and often we find that some situations that may seem innocent enough at the onset end up in a negative light at no fault to the individual involved. The issue of Investments in Conflict with Official Duties is covered within the ICMA Code of Ethics. Guidelines for the code were revised in July 2004. I would draw your attention to a couple of passages within this section, the first, "A member should not invest or hold any investment, directly or indirectly, in any financial business, commercial, or other private transaction that creates a conflict with their official duties," and second, "Because personal investments may prejudice or may appear to influence official actions and decisions, members may, in concert

with their governing body, provide for disclosure of such investments prior to accepting their position as local government administrator or prior to any official action by the governing body that may affect such investments."

In this case, the administrator simply used bad judgment in entering into this deal with his daughter. First, he should have ascertained from his daughter whether the loan for the condo was simply an investment for purposes of profit or strictly for their personal use.

I believe that this situation would have been a nonissue had the investment been for the couple's personal use. Another way that this issue could have been avoided would have been if the administrator had simply given his daughter the money as a gift. In that scenario the fact that he provided his daughter with the money would have been totally separated from how they invested the funds.

Going back to the issue of the "loan," the administrator could have possibly avoided any embarrassment by initially disclosing the details of the transaction to his commission in order to gauge any concerns or negative feedback that he may have received. Unfortunately, there was no way for him to know about the intent on the husband's part to utilize the funds in a fraudulent manner. I would guess that the daughter was probably unaware of her husband's activities also. Therefore, as innocent as the transaction was between the administrator and his daughter, the connection with the loan to the indictment of the husband definitely resulted in a cause for concern.

In general, as a rule of practice, an administrator should never engage in any type of real estate investments in the area where he or she is employed (bound by either the city or county limits). In addition, contingent on one's relationships (close friendships, etc.) with managers and administrators in neighboring communities, I would also be cautious on entering into any investment deals in those areas.

Sandra J. Reinke, Associate Professor of Public Administration and Director, MPA Program, University of Central Florida:

Do appearances matter? Absolutely! In this case, an administrator with fifteen years of experience in the job let his parental love get in the way of better judgment. Prominent public officials such as the one in this case live in what I refer to as a fish bowl, a place where every action and every word reflects on the quality and probity of government and affects the public's trust in government. It is sad but true that the original charges against the administrator were probably on page one of the local paper, while the news of his exoneration was on page six, next to the picture of this week's featured dog and cat from the local animal shelter. The elected officials in this case clearly understand this dynamic and the importance of appearances. Under pressure from a public that focused on the charges, they felt compelled to "do something" and so they took the only step they could. Since there is no basis for disciplinary action or termination in this case, they engaged in symbolic politics and ordered the administrator to put together a policy on county employees and real estate transactions. We are left to wonder whether the administrator's relationship with these elected officials will be permanently damaged.

Appearances also matter in this case because employees take their cues for what is appropriate behavior from their leaders. And for county employees, there is no more visible leader than the county administrator. This administrator has damaged his or her ability to lead. If this incident is one of a long string of poor decisions, then the county should be prepared to deal with more problems like this from employees at lower levels in the organization as the employees copy their leader's behavior. If this is one bad mistake in an otherwise exemplary career, then the county's employees will likely rally around their administrator and the organization will recover rather quickly.

Author's Note: Story based on articles in the Naplesnews.com (www.naplesnews.com) August 2, September 4, September 30, 2008 and www.icma.org.

4.8 Ethics and Performance Evaluations

Controversies: 3.15, 6.15, 6.16
Key Words: evaluations, city, ethics standards
Case Complexity → High
CD: 3.9 Performance Evaluation for Managers
CD: 4.12 Ethics Management in Cities and Counties

Your city workforce has been experiencing a rash of ethical lapses. It seems as if nearly everyone, from the janitorial staff to the department managers to the deputy directors, has had an ethics miscue over the past year. As the director of human resources, you feel strongly that it is time to put an ethics component in the annual evaluation of hourly workers and managerial/professional employees. You realize, of course, that your boss must agree and begin to think about how you will make the case to evaluate the ethical behavior of employees.

Ah, you have it, why not collect information from cities like yours to identify what others are doing? After a few weeks of telephone calls and e-mails, you discover that very little is being done, but you do find one municipality that has an ethics component in the annual evaluation of the city manager, the city clerk, and the city attorney. The evaluation instrument asks the evaluator to rate the city manager/clerk/attorney as "Excellent," "Fully Satisfactory," "Satisfactory," or "Unsatisfactory" in response to the statement: "Conducts self in accordance with the ethical standards of the office of Charter Officer."

Disappointed by what you learn, you decide to form a committee to draft language that could be placed on the form to evaluate professional/management personnel. You decide to do the same thing with the hourly employees' evaluation language but at a later date. The committee takes their assignment to heart and produces the following set of evaluative statements:

1. Demonstrates an ethical approach in the discharge of duties.
2. Displays ethical behavior—promotes an environment that is open, fair, tolerant, trustful, and respectful. Values public interest over self-interest and is accountable.
3. Clearly understands and communicates ethical practices, policies, and goals relevant to the community.
4. Shows respect for the views of others, takes pride in work products, places public interest over own self-interest.
5. Demonstrates integrity in all aspects of work.
6. Adheres to the city's ethics code.
7. Demonstrates a clear ability to identify, evaluate, and resolve issues related to ethics.
8. Demonstrates sound ethical judgment and encourages ethical behavior in others.
9. Complies with rules and laws defined by the city Personnel Manual and professional standards and conducts self with integrity while avoiding undue influence.
10. Displays proper attitude toward organizational transparency and has sufficient knowledge of city's ethical standards.
11. Demonstrates ethical judgment as defined by the city code of ethics or applicable professional standards.

Discussion Questions

1. Which of these eleven statements do you like the best? Like the least? Why?
2. Rank order three statements, with one being the best.
3. Would the list differ in any significant manner for hourly employees?
4. In forming the committee to draft language to be placed on the performance evaluation, what should be the key criteria for membership?
5. Do you anticipate resistance from the workforce about including an ethics component in the annual evaluation? Why or why not?
6. Do you believe that the ethical performance of an employee can be evaluated fairly and accurately? Why or why not?
7. What do you say to persuade your boss that the city should place your preferred statement on the annual performance evaluation form for managerial/professional staff?

Case Assessment

Karl Nollenberger, Assistant Professor, University of Wisconsin–Oshkosh and former Administrator of Lake County, Illinois:

> The top management of the city needs to clearly articulate the ethical standards that it expects to maintain in the organization. The city is part of the public service that is committed to providing services to all citizens in a manner that promotes equity and fairness with integrity. The city is responsible to the entire citizenry and must forego any appearance of favoring certain individuals or groups in the community.
>
> While all of the committee's suggested evaluation questions are well thought out and of good quality, an evaluation needs to focus on three questions to articulate the importance of the topic area. The following three questions reflect the overall values of the committee and can be addressed in an evaluation annually for each employee:
>
> 1. Demonstrates an ethical approach in the discharge of duties.
> 2. Displays ethical behavior—promotes an environment that is open, fair, tolerant, trustful, and respectful. Values public interest over self-interest and is accountable.
> 3. Complies with rules and laws defined by city Personnel Manual and professional standards and conducts self with integrity while avoiding undue influence.
>
> All employees need to be reminded at least annually of the importance of ethical behavior in the performance of their positions. They are the embodiment of the public trust! An annual seminar for all employees on the significance of the ethical dimension of public service would

also help to emphasize the importance that the management accords to this topic. The communication of values in an organization is the most important element of effective management. Employees throughout the organization are called upon to make decisions daily, and if they are doing so within the values of the organization, the community will appreciate the quality of public service.

Robert Lee, (former) City Manager, Gulfport and Naples, Florida, and Past President of the Florida City and County Management Association:

Although the intentions of the human resources director are good, the approach that is being taken in this case study is destined to fail. First and foremost, it is critical that the agency's CEO (e.g., city or county manager, elected executive, etc.) and not the human resources director, take the lead in changing this culture. The CEO should appoint a committee of employees (with the active participation of the human resources director) and task them with evaluating the agency's existing ethics policies (if any). Are they comprehensive? Are they clear? That is, are they written so the average person can understand them? Do they meet or exceed federal and state requirements? Are they agency specific? That is, do the policies cover situations that employees encounter in their jobs? The CEO should establish a timeline for completing the task and attend some of the meetings to discuss the committee's progress and to answer questions regarding policies discussed. The CEO must evidence he or she is 100-percent committed to this assignment. In evaluating existing policies or in establishing policies, a review of ethical policies established by other agencies is a good start.

Once a fair, understandable, interpretable, and enforceable ethics policy is established, and the employees are recognized for their role in its development, the next important step is training the agency's employees so they understand the expectations therein. Training is a requisite. In addition to formal training (which the CEO must attend as well), daily and weekly reminders via e-mail, at staff meetings, in the organization's newsletter, etc., are necessary to continue to remind employees of their ethical expectations. There should also be one or more people that employees know they can feel free to call to discuss or clarify ethical situations that confront them.

The third step in establishing an ethical culture, in this case study, is to make certain that violators are held accountable in a fair and consistent matter. Employees are always watching how management handles situation that involve policy violations. Fair and consistent action will achieve the balance needed for employees to know that they will be held accountable for their actions, yet also feel free to be innovative and make mistakes (if pursuing solutions in the agency's best interest) without retaliation. By repeating ethical expectations, the differences between a mistake and a conscious decision to violate policies will be clear in most cases.

Adding an ethical section in employee evaluations can now be considered. The section could be applicable to all employees. A suggestion would include: "Promotes and demonstrates the agency's ethical policies in their day to day responsibilities." A section should be available for written comments as well.

4.9 Mired in an Ethics Swamp ...

Controversies: 3.11, 3.18, 4.14, 5.17, 6.13, 6.19
Key Words: county manager, public interest, trust, appearance, scandal, grand jury, sunshine, transparency, news media
Case Complexity → High
CD: 4.11 I Didn't Do Anything Unethical ...
CD: 7.6 Ethical Illiteracy in Local Government
Ethical reasoning questions are included in this case.

This case involves deception and blunder in a modern, progressive, urban county. The county government has a history of stability and professionalism. No county commissioner has lost reelection since 1992, and the current county administrator has been in office for five years, replacing one who served twenty-two years. County employees are treated well and enjoy long careers. Yet, it is a county embroiled in controversy and scandal over an insider land deal.

As the case unfolds, you are asked to assume the roles of the key actors—the property appraiser, the county administrator, the county attorney, and others. One fascinating question threads throughout the story: "How could well educated, politically smart, and experienced public officials have a collective lapse of ethical judgment?"

The Property Appraiser (PA): You were elected nearly twenty years ago and intend to seek reelection next year, having been reelected without opposition in 1996, 2000, and 2004. You enjoy a reputation as a fair, competent public official who is described as "a man of high integrity." Thirteen years ago you purchased a beautiful home site for $15,000. You think of the 1.5 acre parcel in the county as an urban oasis. You tell friends that the site is what the Spaniards must have seen when they first came to Florida.

As the years pass, however, the parcel sits vacant and you reconsider your plan to build your dream house. "Perhaps I should put it on the market," you muse. And, since your daughter is a new real estate agent, let her handle the listing—$400,000. Your office appraised the just market value of the land at $59,400.

Nine months pass and no buyer is in sight. You have personal problems too. Your eleven-year marriage ends in divorce and the $1.2 million house you shared with your former wife belongs to her. Consequently, you decide to purchase a $497,000 house and intend to use the money from the sale of the land parcel as a down payment.

Ahaaaa! It hits you—why not sell the property to the county? After all, county work crews severely damaged the property while engaged in flood repairs following the 2004 hurricanes. Surely the county commission would be sympathetic to your case and they can legitimately claim that the property would be useful to the county in the event of future flooding. And, you suspect, you can expect a fast-track handling of the sale.

You decide to meet with the county administrator to let him know just how unhappy you are with the damage to the property. You also hire an attorney who sends a letter to the county administrator suggesting that the county buy the "destroyed" property rather than face a law suit about the damage. The letter states: "While my client is understandably upset about the ruination of his property, he is not vindictive and wishes to resolve this matter in a fair and expeditious manner … this letter will serve as a request that the county purchase the subject property so that he can have adequate funds to seek an alternative piece of property with a pastoral setting like the one his subject property previously enjoyed."

The County Administrator: You became county administrator five years ago and enjoy a very strong relationship with the county commission. You bring to the job more than twenty-five years experience as a high-ranking county official in a nearby urban county. You have acquired a reputation for high quality service improvement and adopting innovative approaches to county management.

You are very much aware of the property appraiser's desire to have the county purchase the home site and his very strong feelings about the damage the county did to it. In fact, a high-level subordinate visited the site where he encountered the PA who "was unbelievably mad—screaming, yelling, cussing." You are shocked at how upset the PA is and promise to look into the damage. You caution county staff to be very sensitive about the matter, knowing any sign of special treatment given to the PA would raise eyebrows.

You delegate the matter to your assistant county administrator (ACA) who is in his first week on the job. He instructs staff to determine if purchasing the property would be a good acquisition for needed flood control in the area. Staff return with a positive response. The assistant county administrator instructs staff to proceed with the purchase according to county policy, which requires an outside appraisal.

The outside appraiser places a $250,000 price tag on the property but warns that the appraisal does not reflect any water issues (especially flooding, which could devalue the estimate) and recommends that an expert be consulted. You decide not to seek an expert opinion as you wish to get the matter resolved quickly and instruct the ACA to make an offer to the PA of $200,000. The PA counters with $225,000, which you accept subject to approval by the county commission.

It is your practice to discuss all agenda items with each member of the county commission prior to official meetings and this item is no exception. Several commissioners ask about the sale and find your response satisfactory. A few days later, the commission holds its weekly meeting and votes unanimously, with no public discussion, to approve the purchase.

The County Attorney: You were hired more than twenty-five years ago and have been the county attorney for twenty years. You enjoy the full trust and confidence of your elected bosses. A former commissioner describes you as "a woman of high integrity and ethics and is always on the side of caution."

The PA asks you to represent him and, as a long-time friend and colleague, you agree to do so without compensation. You understand that dual representation, representing the PA as a private citizen and the county, is not illegal but could be a slippery slope. You decide to seek a conflict of interest waiver which requires the chair of the county commission to sign off. You send the waiver to the county chair with a cover memo but the memo does not detail the scope of possible work for the PA. The chair signs the waiver. You do not inform the county administrator or the county commission that you are representing the PA in the sale of the property to the county.

The County Commission: By most accounts the county commission is a collegial group that works as a team with the county administrator and the county attorney. No commissioner judges the purchase of the property appraiser's vacant lot to be a big deal as the county quite frequently purchases property for flood control. Not all agree—especially the local media.

The Newspaper Reporter: You routinely attend county commission meetings and read each week's agenda carefully. The county's purchase of the PA's property gets your attention because it moved along so fast and was quickly and silently dealt with by the county commission. You suspect insider dealing and begin to ask questions. The more you dig, the more you become convinced that the commission was asleep on its ethical watch. The story breaks and the county scrambles. All seem complicit—the PA, the county administrator, the county attorney, and the county commission.

Your newspaper lambastes the commission in the local media for a "conspiracy of silence" as a member of the "courthouse gang." One columnist claims that that county commission is embarrassingly complacent and deferential and should at least fire the county attorney who led them astray. Letters to the editor and blog postings are consistently critical of the commission. One writer asserts that "this is only the tip of the iceberg in county corruption." Another asserts that this "sort of back-door deal causes residents to distrust the commission … a wink and a nod won't do."

The public uproar grows when it becomes public that the county used money from a recently voter-supported referendum called Penny for Prairie County to purchase the vacant lot owned by the PA.

The local newspaper editorial calls for the PA to resign and the county commission to fire the county attorney. The PA loudly proclaims his innocence and asks the state attorney to convene a grand jury to investigate the matter. The state attorney rejects the PA's request, but as more details are published in the newspaper he changes his mind.

County Chair: As chair of the county commission, you never imagined that you would be hauled before a grand jury and suspected of going along on an insider land deal. "I cannot tell you how disturbed I am to be facing a grand jury," you tell your friends, "because the county attorney failed to disclose information." You decide to raise the matter of what to do with the county attorney. Should the commission fire her? Suspend her with or without pay? Neither until the grand jury finishes its investigation?

The Grand Jury's Findings

The grand jury heard forty-one witnesses and reviewed numerous charts and references provided by the witnesses and both public and private entities. The key findings in the presentment were:

1. There is no evidence that public officials "maliciously abused" their positions.
2. Several officials, including the county commissioners, helped foster the "clear public perception" that the PA received favorable treatment because of his status.
3. Several commissioners were completely unaware that the decision to purchase the PA's property had been preceded by a threat to sue the county.
4. The county attorney's actions were "perplexing and misleading."
5. The normal objective appraisal process was rushed by the county administrator.
6. The county violated the PA's property rights by entering the lot, but there was no credible evidence that the work crews were responsible for the devastation claimed by the PA.
7. County officials failed to conduct any public discussion of such a sensitive purchase by a fellow elected official.

The presentment concludes with this statement:
"In closing, the grand jury notes that it is unfortunate that the cumulative omissions of a relatively small number of officials and employees may cause the claim of improper favoritism to stain the reputation of the thousands of dedicated county workers, both in the County Administration and in the Property Appraisers

Office, who work diligently on a daily basis to improve the services provided to the citizenry and as a result improve the quality of life in Pinellas County. Thus, the significance of this incident should be placed within the perspective of over three decades of scandal-free governance. Compared to those prior incidents, in which elected officials solicited or accepted bribes and went to prison for their conduct, the mishandling of this transaction might seem to be relatively minor. It, nonetheless, should serve as a reminder to all officials and public employees that every citizen is entitled to prompt, fair, and unbiased treatment and that maintaining both the integrity of government and the public's perception of that integrity will require continuing vigilance.

All public officials should be keenly aware that in current times the public's trust in government is particularly fragile. The breath of scandal surrounding this affair we believe will, unfortunately, have a lasting impact on how the citizens of Pinellas County view its officials and government. It is incumbent on all county officials to take all steps necessary to restore confidence in our government."

Author's Note: The full report is at http://www.sptimes.com/2007/08/28/images/tb_presentment.pdf

The Property Appraiser's Response

"I went through the grand jury process and nothing was found there. The presentment was fair but incomplete. It was evident to me that the grand jury had been influenced by news media articles about the case and had made up their minds about my guilt. Where did I do something wrong? I fail to see it."

The County Attorney's Response

"I am very pleased that the grand jury has completed its work and has determined that no criminal wrongdoing was involved in the county's purchase of the PA's property. It is in everyone's best interest to have a conclusion to this matter. The grand jury's recommendations are well taken. I welcomed any fair minded inquiry into these facts to dispel the many misperceptions reported over several weeks by the local newspaper.

It is now evident that I did not represent the PA personally or individually or agree to represent him in this matter. My actions were taken in order to authorize the county administrator to deal directly with the PA himself on the issue of his property. I knew that the county administrator's communications were directly with the PA and the PA's communications were directly with the administrator and his staff. They met on the property, discussed various options, concurred on the sale of the property, and negotiated the sale price and the closing contract without my input. My function was to advise the county on legal issues. Based upon the facts presented to my office, I advised the county administrator that the county staff clearly had no right to enter the property and that doing so unequivocally impinged on the PA's property rights. While the extent of the damage done to the property was not addressed by my office, our research found no substantial arguable basis for these actions. This involvement was well within my charge as county attorney, and was understood to be in my role as the county's legal officer. Providing this legal advice should have been an aid to the county administration in determining how to deal with the PA's claim, as well as providing guidance for their actions in the future, it was not a directive to purchase the property, which the county administrator was free to choose not to do so.

Although I did not provide legal representation to the PA, apparently the administrator and others perceived that I did. Although my actions were clear, there was apparently confusion and ambiguity surrounding them. I understood my role and intent, but apparently failed in my attempt to explain it clearly to the administrator. Although at all times my conduct was open and ethical, the perception remained that it was not. My only desire was to allow the parties to negotiate between themselves to save the substantial expense of dealing with a well-founded property rights violation. The waiver of conflict letter was consistent with my course of dealing over twenty years as county attorney in these situations. The chair has executed such waivers because he or she is the "client," not the county administrator. Pursuant to a protocol which has been in place since before my association with the County Attorney's Office 26 years ago, perceived, or possible conflict situations are handled on a rather routine basis by presenting a waiver letter to only the chairman of the Commission. Although the letter implies that I could represent PA, the purpose of the letter was to advise the chair that I would not continue to represent Pinellas County, the only client I was representing, if the dispute continued into litigation. Had the matter moved to litigation, the value of the property would have been an obvious issue, and as proof of value, one or both sides of the dispute would refer to the value placed on the parcel by the property appraiser in his official capacity, thus raising the issue of conflict. The fact of the matter is that the county administration recommended the purchase of the property not because of the legal issues referred to me for opinion, but because the county apparently believed that the land was needed for future flood control activities. The end result is that the county administration acquired property it said it needed for $25,000 less than its appraised value and the county avoided the costs and expenses related to the inverse condemnation claim which the county probably could not successfully defend against based upon the county's prior actions. This was clearly pointed out in the presentment returned by the grand jury in this matter.

I welcome further scrutiny of the events surrounding this matter. I have cooperated fully and testified truthfully. Over the past twenty-seven years, I have put the best interests of the county first and will continue to do so if given the opportunity. I believe that this transaction was in the best interest of the county. I regret any confusion, misunderstanding, or ambiguity regarding this matter."

Author's Note: The complete text of the county attorney's response can be found at http://www.sptimes.com//2007/08/30/images/churuti_letter.pdf (accessed November 30, 2008).

The County Administrator's Response

"I accept full responsibility for errors or missteps by me and members of my administration in connection with the PA's property purchase. I will not address issues surrounding the actions of the county attorney or property appraiser. The following are my initial 'after action' conclusions and planned corrective measures within my purview which I intend to discuss with the Board of County Commissioners. Our public works crews should not have entered the PA's property without proper authority. This is what prompted the initial claim. They were trying to do the right thing (clear drainage blockage) with the right intentions (prevent neighborhood flooding), but did it the wrong way.

This transaction was initiated by a tort liability claim for property damages by the PA but was not evaluated thoroughly as such. Instead of performing due diligence on the claim for damages, the Public Works Department recommended purchase of this property for creek drainage maintenance access. This alternative approach bypassed the review that this claim should have received. I will recommend implementation of a practice that requires a review and report of claim resolution alternatives in future circumstances like this.

This transaction was expedited in the interest of trying to protect the public from legal liability exposure. I personally should have slowed things down to ensure that greater care was taken with the analysis supporting the decision and that all questions were thoroughly addressed. In the future, the administration should regard legal guidance as just that and exercise more independent judgment on matters such as this.

While I made it a point to alert every commissioner of the individual elected official involved in this transaction (PA) and the rationale for my recommendations, they didn't know as much about the matter as they should have. While there are a myriad of topics I discuss with commissioners regularly, making it difficult to cover all subjects thoroughly, I should have provided more information to the board on this topic. I pledge that this situation will not repeat itself.

The controversy surrounding this acquisition has been deeply troubling to all of us who have labored hard to cultivate a high-quality government. It has regrettably damaged the image of our organization in the public eye. The grand jury did a commendable job of sorting through the many important facts of this issue and arriving at fair conclusions and constructive recommendations. I wish to apologize to the public, Board of County Commissioners, and our employees for any contribution I made to this controversy. I hold the public trust as my highest professional responsibility and would never intentionally do anything to call that obligation into question or bring harm to the Pinellas County government. Be assured I will do everything in my power to restore any diminished trust in the public's county government."

> **Author's Note:** The complete text of the county administrator's response can be found at http://www.sptimes.com/2007/08/30/Opinion/Apology__and_a_pledge.shtml (accessed December 11, 2008).

The County Commission Acts

Recognizing the need to restore public trust and confidence in county government, the county commission fired the county attorney and publicly reprimanded the county administrator at the conclusion of a two-hour meeting. As one commissioner put it, "We've got some sour milk. You smell it and I smell it, and we've got to do something ... someone has got to pay the price, and that's painful."

In an effort to save her job, the county attorney apologized for not giving the commission more details on the land transaction but said she expected the county administrator to make that kind of disclosure. She denied doing anything wrong. "I always acted in what I thought was the best interest of the county. I didn't do anything unethical, illegal or immoral," she said. One commissioner found her claim of innocence annoying and said, "What I am hearing is that everybody else misunderstood her actions."

She was dismissed without cause and entitled to six months severance pay, approximately $97,000.

The County Administrator Acts

Recognizing that his support by the county commission is in jeopardy, the administrator submits his resignation several days later. He states: "This resignation is submitted with no negativity or ill feeling as I am proud of the accomplishments we have achieved together ... I sincerely believe this course of action is in the best interest of moving the county government forward" (*St. Petersburg Times*, September 12, 2007). His resignation is accepted by a unanimous vote of the county commission and he is eligible for a year of severance pay, $223,476.

Lessons Learned

If he had it to do all over again, what would he do differently? County Commission Chair Ronnie E. Duncan asserts: "I would do two things differently. First, when the county attorney asked me to sign the conflict of interest waiver, I would push back—not just simply acquiesced in her request. Second, I would request a full presentation of the facts about the land transaction before the County Commission. Had these two things been done, the perception of a scandal would never have happened" (Duncan 2007).

Two important, painful lessons were learned by the county administrator: don't rush a deal involving a highly visible public official and push back. In his words, "If I had it to do all over again, I would have stuck with my gut instinct to slow everything down and would have spent more time discussing the matter with the Commissioners" (Spratt 2007). Push back at whom? When asked why he didn't slow the sale of the appraiser's property to the county, he replied, "I relied on the advice of the County Attorney to settle the transaction to prevent potentially high litigation costs" (Spratt 2007). "If I had it to do over," he continued, "I would have pushed back at the County Attorney."

Failure All Around?

Here is how the scandal and its fallout are sized up in a newspaper editorial (*St. Petersburg Times*, August 30, 2007):

> The grand jury report clearly chronicles the many ways county government utterly failed taxpayers in its questionable purchase of private property owned by the PA. Now it is time to hold accountable those who violated the public's trust as they quietly conspired to appease a political insider interested only in personal gain.
>
> There is plenty of blame to go around in the 22-page report, from the PA to the county attorney to the county administrator to the silent, complicit County Commission. Although the grand jury issued no criminal indictments, it was clearly disturbed by the PA's behavior and the county's ill-considered rush to buy his private property—actions that have led to what the report calls the "breath of scandal surrounding this affair."
>
> The grand jury makes clear that the PA has acted in his own best interest rather than the public's for years. The presentment reveals that PA lobbied one of his own staff appraisers to change the amount

of upland assigned to the vacant 1.4-acre parcel he purchased in 1994—a change that lowered the taxable value that year and subsequent years.

The grand jury also seems to doubt the PA's claim early this year that a county crew had "devastated" his property and destroyed its value while cleaning out a creek in late 2004 and early 2005, leading the PA to threaten to sue the county until it agreed to buy his entire parcel for $225,000. While the grand jury said county workers should not have entered the PA's property without his permission, it found no evidence they worked on the upland, or valuable, portion of his parcel. The PA's own office had valued the wetland portion, a little over one acre, at just $5,000 an acre.

As the PA threatened to sue and applied pressure to force the county to buy his land, he had a powerful ally in the county attorney. She represents elected constitutional officers, the PA included, in their official capacities. But she represented the PA in what the grand jury defined as his "private damage claim asserted in his individual capacity against the governmental entity she was contractually and ethically bound to defend." That violates a state law, according to the presentment, and the county attorney's explanation that she merely was clearing the way for others to negotiate rings hollow.

The county attorney had the PA and the county commission chairman sign a waiver so she could "investigate" the PA's damage claim at his request, but the grand jury found she did little investigating. She did not even calculate the county's legal exposure or whether only the inexpensive wetland portion of the PA's property was the only part allegedly damaged. The grand jury found that virtually every week, she asked the county administrator for updates on the PA's deal, leaving him feeling pressured to complete the deal. It calls her behavior "perplexing and misleading," and that sounds generous.

The county administrator also is not without blame. He rushed the processing of the purchase, relied on a faulty appraisal to negotiate the price and did not tell all county commissioners everything he knew about the deal. His actions and judgment fall far below what is expected from a veteran county administrator.

The county commissioners also failed their constituents. The grand jury criticizes them for approving the PA's deal with no public discussion, which the presentment says "could have resulted in the exploration of other alternatives to purchasing the entire property and would have certainly reduced the specter of secrecy."

The grand jury's findings only strengthen the case that the PA and the county attorney are unfit to continue in public service. The PA used his public office for personal gain, and he should resign instead of continuing to make excuses. If he doesn't leave now, it will be up to voters to toss him out next year.

The county attorney also continues to defend her indefensible actions. If she does not resign, county commissioners should fire her and hire a county attorney more sensitive to both real and perceived conflicts.

As commissioners decide what to do with the county administrator, they will have to weigh his serious mistakes against his overall performance and their own failures to scrutinize the PA's land deal. At least the county administrator has written a public apology, taken responsibility, and proposed corrective actions he will take if he keeps his job. Commissioners owe the public an apology as well, because their quick and silent approval of the land purchase confirms some observers' long-held belief that the county government is disinterested in transparency. But they will have to decide whether this incident has so compromised their relationships with the county administrator that they no longer can work together.

Discussion Questions

1. Did the property appraiser do anything wrong? His response: "I did not lean on the county ... I have done absolutely nothing wrong."
2. What was the county attorney's motivation to represent the PA? Her response: "I was trying to save the county money and resolve the issue." Should the county attorney be fired?
3. Was the county administrator blind-sided by the county attorney? His response: "No comment." Should the county administrator be fired?
4. Was the county commission chair duped? His response: "No comment."
5. Was the county commission "the slack-jawed rubber stamp of a bureaucratic, public-be-damned administration?"—as one newspaper reporter claims. What should the county commission do to restore public trust and confidence in county government?
6. Did the county's highly educated, politically smart, experienced public officials have a collective lapse of ethical judgment? Or is this a case of collective bad judgment? Is there a difference?
7. Is firing the county attorney sufficient to restore public trust and confidence in county government? One online commentator put it this way: "So that's it, huh? The county attorney is made to be the villain, in which she did play a part, but the county administrator is too 'important' to replace, and the commission, my goodness gracious, where will we find the accolades to describe their good work. They all have a lot of gall and brass to be sitting up there criticizing both the county attorney and the county administrator and sounding like they had nothing to do with the deal. It is indeed a sad day in county

politics and leadership, but I'm afraid that's what we've come to accept. All of those career politicians should be shown the door. I hope the voters of this county remember this. I really do."

8. Was the county administrator treated too lightly? As one citizen put it, "... as a taxpayer I am appalled and angered at the conduct of such public servants. Their actions are unacceptable and I vote that both of them be fired immediately."
9. Should the county commission chairman resign?
10. What more could the county commission do to convince the public that it deserves their trust and confidence?

Ethical Reasoning Questions

1. Is there an ethical issue facing the county manager? The county attorney? The property appraiser? The county commission?
2. What is the ethical issue?
3. What might be done to resolve the situation?
4. Does the preferred course of action satisfy the needs/preferences of the primary stakeholders?
5. Is the preferred course of action ethical?

Case Assessment by Author

The tale of the county insider land deal scandal raises many intriguing and challenging questions about (1) the circumstances that can lead to an ethical meltdown of a well-managed professional local government whose public officials (elected and appointed) are committed in principle to ethical governance, and (2) what can be done to restore integrity in governance once a serious breakdown occurs.

Circumstances. This case study points to a set of circumstances that may not be altogether different from what might be found in many states and counties across America. First, there is a trigger event. In this case, it is the property appraiser's motivation to sell his vacant lot to the county. Second, the fragmented nature of county governance with multiple actors, each having a high degree of political and organizational independence, can be a critical ingredient in a scandal-to-be. And, it should be pointed out that the county administrator does not enjoy the political independence that the property appraiser does. So, it is not altogether surprising that the administrator would do what he could to facilitate the transaction.

Third, the case clearly illustrates the vulnerabilities that lurk just below the surface when elected officials and appointed high-ranking officials such as the county attorney hold office for an extended period of time. The county attorney and the property appraiser, not to mention the county commissioners, have known each other for a long time. While these circumstances can lead to friendships that can be a precursor to a scandal, they can also result in good intentions gone bad. That is, it may well be that the county attorney's claim that she was merely trying to save the county money by avoiding a law suit is believable and understandable, although perplexing as the grand jury noted.

Fourth, the circle of trust that bound the administrator, county attorney, and Board of County Commissioners together may indeed have been woven too tightly. That is, teamwork, loyalty, and cooperation certainly have a place in good public management, but it can also have a troubling side, as this case illustrates. A degree of healthy skepticism and questioning appears to have been absent.

What to do about an "indelible impression"? *Indelible impression*—these are the grand jury's words to describe the possibly long-lasting effect of the scandal on the "minds of the public." What can and should be done to restore integrity and public confidence in county governance? Let's consider the possibilities.

First, although arguably not as effective as one would first think, is to remove from office those officials who are responsible for the scandal. In this case, the commission dismissed the county attorney. A few days later the county administrator stepped aside. Nonetheless, these dismissals are regarded by some irate citizens as hardly sufficient. As one letter-to-editor writer asserts: "the whole County Commission should resign ..." along with the county administrator and the property appraiser. Sitting public officials are not likely to step aside over a noncriminal act, however unethical it might appear to be. This is not a garden variety, ordinary corruption case of public officials stealing from the county treasury or taking bribes to make rulings favorable to clients.

Second, perhaps the county should adopt term limits for the Board of County Commissioners. While this would curtail some degree of friendship longevity, term limits are blunt instruments. And, the time it would take to put term limits into place, as well as the political muscle needed, would be substantial. Moreover, term limits set for county commissioners would not touch the independently elected constitutional officers. Term limits may be an attractive solution to restoring integrity in governance but ...

Third, the county could adopt a code of ethics that is applicable to all public officials, elected and appointed. As it turns out, the county has a "statement of ethics" that is applicable to employees, presumably including the county administrator, and elected officials. The existing statement of ethics admonishes employees to "neither apply nor accept improper influences, favoritism and personal bias." It is evident that the existing "statement of ethics" did not prevent the problem at hand. Moreover, an indicator of the statement's relevance is suggested by the fact that it is printed on the last page of the Employee Personnel Manual. The county should draft a much stronger code that covers all elected and appointed officials. Such a code, with a credible enforcement mechanism, would certainly be viewed in a positive light by a doubting public. And, perhaps most importantly, the code should contain an "appearance standard," that is, county officials should avoid the appearance of unethical behavior. An "appearance standard" is a very high standard and, in this case, is woefully absent. The county should waste no time in taking these steps to begin to restore integrity in Pinellas County governance.

Fourth, decision-making transparency has long been employed as an effective tool for encouraging ethical behavior and combating unethical behavior. While the county operates in a reasonably transparent environment, frequently described as in "sunshine," the case at hand suggests that more sunshine should be let into the courthouse. Of course, one obvious way to do this is to make sure that *due diligence* is pursued in information provided to the public and its elected officials. The case is a classic example of the failure to practice due diligence by all officials, appointed and elected.

So what is the bottom line in this case? Does the case simply point to a collection of officials with weak characters? Is it a matter of a few "bad apples"? No. Rather, what we have here is governance run aground by public officials who developed an ethical blind spot caused in part by events, circumstances, and institutional weakness fostered by unusually lengthy tenures of high-ranking officials. "Why did the county's well educated, politically smart, experienced public officials fail to exercise sound ethical judgment?" The answer: they did not recognize the ethical maze they were about to enter and eventually become entrapped in. Good apples can be spoiled by a "bad barrel." The Pinellas case is a "bad barrel" case for the most part.

Author's Note: Based on a real case reported in the *St. Petersburg Times*, July 4, 21, 22, 24, 25, 27, 28, 29, August 2, 30, September 5, 2007, and interviews conducted by the author.

Controversies
4.10 Codes and Oaths

Cases: 3.6, 310, 4.7, 5.5, 5.8, 6.8, 6.10

Elected and appointed public officials typically express a very positive attitude toward codes of ethics. The conventional wisdom is that codes have a positive influence in governance, especially in deterring unethical acts by ethically motivated public servants. That is, unethical officials are likely to be unethical regardless of whether a code exists, but those who want to be ethical find a code helpful. Of course, the motivation for adopting a code is often the result of unethical behavior or scandal in the organization.

Oaths are also employed in some jurisdictions to encourage ethical behavior. Here is an example of an oath that one local government requires its employees to sign.

I do solemnly swear that I will support the Constitution of the United States and the Constitution of the State of _____, and faithfully discharge the duties of _____ , and to abide by and adhere to the provisions of the Code of Ethics of the Government of _____. So help me God.

Hard evidence that codes or oaths either encourage ethical behavior or discourage unethical behavior is sparse. Nonetheless, many administrators believe that codes and oaths contribute significantly to an ethical workplace. Some managers even require their subordinates to sign their professional code and hang it on their office wall.

A few years ago, the American Society for Public Administration debated the wisdom of requiring new members to sign the membership application indicating that "I support the ASPA Code of Ethics and will abide by its principles." National Council rejected this pledge and opted for an optional check off on the application form stating that "I have read and agree with ASPA's Code of Ethics."

Discussion Questions

1. Do you agree with a policy that does not require a member of a professional association to sign the membership application that he will support the association's code of ethics?
2. Should renewing members pledge to uphold the code?
3. As a top manager, would you require lower level managers to sign and put on public display their professional code of ethics or oath? Why or why not?

Commentary

Cities and counties can require employees to take an oath or sign a pledge that they will obey the code of ethics. These actions are legal and make it easier for an employer to hold an employee accountable should an ethics violation occur. A professional association is not one's employer nor is it governmental. Membership is voluntary. Still, some associations require members to sign a pledge that they will uphold the association's code of ethics while others do not. In fact, it can even be viewed as "illegal" in some states (e.g., California, Washington) to sign an associational code of ethics that endorses affirmative action—if state law has abolished affirmative action. Thus, one can be put in the position of "breaking the law" by signing an associational pledge.

Karl Thoennes III, Judicial Circuit Administrator, Unified Judicial System, State of South Dakota:

The National Association for Court Management (NACM) just adopted a new ethics code after a long, painstaking process. We did include a nondiscrimination or "fairness" provision but purposely did not refer to affirmative action, in part because of the issue that members could be viewed as violating the law and also because some colleagues saw affirmative action as more a HR/personnel/hiring-practices topic than a broader ethical principle. I suppose that NACM's Canon 1.4 Respect of Others could pretty easily be used to argue against affirmative action.

4.11 Should Professional Associations Censure and Expel Members for Violating Their Code of Ethics?

Cases: 3.5, 5.8

The International City/County Management Association censures and expels members every year as individual cases warrant. The ICMA's code of ethics has long been recognized as a model code for encouraging ethical behavior in the public management profession. Yet, year after year, the ICMA finds that some members cross over the line and must be censured and even expelled from their organization. In 2007, The ICMA Committee on Professional Conduct reviewed twenty-four ethics complaints filed against ICMA members. The review resulted in:

■ One membership bar—failure to keep a commitment when a former member reneged on his written commitment to his employer when he left the organization after serving for seven months to take a more financially lucrative position.
■ Two public censures with membership bar—member pled guilty to six felony and misdemeanor charges of theft of public funds, receiving stolen property, unlawful use of a computer, and misappropriation of government property. The member used approximately $88,000 in public funds for personal expenses, including $4,905 in petty cash and $4,100 in fraudulently transferred leave. Another member pled guilty to a charge of theft of public funds, falsified records, impugned the reputation of other public officials by falsely stating that they attended meetings with him at an adult entertainment club, and brought embarrassment to the community he served.
■ Six public censures—a manager's multiple arrests for driving under the influence undermined the public's trust in his work as a professional city manager. A member pled no-contest to two misdemeanor charges of making terroristic threats. A manager pled guilty to a misdemeanor charge of voyeurism.

■ Eight private censures—a manager signed an invitation to a fundraising event for a candidate for statewide office and made a financial contribution to the campaign. A member made campaign contributions to a candidate running for state office in another state. A manager made a small campaign contribution and displayed yard signs in support of a mayoral candidate in the community where he resided.

■ Seven closed cases.

Source: http://icma.org/main/bc.asp?bcid=75&hsid=1&ssid1=2530&ssid2=2 716 (accessed August 12, 2008).

The American Society for Public Administration (ASPA) has never censured or expelled a member, although the by-laws state that membership can be terminated "when in its sole and absolute discretion the Council determines that any member appears to have acted in violation of the Society's Code of Ethics" (Article 2: Section 5). Given this authority, why hasn't the ASPA code been aggressively enforced? The answer is based on both practical and philosophical reasons.

On the practical side, there's a rather important matter of liability. That is, should a member be expelled he could sue the ASPA and, if successful, this could inflict severe fiscal damage—perhaps even mortal organizational damage as the ASPA does not have liability insurance to cover such a loss. ICMA sources say that their liability coverage is expensive but feel nonetheless that it is important to be able to expel a member. And, rarely, if ever, has ICMA lost because censured and expelled members typically do not sue and if they do, find it is difficult for them to prove to a court of law that ICMA treated them arbitrarily or unfairly in reaching such a decision. ICMA has an elaborate adjudication process that is followed carefully whenever a member is alleged to have violated their code. ASPA has no equivalent set of due process procedures.

On the philosophical side, the argument continues as to whether ASPA's code of ethics is and should be an aspirational document or a practical set of proscriptions. Some members feel strongly that the code's strength is its aspirational qualities, while others feel just as strongly that the code's weaknesses are its absence of proscriptions akin to those found in other professional codes.

Discussion Questions

1. Is a professional code of ethics that is not enforceable a satisfactory code? Why or why not?
2. What would you do if a colleague accused you of violating your professional association's code of ethics?

Commentary

Mark Monson, Deputy Director for Administration, Department of Health
Professions, State of Virginia:

> If ASPA is to stand for something in the eyes of the public and politi-
> cal leaders, we have to be viewed as ethical above reproach. If we aren't
> viewed that way, then we are nothing more than another glorified
> public sector employee association. It seems to me, therefore, that we
> absolutely must be willing to censure and expel members for ethics vio-
> lations. I would even advocate ASPA taking public stands denouncing
> ethics violations in the public sector whenever they occur.
>
> I'm not suggesting that we establish some kind of internal affairs
> organization charged with rooting out violators. But we must not hesi-
> tate to take action when we become aware of problems.

Mylon Winn, Professor, School of Public Policy and Urban Affairs, Southern
University, Baton Rouge, Louisiana:

> The ICMA experience with enforcing its code is a perfect example of
> why ASPA's code of ethics needs to be strengthened. ICMA's experience
> with liability suits and potential legal costs associated with enforcing
> its code has not been a problem. It is, therefore, a specious argument
> to contend that ASPA should not place an enforcement provision in its
> code.
>
> Moreover, the argument that the ASPA code is primarily aspira-
> tional reinforces the contention that individual administrators should
> assume personal ethical responsibility for their behavior. Together these
> two arguments have dominated the literature and informal discussions
> about the code. The ASPA code as revised in 1994 was crafted to serve
> primarily the association and the profession. The code sought to estab-
> lish ethical standards that serve the profession at large. Hence, the con-
> tention that the code's usefulness is based on its ability to first assist
> individual administrators make ethical decisions ignores the code's
> intended purpose. If the focus is serving the public administration
> community, the fact that it is aspirational is a welcomed, but indirect,
> outcome, which can motivate individual administrators to make ethical
> decisions. Conversely, if the focus is on an aspirational code where per-
> sonal ethics is the primary emphasis, there is a limited need for a strong
> and enforceable code. In other words, it is sufficient for each individual
> administrator to self-regulate his or her personal ethical behavior.
>
> The codes adopted by the International City/County Management
> Association and the National Association of Social Workers are light

years ahead of ASPA's code. ASPA's code is where the first two were before 1920 with ICMA and 1940 for social workers. Both periods were the pre-enforcement era for these professional associations. Among social workers, self-regulation is based on having a strong and enforceable code. In this regard ASPA is behind because the aspirational and legal liability arguments have tacitly supported maintaining a weak code that has limited usefulness.

Recent practitioner surveys consistently report that practitioners are embracing ASPA's code. They are defining how ASPA's code is applied in the workplace. Hence, there is hope for escaping the limiting effects of the aspirational code and the legal liability arguments. The efforts of practitioners represent an enlightenment that may eventually cause the code to be revised to promote shared ethics values that can be enforced. Without an enforceable code, we are just a collection of people imposing our personal ethical views on public situations.

4.12 Does Courage Have a Price Tag?

Cases: 3.8, 5.4

Dateline: Nanchong City, Sichuan Province, PRC, July 2002—Frenzied man stabs bus conductor to death with more than twenty passengers looking on. None lifted a hand to help the mortally wounded conductor defend himself. This incident, according to the *China Daily* (the government's English print newspaper), stirred the nation. How could more than twenty people stand idly by and do nothing but witness such a horrific crime?

The answer, writes Xiao Xin in the July 31st issue of the *China Daily*, is straightforward: "Our society has not set up a system to encourage and financially help those who take action to fight against criminal acts." Continuing, the author suggests that a "compensation mechanism for those brave enough to act should be created." Why should someone risk injury or their life to save another if one's livelihood is endangered or one's family impoverished should a hero be maimed or killed?

Discussion Questions

1. How many dollars or Chinese yuans does it take to make a hero?
2. Does courage have a price tag?
3. Would compensation help people "understand the difference between right and wrong"?

Commentary by Author

It is hard to imagine that money can buy courage. Or put differently, can an instrumental value (money) actually produce an intangible value that we often associate with character? However, the example here is China, a country in which many people have no safety net should they be debilitated in some fashion while trying to do good. Still, the idea that courage can be bought is repugnant to most people.

4.13 Do Ethics Codes Make a Difference?

Case: 5.8

As a mid-manager in a mid-sized United States city, I keep a modestly framed copy of the ASPA Code of Ethics cut from the back cover of the *Public Administration Review* on the coffee table in my office. In the last year, three different colleagues from another department, presumably uncomfortable approaching the available leadership in that department, have come to me with ethical concerns. Each time I asked them whether there is a professional code of ethics they prefer to use, and having none, I used the ASPA code as a framework for talking through the issue at hand. Each time I also copied the code for my colleague to take back to the office with her and each was satisfied that it gave her a useful tool she did not have before.

In two cases, we concluded that the employee had fulfilled her professional obligations. In the third case, we concluded that it was indeed necessary to remedy the behavior in question even if that required whistle blowing. We monitored the situation until that happened and the harm was rectified. Our city does not lack for administrative regulations covering gifts and gratuities, nepotism, and similar procedural issues. But, I find such practical guidelines are not a substitute for a statement of principles. The ASPA code has served my colleagues and me well.

Discussion Questions

1. How do you know that a code of ethics prevented a misdeed?
2. How do you know that a code of ethics elicited an ethical behavior?
3. Are codes merely veneers? Shiny on the outside but hollow on the inside?

Commentary

Jeremy F. Plant, Professor of Public Policy and Administration, Penn State Harrisburg:

> Formal codes of ethics have become increasingly common in recent years. Often, a professional association is the source. A good example of

the utility of a professional code of ethics, in this case the code promulgated by the American Society for Public Administration (ASPA), is provided in this case. The mid-level manager (presumably a member of ASPA) has used the ASPA code to provide useful guidance to colleagues in the city government. Having the ASPA code as a set of principles seems to enable the individual to provide ethical guidance with a firm foundation in professionalism. The role played by the manager as an informal advisor on ethical questions is no doubt strengthened by her ability to provide not simply a personal opinion but one grounded in ASPA's professional code.

The ASPA code is designed to provide a set of five canons or principles: serve the public interest, respect the constitution and the law, demonstrate personal integrity, promote ethical organizations, and strive for professional excellence. In each of the five areas, between four and eight specific examples are given to show how the principles are expected to guide behavior. While the two cases in which professional obligations were met are not spelled out, the example of whistle blowing derives from the second canon in the code, respect the Constitution and the law, article 6: "Encourage and facilitate legitimate dissent activities in government and protect the whistle blowing rights of public employees."

As an association bringing together a broad base of public sector practitioners, academics, and students, the ASPA code has been written to provide ethical guidance for a wide variety of settings and professional activities. The code of ethics of the International City/County Management Association (ICMA) provides a code more specifically designed for professionals working in city and county governments. The manager in this case, working in a mid-sized city, might also find it useful to review the ICMA code to see if it provides more specific answers to ethical problems of the sort indicated in the case.

The role played by the manager in this case is a positive one, but it indicates a serious problem if a number of employees from different departments do not feel comfortable going to their supervisors with ethical issues. It seems to be time for the leadership of the city, whether elected or managerial, to provide ethical training or an ethics audit for the city government as a whole. Their practical codes of conduct do not seem to be grounded enough in ethics to provide adequate guidance for the employees. In the meantime, it is providential that there is an ethical exemplar like the manager in the case who takes the time to listen to individuals troubled by what they see as problems of ethics that have no simple or self-evident answers.

4.14 San Diego on the Move!

Cases: 4.9, 5.3, 5.8

The San Diego Mayor's Office of Ethics and Integrity (OEI) opened its doors in early 2006 in response to a string of scandals that brought down top ranking city officials. The city's website states that the OEI has been established to promote a strong ethical work environment for city employees. Operating alongside an existing Ethics Commission, the OEI conducts training for city employees in departments under the jurisdiction of the mayor. The Ethics Commission has no jurisdiction over classified city employees nor do the provisions of the Ethics Ordinance regulate the activities of classified city employees. Investigations of alleged violations of the city's ethics code as well as enforcement of the code are the responsibility of the Ethics Commission, which was established in 2001. Both units conduct training programs, albeit aimed at different audiences. Confusing? Perhaps. Visitors to each unit's website find links that explain "how we differ from the Ethics Commission/ Mayor's Office of Ethics and Integrity."

To its credit, the new OEI contracted with the Ethics Resource Center to assess the ethics culture of city departments. Online and paper surveys were employed to canvass 10,992 city employees. The survey results found that (1) many city employees are unsure about the city's ethics policies and procedures and (2) employees do not trust the city's confidential process for reporting misconduct. Among the other findings, 41 percent report that they had observed unethical behavior at work, a much higher percentage than the 26 percent reported by the Ethics Resource Center's National Business Ethics Survey.

City administrators say they will use the findings to strengthen their ethics cultures.

Discussion Questions

1. Should more municipal governments assess their ethics cultures?
2. What assessment tools other than a survey can be used for this purpose?
3. Are there any "negatives" in conducting an ethics culture assessment?

Commentary

The survey conducted by the Ethics Resource Center points to the clear, if not compelling need for the city of San Diego to monitor its ethics culture. Most local governments spend very little time or money assessing their ethics culture, which can be an important preventive step in avoiding an ethics scandal. Rather, the vast majority of cities ignore ethics matters until a scandal occurs. Why is the learning curve so steep? Mostly because city leaders are busy doing other things and usually do not want to allocate scarce resources to managing ethics in the workplace. After all, governments do not exist to produce a product called ethics. Do they?

Sources: http://www.sandiego.gov/oei/about/index.shtml; www.ethics.org

4.15 An Ethics Test for Local Government Employees

Cases: 3.3, 5.7, 6.1, 6.2, 6.4, 6.6

1. An inspector is asked to approve construction work that does not comply with the city's building codes. In exchange, the contractor offers tickets to an upcoming concert. Should you accept the tickets? Yes/No
2. Your relative wants to set up a snow removal business and in addition to other contracts, they want to have a contract with the city. You work for the department that issues this type of contract, but not in the contract section. Should you declare a conflict of interest? Yes/No
3. You have a business in addition to your job with the city. You spend time on the telephone arranging business deals, contacting suppliers and potential clients. Your work for the city suffers because of the amount of time spent on your private business. Is this ethical? Yes/No
4. You have learned several specialized skills working for the city. Another local government learns of your talent and wants you to work for them, "moonlighting" on the weekends, if you are not called in by your employer to work on an emergency problem. Should you "moonlight"—that is, work part-time for the other city? Yes/No
5. A department head or city council member contacts you for information about how a city service is handled. You provide the information to the department head or the city council member who made the request. You then send additional information directly to the citizen who had contacted the director or city council member. Should you have sent the additional information? Yes/No
6. You spend several hours during the week using the city supplied computer to download information on a relative's medical condition. Is this ethical? Yes/No
7. A health inspector arrives at a restaurant during the start of the lunch hour. Several violations are noted during the inspection. The manager offers the employee lunch in exchange for waiting to write up the inspection, asking for time to make the needed corrections after the lunch hour. Should the employee accept the free lunch? Yes/No

8. You have inspected a building and find items that do not meet the city's building codes. You write up your inspection and then leave. The contractor contacts you, does not like your answer, and asks to speak to your supervisor. They discuss the situation and find another option that will meet the building codes and not cost the contractor a whole lot of money. Is the supervisor's action ethical? Yes/No

9. You inspect a restaurant just after they have had a spill of grease in the kitchen. It has contaminated surfaces and food. The kitchen staff is busy throwing out food and sanitizing surfaces. You tell the manager you will wait until the kitchen order is restored before conducting your inspection. Is this ethical? Yes/No

10. You are asked to provide a special service to someone, for example, to just let him or her ride with you, in your city vehicle, for a private (not city related) purpose. Is this ethical? Yes/No

11. A manager in another department comes to you and asks that you handle a matter outside of the normal process and it is a service that not everyone in the city would get. The manager states that the person needing help is a very important person and the normal rules and procedures don't apply to their request. Should you handle the matter as requested? Yes/No

Answers

> **Author's Note:** This test was developed based on scenarios published in an ethics training handbook used by the Kansas City, Missouri, Education & Development Office.

1. no
2. no
3. no
4. yes
5. yes
6. no
7. no
8. yes
9. yes
10. no
11. no

Commentary by Author

Ethics tests may be helpful in informing employees of basic "dos" and "donts" in a specific jurisdiction from the perspective of "how to stay out of trouble." But they do little to help employees resolve challenging ethical dilemmas. A very different kind of experience is needed for this purpose.

4.16 Learning Ethics Online

Controversial? Perhaps, depending on what it means to "learn" ethics. If learning ethics means adopting behavioral practices advocated by a professional association, then learning ethics online might work. Consider the online ethics course prepared by the Florida City/County Management Association (FCCMA). (The FCCMA website is at http://www.fccma.org/.)

The FCCMA has placed online a set of cases linked to the twelve tenets in the ICMA code along with a set of questions asking the learner to select the "right" choice. Here's a case example.

The recently hired, first-time city manager of a "university town" and his wife are invited by the president of the university to join him in the president's suite at the upcoming football game as a way to introduce the manager to the university. The university president indicates that they will also be joined by the mayor, the president of the Chamber of Commerce, the CEO of the regional power company, and several other community leaders who are football fans and supporters of the university. Even though the city manager is not a huge football fan, he feels that it is important that he establish a positive relationship with the president and community leaders.

The city manager checks the city charter and state law and does not find any guidance as to any restrictions that would prohibit him from accepting the invitation. The university and the city have enjoyed a great relationship over the years and there are no pending projects between the city and the university.

The manager considers a number of factors regarding a decision to accept the invitation to attend the football game: (1) The manager wants to get to know the university president better (as well as other community leaders) and make a good first impression. (2) The "first" city manager's position salary does not afford the manager with much disposable income to afford tickets to the football game. (3) The manager is concerned that not accepting the invitation could damage the positive "town and gown" relationship that exists. (4) The mayor stops by to see the manager to let him know how much he is looking forward to introducing him to the college football weekend experience. (5) The manager's wife really wants to attend a big-time college football game and sit in the president's skybox.

Discussion Questions

1. What should the manager do?
2. Should he accept or not accept the tickets?
3. Can one learn ethics from online courses?

Commentary by Author

Ethics are often regarded as a very personal set of values or principles that are acquired early in life from one's parents, friends, church, or community. By adulthood, it is suggested, one's ethical worldview is in place and little can be done to change it. This view is contested by those who contend that human beings experience different levels and stages of moral development. Kohlberg (1981) posits three levels with six stages. The three levels are pre-conventional, conventional, and post-conventional. At the pre-conventional level, typically exemplified by children, "right" and "wrong" are defined by punishment and obedience. At the conventional level, where most adolescents and adults reason, one judges the morality of action in response to societal views and expectations. Social norms and group values such as following the Golden Rule and obeying the law are important. At the post-conventional level, one engages in abstract moral reasoning. Mahatma Gandhi and Martin Luther King, for example, are examples of individuals who embraced universal ethical principles that justified disobedience to laws.

Learning ethics online? Not likely if one accepts Kohlberg's theory of moral development.

References

Ashworth, K. 2001. *Caught between the Dog and the Fireplug or How to Survive Public Service.* Washington, D.C.: Georgetown University Press.

Duncan, R. 2007. Interview conducted by author on October 11, 2007.

Kohlberg, L. 1981. *The Philosophy of Moral Development, Moral Stages and the Idea of Justice.* New York: Harper & Row.

Spratt, S. Telephone interview conducted by author on December 14, 2007.

St. Petersburg Times, September 12, 2007.

Chapter 5

Building Organizations of Integrity

> I seen my opportunities and I took 'em.
> **Senator George Washington Plunkitt** *of Tammany Hall explaining the difference between honest graft and dishonest graft.*

Cities and counties have a long and all-too-often tarnished history of unethical governance. The nineteenth-century era of Tammany Hall politics in New York City have historical counterparts in the Pendergast machine of Kansas City, the boss Daly political dynasty in Chicago, and the feudal barons in Philadelphia. In more recent times, the cities of Detroit, San Diego, Washington, D.C., Minneapolis, Newark, Pittsburgh, and Spokane, among others, have suffered from errant behavior by public officials. The times change, however, and the more flagrant offenses of years past have largely given way to a host of more subtle but perhaps just as pernicious challenges dealing with human rights, justice, duty, fraud, abuse of power, advocacy, hierarchy, and more.

Nonetheless, the task of strengthening ethics in local governance remains a "work-in-progress." The strides made in recent decades are noteworthy and include curbs on nepotism, financial disclosure, conflicts of interest, post-employment relationships, secrecy, use and abuse of equipment and property, and other measures. These "don't do" admonishments, along with the establishment of a galaxy of state-local ethics laws and regulatory commissions, have done much to improve local governance.

Yet, lapses are not uncommon and, some would argue, are occurring with increasing frequency. The 2007 survey of ethics in government by the Ethics

Resource Center (ERC) supports this view. The ERC report finds that six of every ten local government employees say they witnessed misconduct at work over the past twelve months, with abusive behavior and placing one's own interests ahead of the organization leading the way. Additionally, the survey found that one of every four local government employees say they work in environments conducive to misconduct. Other surveys report lower levels of misdeeds but still underscore the need to strengthen the ethics culture of the local government workforce (Menzel 2008).

The Ethics Resources Center study points to a glaring information gap between top management and employees regarding the extent of misconduct (see Figure 5.1). Organizational leaders just don't know how much misconduct is occurring. This situation in combination with a nonconducive work environment and ineffective intervention contributes to a high rate of misconduct that places the public trust at risk.

Practicing public managers, especially in local government, have become increasingly drawn into the world of policy making and community development. Public managers are expected to be leaders, not just implementers of policy handed down by their elected bosses. Consequently, they face the challenge of leading "without fear or favor"—an enormous challenge.

The cases and controversies that follow are illustrative of the contemporary nature of ethical challenges faced by local governments—human rights, justice, duty, fraud, abuse of power. The lead case presents a most unusual situation in which the city manager of an urban community decides to have a gender

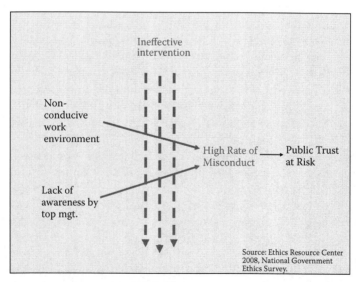

Figure 5.1   A high rate of misconduct is a result of a nonconducive work environment, a lack of awareness, by top management, and no effective intervention.

reassignment, that is, change his sex. As the case progresses, the reader will find that this decision leads him down a path of surprises and disappointments, and eventually he is abandoned by the community he served for many years. While the case is unusual in the history of city management, it describes a complex ethical environment in which the city manager believes that he is in a "city of progress."

The cases in Chapter 5 are cross-listed in a matrix with the ethical competencies in Appendix 3. The matrix cells enable the reader to identify specific cases with specific competencies. For example, the competency "*refuse to do something unethical*" is highlighted in two cases: 5.4 "What's a Whistle-Blower to Do?" and 5.5 "When the Chief Asks You to Lie."

5.1 What Would You Do if You Were the Sheriff?

Controversies: 3.13
Key Words: county, loyalty, cook the books, leadership
Case Complexity → Moderate
CD: 4.34 Citizen-Client-Customer
CD: 4.35 Ethics Management for Public Administrators

Imagine that you are the county sheriff in a large, urban, high-growth county where you have served as a popular elected county sheriff for twenty years. To your dismay, you are informed that one of your sergeants who has served the county for many years is charged with 129 counts of falsification of official documents, 144 counts of failure to follow standard operating procedures, and conduct unbecoming a member of the sheriff's office—charges made by your internal affairs investigators. The deputy, as it turns out, coordinates all the work at the port authority and is in a position to log off-duty assignments for himself at the port that far exceed regular work week hours. The investigators charge that the sergeant knowingly cooked the books and over-rode computer programs to prevent others from knowing what he did.

Discussion Questions

1. What would you do with the sergeant?
   a. Put a letter of reprimand in his personnel file?
   b. Ban him from working any off-duty assignments?
   c. Suspend him, reduce him in rank, fire him?

The sergeant's supervisor wants him suspended for thirty days and reduced to the rank of deputy. The disciplinary review board wants him fired. You are about to retire and don't need to worry about being reelected any more. The allegations against the sergeant have been published in the local newspaper. What would you do?

Results

The sheriff placed the officer on a twenty-day suspension without pay, banned him from working off-duty assignments for two years, and ordered him not to coordinate any off-duty work for the rest of his career.

Case Assessment

Mary Delano, New Jersey Institute of Technology, Center for Architecture & Building Science Research, Newark, New Jersey:

> As managers of public agencies and publicly funded organizations, we have an obligation to perform our jobs with the highest of ethical standards in regards to behavior and financial responsibility. The deputy abused both. His abuse was not minor, it was to his own benefit and at the expense of the tax payer, and therefore he should have been fired for cause. The punishment did not fit the crime. In the public sector we are obligated to make decisions and act based on what is right and appropriate within the framework of what we are entrusted to do on the public's behalf or we risk losing the public trust and support.
>
> I say the sheriff responded in a way that was convenient, perhaps, but not in a way that was justifiably called for and appropriate. He therefore misused his power for convenience and this is wrong. We are betraying the public trust by making decisions based on convenience or politics or expedience, or what have you (because we have the power to). We should make decisions based on what is right and appropriate within the framework of what we are entrusted to do on the public's behalf.
>
> This is what ethics is about—doing what is right as opposed to what we can get away with for self-serving reasons.

Mark Monson, Deputy Director for Administration, Department of Health Professions, State of Virginia:

> If I were the sheriff, I would immediately suspend the deputy pending a review of the Internal Affairs report. (Whether he is placed on paid or unpaid suspension would depend on the internal policy regarding such suspensions. If there is no policy, I'd place him on unpaid suspension.) If the review of the investigators' report shows that he is guilty of the

allegations, I would immediately fire him. Moreover, I would refer the matter to the local commonwealth attorney for criminal prosecution.

My logic ... This is not an ordinary bureaucrat. This is a person who took an oath to uphold the law and has the authority to arrest those who do not. He violated that oath. Punishment for such a violation must be clear, swift, and unequivocal. The public deserves nothing less. Moreover, failure to take strong action could cause all the members of law enforcement in that community to be tainted by his actions. Law enforcement officers already have a tough enough job. They don't need that burden, too.

Author's Note: Based on a case reported in the *Tampa Tribune*, June 9, 2004, Metro p. 2.

5.2 A New City Manager's Dilemma

Controversies: 6.12
Key Words: confidential information, trust, city manager, privacy
Case Complexity → Low

Assume that you are a brand new city manager on the job for only a couple months. Alas, you find out that your administrative assistant is dating a firefighter who is currently the president of the local firefighter's union. While there is no city policy that prohibits dating among employees, you are nervous about the situation and concerned that the relationship could result in a compromised (real or imagined) ethical issue. What should you do to be confident that the relationship will not be a problem?

Discussion Questions

1. Is this an ethics issue? Management issue? Both?
2. Should you have a private counseling session with each employee encouraging them to end the relationship?
3. Should you speak only to the administrative assistant? Why or why not?
4. Does the city manager have any "right" to intervene in a private affair?
5. As there is no direct supervisor-subordinate relationship, should you simply ignore the situation?

Case Assessment

Jim Drumm, City Manager of High Springs, Florida:

> I would sit down with the administrative assistant and explain the confidentiality of the administrative assistant's job and explain that there could appear to others in the organization to be a conflict of interest due to this situation. Explain that trust to all involved is imperative. Explain that for her protection you may have to use other administrative staff to prepare any union documents. I would also warn that if this does cause performance issues with her work, she may have to be transferred to another department.

Vincent Long, Deputy County Administrator, Leon County, Florida:

> Well, employees are people, and people have relationships. There is no reporting relationship between your administrative assistant and the firefighter, so I doubt your HR policies prohibit this relationship. However, there are some things that are just very good to know, and this is one of them. Judgment and discretion are more important than any clerical skill for the successful administrative assistant to a city manager. However, knowing what you now know, your judgment and discretion will serve you well in handling this hot potato. There is certainly no need to overreact or perhaps to do anything immediately. After you get to know your administrative assistant better, let her know that you are OK with her relationship, but discuss possible scenarios where she might be "conflicted" in her role vis-à-vis the role of her boyfriend and discuss how the two of you should deal with any of those should they arise. This conversation is a great opportunity to establish trust and respect with your new employee as well as to establish some important professional expectations.

Carl Harness, Assistant County Administrator, Hillsborough County, Florida:

> Although this situation appears to be quite sticky, I feel that the solution is relatively straightforward. You obviously cannot suggest to your administrative assistant that she stop dating the firefighter (who also happens to be the local firefighter's union president), but the opportunity for personal versus professional conflict could exist in this current state of affairs. First, you should have a very serious discussion with her concerning what you expect from her as a member of the city manager's team. Second, discuss the importance of confidentiality that

comes with this position, and hopefully through that conversation you can determine if she can handle this situation in a professional manner. Should you both agree to give this working relationship a try, you need to be clear that any breach of business-related information (especially any information related to the fire department) will be grounds for serious disciplinary action. On the other hand, if you find that this individual cannot handle her responsibilities in a professional manner due to the fact that you are the "brand new" city manager, you are not obligated to keep this individual in her current position. I would recommend that you discuss the situation with her (recognizing the conflicts that could arise within your working relationship) and transfer her to a similar position within the organization with no adverse changes to her rate of pay or job responsibilities. Once the transfer has been completed, you can implement a recruitment process to fill the open position.

5.3 Commercializing a City's Website

Controversies: 4.14, 6.14, 6.17
Key Words: city, home page, advertising, fairness
Case Complexity → Low
CD: 4.16 Cities-Counties Ethics Issues

As the newly appointed city manager of Anytown, USA, you are determined to bring your city into the Information Age as quickly as possible. Within two months after taking your new post, you establish a Division of Information and Technology Services and order the director "to get all city agencies on the Internet within six months." The director took her charge seriously and formed a task force to determine what would be needed to bring the city online. After three months of discussion, the task force reported to the director the city should develop a home page with links to each city agency. Additionally, the task force recommended that the city sell advertising space on its home page. Task force members felt that this would be a good way to help recover the costs of acquiring new computer hardware and software needed to go online. Moreover, you have made it clear that you strongly favor public-private sector partnerships, especially if they promote economic development.

The director asks you, the city manager, how she should respond to the questions that follow. What would you say to her?

Discussion Questions

As the director of ITS began to mull over the recommendations of the task force, she asked herself:

1. Are there any ethical or legal issues in selling advertising space on the city's home page?
2. Do government agencies accept advertising on print publications such as annual reports, tax forms, etc.?
3. Is selling commercial advertisements on the city's home page any different than, say, placing commercial ads on municipal buses?
4. Can the city refuse to advertise some products or services?
5. Would a company bidding on a city contract be allowed to place an advertisement on the city's home page?
6. Would such an ad create the appearance of a conflict of interest?
7. Would political ads be forbidden?
8. How would the city set advertising rates and choose between competitors?
9. Should a disclaimer be placed on the home page stating that the city does not endorse the products or services being advertised?

Case Assessment

Liangfu Wu, Director, Information Services, Village of Downers Grove, Illinois:

> The issue that the city manager faces deals with a fundamental question concerning the role that government plays in the society. As it is important for a city to maintain adequate revenues to support its services to the community it serves, which is the main goal of this new city manager, public agencies need to realize that not all revenue sources available today can be considered a financial solution for the agency.
>
> For a municipality, two major funding sources are service-based fees and tax. Both are considered public funds. Attached to the public funds are two principles underlying any decisions the city manager makes. First, whether a municipality that operates based on public funds can compete in the market place against other private business, in this case, those marketing and advertising firms. A website owned and operated by the city is basically a public service. To sell advertising space on the website clearly constitutes unfair competition between the city and private advertising firms. The private firms could argue that the city uses their tax dollars against private businesses that pay the tax to the city.
>
> Second, due to its funding sources, the city, when providing services, cannot discriminate against one or more groups because of their social status. It is the principle of fairness in government

services (Klosko 1992). Based on this principle, if the city were to start selling advertising space on its website, it would have to offer the same space and price to all private parties, including political organizations and those whose contents may not fit the image of a public agency.

Although the city could technically claim that its website is totally funded on the revenue generated from the commercial space, the ownership of the website links the contents back to the city.

Stephen K. Aikens, Assistant Professor, Public Administration Program, Department of Government and International Affairs, University of South Florida:

> AUGUST 8, 2008
> FROM: THE CITY MANAGER, CITY OF ANYTOWN
> TO: THE DIRECTOR OF INFORMATION AND TECH-
> NOLOGY SERVICES
> RE: SELLING OF ADVERTISING ON CITY WEBSITE

If done properly, the selling of advertising on our city website can generate a stream of revenues that can reduce the cost of providing government information and services online and save taxpayers some money. Another way of reducing the cost of our city government services online is through sponsorship, whereby sponsors fund parts of the city's web presence, or support this effort by providing services or equipment in exchange for visible acknowledgement. Although either approach can be legitimately used to finance our government's web presence, serious ethical consequences regarding appearance of favoritism and conflict of interest can arise if appropriate guidelines are not developed and strictly enforced. Regardless of the form of revenue generation utilized, we must exercise due care to retain our government's independence in the eyes of citizens. The management of our advertising or sponsorship can be done through in-house management of web space or through the use of a third-party supplier under appropriate agreement. Cost and benefit considerations, coupled with the availability of internal expertise, must be carefully weighed in deciding the most appropriate route for our city, and must be included in the evaluation of the business case for making use of advertising or sponsorship on our city website.

Considering the potential ethical implications and controversy surrounding the commercialization of government websites, we must ensure we have the trained resources to manage, promote, and sell the advertising services. The Division of Information and Technology Services must carefully judge the balance between the effort required to achieve the maximum value from advertising, and the income that is earned. In designing the advertising or page, we should ensure the advertiser's brands do not compete with or detract from the effectiveness, integrity, and appearance of our government, and attention should be given to avoid any implication of endorsement of products or services. We must also ensure we have a published privacy statement on the website and must adhere strictly to this statement if we choose to use information about user behavior in selling advertising space.

In order to avoid appearance of favoritism and conflict of interest, the city website should not accept political advertisements. In addition, all advertising space should be promoted at arms length, and any sponsorship be sought in an open and even handed manner using the appropriate public sector procurement methods to secure contract agreements. Furthermore, we should seriously consider prohibiting companies or firms involved in significant commercial or contract negotiations with our city from sponsoring or advertising on our city website, and we should develop and document strict standards as to the nature and type of products and services that will be accepted for advertisement on our website. In whatever we do, we must remember that our government exists to serve the public interest, which implies the need to balance our online services revenue needs against the public trust and citizens' confidence in their government.

Author's Note: Case based on an Internet listserv discussion. Names and places are fictitious.

5.4 What's a Whistle-Blower to Do?

Controversies: 3.11, 3.15, 3.19, 4.12
Key Words: whistle-blower, nonprofit agency, city, federal grant, abuse of power
Case Complexity → Moderate
CD: 7.5 Why are people (un)ethical?

You recently retired from the U.S. Air Force and go to work for a nonprofit agency that works with the city's low-income housing program, which is funded by a federal grant. On four separate occasions over the next few months you are told by the city program administrator to use money from one federal grant to pay for a project that wasn't covered by the grant. At first you follow orders and then begin to realize that if anyone objected, you would be vulnerable to charges of misusing federal funds. So what do you do?

You put your objections in writing and call the regional headquarters of the U.S. Department of Housing and Urban Development, identifying yourself as a whistle-blower. In the meantime, you are asked to approve the expenditure of $87,150 on a private residence that would sell for $70,000. You resist, asserting that federal guidelines prohibit the city from spending that much money on any low-income housing. The program administrator complains to your boss that you are not attentive, productive, or responsive to city staff. Your boss removes you from the project. Frustrated but convinced that you did the right thing, you quit your job and write a letter to the mayor detailing your concerns about the misuse of federal funds. The mayor never responds.

A few months later, HUD officials admonish city officials about using low-income housing funds to help residents who did not qualify. Fast forward two more years— the city's internal auditing staff reports to the mayor that the housing administrator has issued questionable loans, kept poor records, and awarded noncompetitive bids. HUD officials also warn the mayor that the administrator may have misused $1.4 million in federal funds. The mayor dismisses the criticism by HUD officials, saying that he has made changes in response to the internal audit report.

Federal auditors are still not satisfied and warn that the city may have to repay the $1.4 million. The administrator claims that the feds are applying ridiculous rules. The mayor backs him. The administrator appears before city council and asserts that "we do not intend to follow HUD's direction at this point." All but one member of city council praises the administrator.

Fast forward two more years—a federal indictment charges that the city housing administrator used government jobs to reap thousands of dollars in gratuities for seven years. The city is required to wire transfer the U.S. Treasury a total of $1,402,650.

Discussion Questions

1. Is the whistle-blower guilty of "going along to get along"? After all, he did not contact HUD until after he had approved four contracts.
2. Should the whistle-blower have stayed within the organization and tried to change the practice of "fudging" federal funds?
3. Should he have leaked the story to the media?

Case Assessment

Roberta Ann Johnson, Professor of Politics, University of San Francisco:

> The whistle-blower in this case could rightly feel a sense of satisfaction that the wrongdoing he witnessed and tried to stop was exposed and addressed. The city program administrator was indicted and the city

was required to return the federal dollars that were spent inappropriately. But it took seven years to expose the wrong doing and it cost the whistle-blower his job. How might he have protected his job and how might he have been more effective as a whistle-blower?

Systemic problem: Let's call the whistle-blower Larry. He found himself in a situation where corruption was tolerated, where a public agency was bending and breaking rules, where watchdog mechanisms were not working in a timely way, where elected officials ignored the problem, and where federal oversight was moving at a snail's pace.

What to do: Larry worked for a nonprofit organization that administered the city's housing programs. (1) It would have been useful for him to try to find allies in his organization. If he talked informally to other employees about his concerns he might have found out that they were shared. He might have been a more effective whistle-blower if he had blown the whistle with others. With a group of whistle-blowers, it is also less likely that he would have left and lost his job.

(2) It was important for Larry to keep accurate records of all the questionable exchanges—recording the times when he accommodated his supervisor's requests and the transactions when he refused to comply would provide the kind of information that a comprehensive investigator needs. (3) When Larry decided to blow the whistle, he had choices of how to tell and whom to tell. He could have remained anonymous when he contacted HUD officials and the mayor's office, but this may have been difficult working in an apparently small organization in which his identity could have been recognized. The Washington, D.C.-based whistle-blower organization, the Government Accountability Project (GAP), suggests that whistle-blowers who want to remain anonymous should consider providing information to nonprofit advocacy organizations that blow the whistle for them. GAP recommends the Project on Government Oversight (POGO), a group that has skillfully assisted whistle-blowers in this way for years.

But Larry chose to divulge his identity. He contacted the regional headquarters of the U.S. Department of Housing and Urban Development (HUD), the agency that was providing the funding. He also tried to expose the wrongdoing to the mayor of the city. Neither of these efforts brought timely or effective relief. The mayor supported the corrupt city administrator, and while HUD found fault with the corrupt administrator's actions, HUD merely admonished city officials who then ignored the federal agency.

The city's internal auditing staff remains a bright light in this story. The city auditors did their job and reported to the mayor. They found the problems and did not cover them up or blow them off. The whistle-blower might have provided his records to assist the auditors. Unfortunately, with an unresponsive mayor, the auditors were powerless.

One avenue that is often used by whistle-blowers, and was not used in this case, is the news media. Using newspaper and local television outlets to expose the wrongdoing might have been useful as a means to embarrass the mayor and city council into action. Whistle-blowers and their issues are often featured in news stories. But, there are no guarantees of publicity or success. This may not have been the kind of story that garners enough public attention and creates public anger. Stories about administrative rules and financial technicalities are often not sexy enough or sufficiently riveting to excite the public. Unfortunately though, without public outcry, these elected officials did not feel any pressure to change.

When nothing changed, Larry felt and became more and more disempowered. This situation is the most challenging for a whistle-blower. Clearly, the problem was not just one corrupt individual, but was the elected officials who were indifferent in a political environment that tolerated wrongdoing.

Posted on ETHTALK listserv by Mark G. Michaelsen:

Whistle-blowers are motivated by many things. Some are narcissists who crave attention. Some are following through on threats made at work: Do it my way or else.

However, some whistle-blowers come forward because they know right from wrong. They come forward out of sense of civic responsibility. Public servants who are discharged for blowing the whistle on public wrongdoing are protected under many laws. If a whistle-blower faced grave personal risk, that might change the equation.

Consider the motivation of whistle-blower Peter T. Scannell. Promoted from an entry-level customer service representative for mutual fund giant Putnam Investments, Peter Scannell noticed some large clients, including some unions, were using international time differences to make big money in buying low and selling high. That's called market timing. While not illegal per se, liquidating securities to pay withdrawals of market timers cost long-term small investors. Putnam mutual fund prospectuses said market timing wouldn't be tolerated.

Scannell went to his supervisors, who brushed him off. So, he started to keep a record of market timing transactions he personally processed. He took the records to the Securities and Exchange Commission, which didn't act. Then he went to Massachusetts regulators, who did act. It resulted in charges against Putnam, which settled for $110 million. On February 1, 2005, an independent consultant determined Putnam owed another $100 million in damages to small investors.

What did Scannell hope to accomplish? He wanted to do the right thing. What did he get for blowing the whistle on market timing at Putnam? He got death threats from union members. Scannell was almost beaten to death, too.

It's a sad, but inspiring, story. How many of us would have the courage to blow the whistle on wrongdoing when it threatens us or our family personally, not just our livelihood?

Author's Note: Case based on a story reported in the *St. Petersburg Times*, March 8, 2004, B1. Peter T. Scannell testified before the Subcommittee on Financial Management, the Budget, and International Security, U.S. Senate Committee on Governmental Affairs. His testimony is available at www. senate.gov/~govt-aff/_files/012704scannell.pdf

5.5 When the Chief Asks You to Lie

Controversies: 3.12, 4.10, 6.19
Key Words: truth, abuse of power, city, loyalty, family, annual evaluation
Case Complexity → Moderate
CD: 7.13 Public Service Ethics and Professionalism

You are the captain of one of the city's fire stations. The fire station is in serious need of repairs as a critical portion of the station has settled, causing it to become unusable. A tropical storm has blown across the city, causing heavy damage and flooding. The area in and around the city has been declared a disaster area and both state and federal disaster officials are assessing damage for emergency relief. The fire chief has advised federal and state officials that the damage to the station was caused by the storm. Prior to relief officials arriving to assess the damage at the station, the fire chief calls you to advise you of their impending arrival and tells you to inform the relief officials that the damage is a result of the storm.

Although this is not stated, annual evaluations are due next month and the chief is known to use the evaluations to reward loyalty and punish those who do not follow his wishes. Due to a previous illness in the family, you are very dependent on his annual evaluation to keep your salary up with inflation.

Discussion Questions

1. Should you lie for the chief?
2. Should you complain to the chief that you are being put in a position that you cannot agree with?
3. Should you pass the lie on to another staff member by asking him or her to deceive the assessment team?

Case Assessment

Chris Bosch, Fire Chief, Tracy, California:

> I believe that you should stand behind the truth regardless of the fire chief's request or the potential outcome. To mislead the federal disaster officials would be a complete breach of ethics and could cause you to lose the respect of your staff and could cost you and the chief your jobs. Chances are, if your chief was at all credible, he would never have placed any of his staff members in this position.
>
> You should attempt to discuss this issue with the chief, clearly state your position on the issue and make it clear that you will not mislead the federal officials. You should document your discussion with the chief as well as the outcome and maintain a copy of that information for your files. Chances are, you have not heard the end of this issue. If the chief causes you to miss your annual merit increase as a result of your position on this issue, you would be justified to seek counsel and take this matter up through the courts.

Randy Deicke, Deputy Fire Chief, Batavia, Illinois:

> First off, any officer with integrity would not lie or ask someone else to lie. That would never be in the best interest of the department or the individual. But, the question is what steps should be taken and the rationale behind them.
>
> First, you have to take a close look at all the facts. This often involves physically listing them so they can be evaluated. The facts are:
>
> ■ A portion of the fire station has become unstable.
> ■ The chief claims the damage is due to the recent storm.
> ■ He wants you to inform federal officials that the damage was caused by the storm.
> ■ Your evaluation is due next month.
> ■ You believe the chief evaluates based on loyalty.

■ You need a good evaluation because monetary issues have put a great strain on you and your family.

The assumption is that you do not believe that the damage to the fire station was caused by the storm. Therefore, you feel that the chief is asking you to lie for him.

I would let the chief know that I feel that the damage was not caused by the storm, but rather by the settling of the building. Then, I would suggest a city engineer come out and give their impression of what caused the damage. A good chief would agree to a professional opinion and stick by it either way. That should be the end of the story.

But, what if the chief says no to an engineer and you feel strongly that you would be lying if you told the federal officials the damage was caused by the storm?

At that point, I would let the chief know my feelings and recommend that he have someone else talk to the federal officials. I would also explain that if I should find definitively that the damage was not caused by the storm, it would be my obligation to let the appropriate authorities know. It would probably not go well on my evaluation, and I may not get that cost of living increase. My family and I would have to survive, but I should not let my personal life get so dependent on my job that it could compromise my integrity.

The solution was somewhat easy because firefighters are usually well protected from being fired for arbitrary or deceitful decisions. In this case, the most I was at risk of losing was a cost of living increase or perhaps a future promotion. None of those would mean the end of the world. But, without that protection or if this was the private sector, the situation could have a much larger consequence. If I was in jeopardy of losing my job and maybe eventually my home or family, the decision is no longer as easy to make. But, that is for another case study.

5.6 To Obey or Not to Obey!

Controversies: 3.19, 5.17
Key Words: village, insubordination, chain of command, equity, lying
Case Complexity → Moderate
CD: 3.8 Ethics Test
CD: 4.16 Cities-Counties Ethics Issues

Imagine you are an inspector in the Village Engineering Department and have the responsibility to inspect the sidewalks of residents whose streets are being resurfaced. The village policy is clear—residents who live on streets that are partially resurfaced must pay up to $1,000 per home for their sidewalks to be replaced. But, residents on streets that are fully resurfaced are not required to pay. Your job is to determine how much a resident who lives on a partially resurfaced street must pay to replace the sidewalk. Sounds straightforward enough, doesn't it? Not so. Why? Because the technical criteria for determining the difference between a full resurface and a partial resurface are murky. Moreover, as the inspector, you have suffered for many years trying to explain the system to residents who are impacted. And, it is your strong belief that the required fee is too great of a burden, particularly as it is not applied in all cases and a large percentage of the residents are retired. After years of expressing your concerns to the director of the engineering department and having them ignored, you decide to take the matter directly to the mayor.

The engineering director does not find your conversation with the mayor amusing. Indeed, he becomes quite angry with you for going to the mayor and having his policy decision questioned. He instructs you to proceed with collecting money from residents and lobbies the mayor to support the current policy. You continue collecting checks and contracts from residents but decide not to cash them or process the contracts because you feel the mayor will rule in your favor. And, you are right. The mayor concludes the system is unfair and resident contributions are eliminated for all sidewalk replacement projects.

Upon hearing the mayor's decision, you return the unprocessed checks and destroy the contracts. The director, not having budgeted for the change, instructs you to continue with the old policy for the upcoming construction season and to initiate the new policy the following year. Concerned about losing your job, you lie and say that you had not collected any money. You feel it would be impossible to collect the money for the upcoming project year as the change in policy had already been announced in the local press.

In the meantime, the director investigates and finds that the money has indeed been collected and subsequently returned. In his opinion, this was contrary to a direct order. You admit lying but claim that you had merely followed the wishes of the elected officials. The director gives you a pink slip, thus terminating your employment with the village. You decide to appeal the decision to the assistant administrator.

Now imagine you are the assistant administrator. What should you do?

Discussion Questions

1. Was the director right to fire the employee for her behavior?
2. Was the director acting out of his anger at having his decision overturned?
3. Was the employee acting in the best interest of the community?

4. Is it sometimes ethical to disobey an order when you feel it is the right decision?
5. Should the employee be disciplined?

Case Assessment

Michael Bonfield, City Manager, St. Pete Beach, Florida:

> At first, this case appears to be pretty straightforward: (1) the employee does not believe a written policy is fair; (2) he goes outside the chain of command by approaching the mayor with his concerns about the policy; (3) he later does not follow a direct order from his supervisor to follow the policy; and (4) he is terminated.
>
> In assessing this case, my initial concern would be the intent of the employee in the actions he took. The records relating to sidewalk assessments need to be reviewed to determine if, in fact, the policy is "murky" and resulted in disparate treatment of the residents. Assuming that is the case, the employee's initial concerns do not appear to be from any self-interest, rather an attempt to fix something wrong with the system. His intent appears to be to look out for the best interest of the residents and potentially save the village from embarrassment should the policy and its implementation become an issue in the future.
>
> Once the employee's intent was determined to be "for the right reasons," my next concern would be the approach he took to bring his concerns to his superiors. An interview with the employee and department director is needed to confirm if this matter had been brought forward to the director and what, if any, action was taken. If, in fact, the employee had brought the matter to the director's attention and it was ignored, approaching the mayor may have been an acceptable step. This is the type of issue that could easily create bad publicity for the government and needed to be brought to the attention of someone with authority to act.
>
> Although the employee's actions did not follow the traditional chain of command, all indications are that they kept a potentially bad situation with the sidewalk assessments from getting worse. The biggest problem with the employee's actions appears to be when his director instructed him to ignore the mayor and follow the policy as in the past. He should have confronted the director and, if necessary, the mayor, rather than collect contracts and checks from residents and fail to process them in the normal manner. His action to later return checks to residents and destroy contracts was clearly outside any acceptable operational practice. To later lie to the director only compounded the problem. Assuming the employee had a good work

history, I would overturn the termination and institute a short-term suspension without pay as discipline for his actions with very clear counseling on following the appropriate chain of command to have concerns addressed.

I do not agree with the actions taken by the director. First, the fact that this policy has been implemented in this manner in the past and employee concerns were ignored indicates a severe lack of communication and teamwork within the engineering department. Certainly, follow-up and training are needed in this area. Second, the fact that the director instructed the employee to ignore the mayor's directive is a significant problem. If the director did not agree with the mayor, further discussion is necessary. In any case, the final decision needs to be followed and directing an employee to the contrary is clearly an insubordinate act. Assuming this was the first incident with the director in this type of matter, a short suspension without pay would be in order and management training is in order to better establish working relationships in the department.

5.7 Let the Sunshine In ...

Controversies: 4.15, 5.20
Key Words: open meetings, sunshine laws, city, request for proposal
Case Complexity → Moderate
CD: 4.32 Leading with Integrity

Assume you are the newly appointed interim city manager of a community of 23,000. You have a PhD in civil engineering and have worked for the city for ten years. Seven years ago you were appointed the city engineer.

The city has issued a Request for Proposal to modernize the airport plan and you are in charge of the selection committee that consists of the mayor, the finance director, the airport manager, and the public works director. There are eight competing consultant firms and a tight deadline to recommend three to city council.

Concerned that you will not be able to get the job done by the deadline, you decide to call a "staff meeting" to short-list the top three consulting firms. Neither the mayor nor the finance director can be found and are therefore not notified of the meeting, which you decide to hold at your home. When questioned by the news media why you decided to hold the meeting in your home rather than city hall, you explained that the managers were in different parts of the county and "that ended up being the easiest way to do it."

Under the state's Sunshine Law, any committee or ad hoc advisory group that makes recommendations to elected officials is required to meet in public.

An apparent violation of the Sunshine Law, the meeting was held at the same time that nine former and current council members were involved in a lawsuit over allegations they violated the Sunshine Law.

Questions

1. Is this a matter of ignorance of the law and therefore excusable?
2. Is the claim that it is only staff work and therefore there isn't anything wrong about holding the meeting in your home defensible? Why or why not?
3. What steps would you take to ensure that your management team is fully aware of the provisions of the Sunshine Law?
4. Would this incident discourage you from seeking a permanent appointment as city manager? Why or why not?
5. If you were the mayor, would you write a letter of admonishment to the interim city manager? Would you discourage her from seeking the city manager's job?

Case Assessment

Sandra J. Reinke, Associate Professor of Public Administration and Director, MPA Program, University of Central Florida:

> In this case, a new interim city manager (but an experienced city engineer) holds a meeting to eliminate six of nine bidders on a major contract in his home without notifying two of the four members of the selection committee. Public law requires that this be a public meeting, and common sense would dictate that no bidders should be eliminated in the absence of half of the selection committee. Since this is someone who has been city engineer for seven years, this is not likely to be an honest mistake or the result of ignorance of the law (in this case, the state's Sunshine Law). Rather, this problem seems to be a product of an organizational culture that does not respect the public's right to know. Given that a significant number (including four current) of council members have been sued for violations of the Sunshine Law, one can only conclude that this is a local government that does not think the public needs to know, or has a right to know, what is happening in the community.
>
> If I were the mayor, I would definitely write a letter of admonishment to the interim city manager for violating the Sunshine Law and cutting half the selection committee out of a major part of the selection

process. In addition, I would privately suggest that he or she not compete for the post of permanent city manager. This is not someone I would trust and, as mayor, I need someone I can trust to manage the day-to-day business of the city.

Bruce Haddock, City Manager, Oldsmar, Florida:

I would conclude that a violation of the Sunshine Law did occur. As an advisory group making a recommendation to the elected body, their meetings would need to be open to the public, held at a public place, with proper notification given in advance. In this case, none of these things occurred. Further diminishing the validity of any action or recommendation resulting from the meeting is the fact that two of the five members of the committee were not even available!

Given the fact the interim city manager has worked for the city for ten years and served as the city engineer for the past seven years, she should be aware of Florida's Sunshine Law. I don't think pleading ignorance of the law would be acceptable to most people, especially in light of the current lawsuit regarding alleged Sunshine Law violations. Also, claiming it was staff work would be somewhat misleading as the mayor is a member of the committee, and the mayor is obviously not part of the staff.

The action I would recommend would be for the interim city manager to remove herself from the selection committee, have the appointing authority name a replacement, and restart the selection process. It would be best to start from the beginning, with re-advertising, but it might be possible to have the committee start afresh with the eight proposals they had received.

I would discourage the interim city manager from seeking the appointment as city manager. Given the existing lawsuit, involving nine former and current council members, it is imperative to reestablish accountability, transparency, and trust with the public. This incident would have a significant negative impact on the interim city manager's ability to do that.

If I were the mayor, I would not write a letter of admonishment to the interim city manager, but I would discourage her from seeking the city manager's job and tell her my reasons as outlined above.

Information Source: *Sarasota Herald-Tribune*, September 26, 2008.

5.8 Escape from an Ethics Swamp

Controversies: 4.10, 4.13, 4.14, 4.16, 5.18, 5.19, 6.15
Key Words: city manager, whistle-blower, loyalty, EPA, values, public interest, code of ethics, professionalism
Case Complexity → High
CD: 3.5 Leading with Integrity
CD: 7.2 Strengthening Ethics in Local Government
CD: 7.7 Local Governments in Florida

Author's Note: This case is different than others in that it puts the reader in a situation that challenges him or her to think through the steps that could be taken to restore trust and confidence in city government following several ethical lapses.

As the newly appointed city manager of Venice, you are keenly aware of the challenges you face in restoring public trust and confidence in city government. You inherited a government that had waded deeply into an ethics swamp and your job is to get it back on the right track. What should you do to restore integrity in your city government? But first—let's fill in the background.

The City

The city of Venice was incorporated in 1927 with a mayor-commission form of government. In 1977, the citizens voted to change the structure to a council-manager government. The seven-member council is elected for staggered three-year terms on a nonpartisan ballot. The mayor is elected at large.

The city's population in 2007 was 21,584, with another estimated 4,000 snow birds (people from cold Northern states) taking up winter residency. The city employs 296 full-time persons, with an operating budget of $24.2 million and an all funds budget of $68 million. The city workforce has been downsizing over the past five years.

Into the Ethics Swamp with Eyes Wide Closed

The disposal of treated water from the city's sewage treatment facility has been a long-standing problem. Consequently, the city has been forced to dispose of this treated water (also known as reclaimed water) from the city's facility into a variety of locations as permitted by state and federal regulatory agencies. Alas, the city manager and the director of utilities decided to save the city money by disposing of the wastewater in violation of these regulatory operating permits. This practice continued several years until an employee blew the whistle (let's call him Ed), and reported the dumping to the U.S. Environmental Protection Agency (EPA) and the Florida Department of Environmental Regulation (FDEP). The EPA and FDEP launched a joint investigation.

The city manager was not pleased with the whistle-blower. Indeed, it can be imagined that he called him into his office and read him the proverbial riot act. "Why would you do such a thing? Where is your loyalty?" As the EPA and FDEP investigation continued, the city manager decided to discipline the whistle-blower. Convinced that he had been wronged, the employee charged the city manager with retribution and sought relief under the state's whistle-blower protection law. Prior to going to trial, the city settled the lawsuit with the whistle-blower for $40,000.

The EPA brought formal charges against the city for illegal spills and the falsification of documents in violation of the federal Clean Water Act. The evidence was so overwhelming that the city did not fight the EPA, entered a guilty plea in federal court, and paid a $110,000 fine. The settlement reflected a significant reduction in potential multi-million dollar penalties, partly because new city management and philosophies were embraced that included a goal of 100-percent compliance and 100-percent reporting of noncompliance. This new approach included reporting to the public, media, and regulatory agencies of even the smallest of immeasurable spills.

Wastewater dumping was not the only unethical and illegal act experienced by the city during this period. The city's director of Information Systems, who owned a software company, decided to do business with the city, always a tricky matter. Sure enough, he bought software from his company with city funds. An ethics complaint was soon filed with the Florida State Ethics Commission which, after an investigation, found that he was in violation of state ethics laws for doing business with the city. He received a $12,400 fine and was publicly censured and reprimanded. His employment with the city was ultimately terminated.

Discussion Questions

1. Assume it is your first day on the job as the new city manager, how would you use your time?
   a. Would you call a meeting of your management team (budget director, assistant city manager, human relations chief, police and fire chiefs, and other department heads) and announce your intention to clean house?
   b. Would you appoint a staff member to investigate the ethics culture of the city workforce?
   c. Would you call a press conference to lay out a recovery plan for the city?
   d. Would you fire the public works director?

2. By the end of the second week on the job, you decide that you must transform the culture of the city workforce, changing it from a self-serving, risk adverse culture to one that emphasizes pride and integrity in the workplace. What would be your plan of action?

Outcome

Your organization is facing a values crisis. It is evident that whatever passes for mission is lost on the city workforce. Therefore, you decide that the first thing you must do is to develop a mission statement that city employees, members of the city council, and the public can understand and, hopefully, take ownership of. You form a ten-member committee composed of a cross section of employees and charge them with the responsibility of soliciting ideas and suggestions. The committee is chaired by the HR director and is to report back to you within the next three months.

The committee applies itself diligently and surprises you by concluding its work a month early. The result is a mission statement that asserts: "The mission of Venice City Government is to provide exceptional municipal services through a financially sustainable city with engaged citizens." The core values that underpin the mission statement are reflected in the acronym PRIDE—Productive, Responsible, Innovative, Dedicated, Ethical.

The committee recommends that a code of ethics be adopted that incorporates the core values. You wholeheartedly agree and ask the committee to continue its work by developing a code of ethics that strikes a balance between a "gotcha" compliance approach and an integrity approach that encourages each employee to embrace "doing the right thing." On the one hand, you feel that the code must enable employees to know what is acceptable and unacceptable behavior. On the other hand, you feel strongly that true integrity in the workplace can only be achieved by employees who celebrate values such as trustworthiness, honesty, impartiality, fairness, and respect for others.

Six months pass and a code is finally submitted for your consideration. After carefully reviewing the code, you approve it and present it to city council for approval. Your presentation to council begins with the statement: "Unlike some other codes of conduct or ethics, the city policy emphasizes those activities and approaches that will be valued and encouraged, while also identifying those behaviors that are not acceptable."

Central features of the code are:

1. All employees, volunteers, elected and appointed officials shall maintain the highest standards of personal integrity, truthfulness, honesty, and fairness in carrying out their public duties, avoid any improprieties in their roles as public servants, including the appearance of impropriety, and never use their city position or powers for improper personal gain.

2. Identification of appropriate behavior consists of being:
   a. Productive—apply knowledge and expertise to assigned responsibilities and activities, and to the interpersonal relationships that are part of providing service to the community in a consistent, confident, competent, and productive manner.
   b. Responsible—make decisions after prudent consideration of their financial impact, taking into account the long-term financial needs of the city, especially its financial stability, and demonstrate concern for the proper use of city assets, including personnel, time, property, equipment, and funds.
   c. Innovative—display a style that maintains consistent standards, but that is also sensitive to the need for compromise, "thinking outside the box," and improving existing policies and practices when necessary.
   d. Dedicated—convey the city's care and commitment to its citizens, communicating in ways that demonstrate being approachable, open-minded, and willing to participate in constructive dialog.
   e. Ethical—be trustworthy, acting with the utmost integrity, truthful, and dependable. Make impartial decisions, free of bribes, unlawful gifts, and financial or other personal interests that impair judgment or action and demonstrate respect for all persons.

   Productive, responsible, innovative, dedicated, and ethical are highlighted by the acronym PRIDE.
3. Identification of inappropriate behavior consists of:
   a. Benefiting financially from a city contract.
   b. Representing a private person at a city proceeding.
   c. Engaging in private employment that is incompatible with the proper discharge of one's official duties.
   d. Disclosing confidential, privileged, or proprietary information.
   e. Receiving gifts, favors, gratuities, compensation, or rewards that are connected or related to individual services with the city.
   f. Participating or assisting individuals in city matters after leaving city service less than two years.
4. Description of a complaint process that preserves due process and ensures confidence in investigations of alleged violations.
5. Identification of penalties for noncompliance, which includes a range of alternatives from reprimands to termination of employment, with civil penalties up to $10,000.

City council votes unanimously and enthusiastically to adopt the code of ethics. Your next task is to implement it. What steps would you take to implement the code?

1. Would you publish it in the city's newsletter with the warning "read and obey this code if you want to stay out of trouble"?
2. Initiate a series of departmental meetings to discuss the code?

3. Hire a consultant to conduct ethics training?
4. Conduct ethics training yourself to demonstrate to employees just how important you feel the code is to the well-being of the organization?

You conclude that the first suggestion has merit if the "read and obey" language is omitted. This language is classic "gotcha" stuff and can lead to a low-road approach to building an ethics culture. Suggestion 2 is also merit worthy but you feel that suggestion 4 is the best because it demonstrates your commitment to restoring integrity in city government.

One more task is necessary, however, before you can become confident that you are on the right road out of the ethics swamp. You ask yourself, "How will I know if we are making progress?" "I know that an organization of integrity cannot be built overnight," you muse, "so I must have some way to benchmark the change I am seeking." Alas, you decide to hire an organizational consultant to conduct an ethics culture survey of employees. The survey results will be a benchmark that can be revisited in a year or two to determine if the ethics culture has improved.

You meet with the consultant and he asks, "What are the objectives of the ethics culture survey?" You reply that there are three objectives: (1) to establish a benchmark for tracking the culture over time, (2) to assess the ethics culture of the city workforce, and (3) to strengthen the ethics culture. You tell the consultant that you want the survey results to provide information about (1) how strong or weak the ethics culture is, (2) the factors that contribute to a strong culture, and (3) document the relationship between the strength of the ethics culture and workplace values such as efficiency, effectiveness, quality, teamwork, and excellence.

Now assume that you are the consultant. Your task is to develop several items consistent with those below that could be placed on the survey to provide information about the ethics culture.

1. I am encouraged to speak up about any practices and policies that are ethically questionable.
2. My supervisor encourages employees to act in an ethical manner.

You decide that you want at least five items with a five-point scale that ranges from "strongly disagree" to "strongly agree." Develop three more items.

Case Assessment

Kevin Duggan, City Manager, Mountain View, California:

> This case reviews a variety of techniques and strategies to establish and maintain an organization that conducts itself consistent with ethical

principles. One of the significant challenges for the leader of an organization is the realization that he or she will be judged as much on the ethical performance of the organization as his or her own personal ethical conduct. The difficult reality is that even a CEO with the highest personal ethical conduct will be considered a failure if the organization does not perform at an acceptable level ethically. The case points out a number of alternative courses in how to establish and maintain an ethical culture, including:

- "Top down" directives versus collaborative development of ethical expectations
- External sanctions versus personal responsibility
- Measurement/assessment of performance versus "benign neglect"
- Punitive enforcement versus education and value development

Among the key factors in establishing and maintaining an ethical culture in an organization are:

- While rules and guidelines are important, since rules will not cover all ethical dilemmas, a "value-based" ethical culture needs to be developed.
- Organization members will only "internalize" ethical values if they participate in their development.
- Regular education and reinforcement are critical—never "rest on your laurels."
- The need for a clearly stated organizational statement of ethical expectations.
- Ethics need to be ingrained in key aspects of organizational life, including:
  - The hiring process (have ethics be a factor in hiring decisions)
  - The performance evaluation and compensation process (it will be taken seriously—it is either a key area of performance, or it is not)
- Regular assessment/monitoring.
- Personal modeling of the highest ethical conduct by the organization's leadership.
- A demonstrated willingness to tackle the hardest ethical challenges even when the consequences in doing so may be quite negative.

In Venice, as is all too often the case, the need for an ethical revival was born out of a scandal. While even the most effective leaders of organizations cannot guarantee that an organizational ethical lapse will never be experienced, taking steps to prevent an ethical failure is much more effective than reacting once it occurs (and a lot less painful).

5.9 City of Progress I

Controversies: 3.11, 3.12, 6.12, 6.18
Key Words: city manager, public interest, news media, trust, moral courage, community
Case Complexity → High
CD: 6.2 International City/County Management Association Code of Ethics
CD: 7.1 City of Progress
Ethical reasoning questions are included with this case.

Suppose you are the city manager of a thriving community of 67,000 whose motto is a "City of Progress." Let's call you Steve. You have received outstanding performance evaluations over the fourteen years you have served as the city manager. Indeed, the city commission was so pleased with your performance over the past year that they awarded you with a 9-percent pay raise. You regard members of the city commission and high ranking appointed officials such as the police chief and fire chief as good friends and colleagues who, like you, have the best interests of the community at heart. You truly love your job and want to continue as city manager until you retire, some twelve years from now.

Situation 1

Alas, you have a long hidden personal secret. Since childhood, you have felt more like a woman than a man and have cross-dressed for years when vacationing out of state. Your wife is aware of your gender challenge, but your thirteen-year-old son is not. You are, of course, deeply concerned about how your son will be treated if it becomes known in the community that you are transgender and may even become a woman. After much anguishing about the situation, you decide to begin gender reassignment discreetly. The hormone treatments go well, but the change in your body begins to be evident when you find that you can no longer keep up with the police chief during your weekly jogging with him.

What should you do? Should you bring the police chief into your confidence? What about the mayor, who has always been a good friend and strong supporter? Should you approach other members of the city commission? The deputy city manager?

Since you manage a self-proclaimed city of progress, you are confident that city employees and the community at large will accept you as a woman if that moment arrives. Still, as an intelligent, high-profile public official, you worry that the media may discover your secret before you have had time to educate your friends and city employees about transgender challenges.

What should you do?

Situation 2

Feeling confident that you have the trust, loyalty, and respect of your mayor and colleagues, you decide to quietly let them know about your forthcoming gender reassignment. Privately, you inform your colleagues, including the mayor, that you will go public with your intentions to become a woman four months from now when your thirteen-year-old son is away from the community. The circle of trust you have created involves about five people and, as it widens, you are increasingly concerned that you may not be able to keep your intentions out of the public eye until June. Alas, you discover that the circle is broken when a local newspaper reporter confronts you with the rumor that you intend to become a woman.

"Yes," you reply, "I will undergo gender reassignment and will begin dressing as a woman in a month or so. I will change my name from Steven to Susan." The story becomes headline news. Letters and e-mails pour into the mayor's office, with many calling for your removal from office. One local newspaper prints a full page tabloid picture of you with the subtext "a boy named Sue."

City commissioners decide to schedule a public meeting to hear from citizens. Before the meeting takes place, the mayor defends you as does city manager colleagues in neighboring communities. Your supporters claim that merit, not personal issues, should matter the most. The city charter stipulates that you can be dismissed without cause but only by a super majority vote (five of the seven of the city commissioners).

Sixty persons speak at the four hour marathon meeting while nearly 500 more flood the city hall chambers and corridors. One resident contends, "The issue is not the gender change here. It's the fact he deceived people. He wasn't honest with us." Another angry citizen exclaims, "His brain is the same today as it was last week ... he may be even able to be a better city manager. But I sense that he's lost his standing as a leader among the employees of the city." Other speakers were demeaning in their language and accusations.

Humiliated by the spectacle, you decide to leave the meeting. A reporter corners you and asks, "How do you feel about what you heard?" You respond, "It's just real painful to know that seven days ago I was a good guy and now I have no integrity, I have no trust and most painful, I have no followers."

The city commission votes 5-2 to put you on paid administrative leave while your departure is made final. Your contract calls for twelve months severance pay ($140,234) and other benefits during this period.

The lead editorial in the local newspaper exclaims, "Officials bow to mob, prejudice ... the community and most elected officials turned on the city manager and kicked him to the curb."

Discussion Questions

1. Did you exercise moral courage? In hindsight, is there anything you should have done differently?
2. Was it realistic of you to believe you could keep your job and everything would be just fine? Were you naïve?
3. Did the city commission treat you fairly? Was the community's best interest served by your dismissal?
4. Should you sue the city for a human rights violation?
5. Is your professional code of ethics of any assistance?
6. Is your career as a city manager ended?
7. Does your dismissal fly in the face of the city's motto—City of Progress?
8. Was the newspaper sensationalism fair to you? The community?

Ethical Reasoning Questions

1. Is there an ethical issue facing Steve? The city commission? City employees? The community?
2. What is the ethical issue?
3. What might be done to resolve the situation?
4. Does the preferred course of action satisfy the needs/preferences of the primary stakeholders?
5. Is the preferred course of action ethical?

Case Assessment

Vince Long, Deputy County Administrator, Leon County, Florida:

> I can remember reading one of those articles not long ago which identified a laundry list of the most important characteristics of highly effective managers. This article was geared toward corporate managers, but its findings really stuck with me. It suggested that the most important characteristic of the highly effective manager was not their leadership, innovation, or know-how, but their ability to personify the culture of their organization. Even when these CEOs left one organization to lead another with a corporate culture that was quite different than their previous job, they found success because of their ability to adapt to and epitomize the most important values of the corporation and those of their customers.
>
> For many reasons, this characteristic may be even more important for the top manager of a local government. As opposed to the private sector, in local government, your customers do not generally choose

you. Consumers of local government as a whole cannot "take their business elsewhere," unless they move. In addition, the services provided by local government are highly personal—often directly impacting people's property, their neighborhoods, and their very health, welfare, and safety. Add to this the fact that *everything* that local government does is highly visible, especially in Florida where all local government business must occur in the sunshine. As such, the local government CEO is under tremendous scrutiny in the community he serves. The public image of the local government CEO is considered a reflection of the community and is very fragile. Few, if any, corporate managers could expect that any decision they make could be immediately reported on and delivered to the front steps of their customers to read about the next morning.

In this case, the city manager has a proven track record as a "high performer." However, the political skill of the local government manager is as important as any managerial acumen. Most effective local government managers recognize that their ability to deflect the glory to the elected officials when things are good and to take the heat when things turn bad is a key to their political success. In addition, the effective local government manager makes every effort to stay clear of those issues perceived to be "political." In this case, the manager became the "political issue."

This case is not about any nuance associated with the manager's gender issue becoming public. There is arguably nothing that the city manager could have done better to influence the outcome of this situation. This case is not about the many good reasons that his gender reassignment may have been the right thing to do. Furthermore, this case has nothing to do with the manager's ability to perform as a professional local government CEO. This case demonstrates the impact of a large and vocal segment of the community's disapproval with the city manager's decision and its reflection on their community. To this constituency, the city manager's gender reassignment will serve as a constant and highly visible ("in your face") incongruence with their community "values." Despite the city commission's support for the city manager, by becoming a political issue he has put the commission in a politically untenable situation. This case is an extreme example; there are many more common and much more subtle cases that occur everyday, which prove the relatively low political pain threshold that the elected body is willing to endure to defend the local government manager whose effectiveness has become a political issue. The local government manager in this case should have been very well aware of these dynamics.

Robert C. Chope, Professor and Chair, Department of Counseling, San Francisco State University:

> Transgendered people are widely dispersed in any community, so in a relatively small city of 67,000, there undoubtedly is not a large degree of support for Steve. Historically, most trans-people have been discriminated against when they let their transgender status be known. There are, however, examples of individuals who have fared reasonably well in the workplace after becoming a trans-individual. In hindsight, Steve would have done well to research information and sought support from the many virtual communities of trans-people on the Internet prior to announcing his intentions to undergo sexual reassignment surgery and become a woman. Virtual transgender neighborhoods exist on the Internet serving to bring people together to discuss issues that include the reassignment surgery, work, family, and friends as well as adjustment and communication.
>
> Presently, there are anywhere from one to three million transgender people, and in San Francisco there are an estimated 19,000. Accordingly, there have been a number of well-documented cases regarding workplace discrimination against transgender people. With the appropriate information, Steve should not have quit his position but, instead, relied on his years of success to shore him up. Since he was placed on paid administrative leave for what appears to be discrimination, he could seek redress and support from organizations like the Transgender Laws Center (www.transgenderlawcenter.org) and the National Center for Transgender Equality (www.nctequality.org). The Sixth Circuit Court has decided two discrimination suits in favor of transgender clients.
>
> It is clear that the commission did not treat Steve fairly. But then again, the city commissioners are elected officials, and while most people like to believe that politicians make decisions on the merits of a case, typically the decisions are made on the politics. It is unfortunate for the community to dismiss a competent manager like Steve because it serves as an example to everyone that good work and positive results don't necessarily carry the weight that they should. Prejudice has been known to rule in the past and in this case, it still does.
>
> The code of ethics of any professional organization does not necessarily have much in the way of legal teeth. But the code does reflect the interests of the organization and the national or state or local affiliate might be useful in becoming involved in mediating any legal dispute or serving to assist Steve in finding another job placement.

It is quite conceivable that Steve could work as a city manager again. The current police commissioner for the city of San Francisco is a trans-woman. The report in the newspaper of the proceedings of the meeting attempted to be clever in its word use and bordered on sensationalism. But newspapers are hurting now and they will try any number of activities to sell papers. Conservative talk shows are often quite sensational and they appear to be extremely profitable. In most cities, mottos are not always consistent with practice. There are many police departments with the motto "To Protect and Serve," and yet those who have been discriminated against believe that the departments do neither.

Author's Note: Based on a real case, published in the *St. Petersburg Times*, February 28, March 1, 2007.

5.10 City of Progress II

Controversies: 3.11
Key Words: leadership, change, city management, team
Case Complexity → Moderate
CD: 6.2 International City/County Management Association Code of Ethics

Consider an alternative outcome to the case "City of Progress I": What if you succeed in persuading three commissioners to support you? Let's imagine.

You (now Susan) report to work dressed in female clothing complemented by feminine styling and makeup even though you have not yet completed gender reassignment. Your first days on the job evoke some stares, some evasiveness, and some smirks by city employees, all which you politely ignore. As days pass, city employees appear to adjust. You are no longer a physical oddity in city hall.

Nonetheless, you recognize that you have a leadership challenge.

Discussion Questions

1. What should you do to alleviate the anxiety still felt by some rank-and-file city employees about their "new" boss? For example, from a practical perspective, should you use the men's or women's bathroom? Neither?
2. What should you do to ensure that the management team stays a team?
3. What should you do about the commissioners who voted to dismiss you?

4. What should you do to persuade a doubting community about your commitment to the well-being of the city?
5. What leadership style or approach should you assume toward city employees? Your management team? The community?
6. Is it hypocritical to believe that you can lead with integrity? Why or why not?

Case Assessment

Robert C. Chope, Professor and Chair, Department of Counseling, San Francisco State University:

> There will be individuals who yearn for things as they were and will never feel comfortable in Steve's presence. That was true for multiethnic, multicultural, and diversified people who had to work closely with an entirely Caucasian workforce in their place of employment. Neither group necessarily felt comfortable. But teams can develop as individuals and work toward common goals with no direct competition with each other.
>
> The use of bathroom facilities comes under the rubric of the "Principle of Least Astonishment," which suggests that a person who presents as a woman should be least astonishing to others and should use the women's bathroom. Steve should know that an employer has the right to instruct transgender employees to use the facilities that match their presentation. So when Steve becomes Sue, she should use the women's bathroom.
>
> Regarding the commissioners, there will always be opposing sides in politics. Steve might consider meeting with the opposing commissioners and point out their history together and that they should work for the betterment of the city. He would, of course, expect them to represent their constituencies and vote according to issues. Much of the council legislation will require that the city managers carry out their wishes, and Steve should ensure that he would continue to act as he always has for his many years of successful management. He serves at their pleasure and he should be attuned to the politics that push commissioners away from him because of the feelings of the constituents.
>
> City commissioners address the business of the city and the city manager makes it all work. Most residents have little contact with their city manager and it is an appointed, not an elected, position. While the mayor of a city is regularly in the spotlight, the city manager is not. Steve has worked successfully for fourteen years and the residents will probably need some time to adjust because of their own discomfort. If the city is operating well, they can be expected to move on when his transgender story is off the front pages.

The head of the police commission in San Francisco is a trans-woman and yet if asked, most citizens of San Francisco would not know who was the head of the police commission and fewer would know that she is a trans-woman. She is often on the news and while her voice belies her dress, most people in San Francisco are unaware of her gender status.

It is said that adversity often makes winners out of potential losers. The adverse circumstances that Steve experienced could very well make him, as Susan, a more sensitive, respected, and powerful city manger. If Susan is able to retain her integrity, energy, playfulness, and eagerness as she has in the past, her story may turn out to be ok.

Author's Note: Based on a real case published in the *St. Petersburg Times*, March 24, 2007.

Controversies

5.11 A Slippery Slope?

Cases: 3.6

It is common practice for developers to seek neighborhood support for rezoning property. Developers often agree to make improvements in the neighborhood or provide for mitigation when a project is potentially threatening to a neighborhood's esthetics, traffic flow, or natural environment. Typically this is done through a public hearing process and mitigation is financially handled by an appropriate local government agency.

But what happens when neighborhood associations (NA) decide to "encourage" developers to provide them with cash considerations? Can developers become the "victims?" Possibly, maybe even absolutely.

Here's what one developer, who is building nearly 100 homes in West Tampa, has to say about cash deals: "It's kind of a standard practice. Where do you cross the line here? I don't know. It puts everyone in a very difficult position and it's hard to tell where legitimacy ends and impropriety begins."

Another adds: "This happened because small groups of people are basically trying to use their influence to shake down builders. It's wrong."

Is there a slippery slope here? Perhaps, but in my neighborhood?

Discussion Questions

1. Is there anything wrong with getting developers to improve one's neighborhood? Does the improvement have to be related to the potential harm caused by the development?
2. What happens when a developer doesn't go along to get along? Will the neighborhood association work hard to ensure that the developer doesn't get his way?
3. Do city ethics codes deal with this situation? Do any ethics codes deal with this situation?

Commentary

Regina Williams, City Manager, Norfolk, Virginia:

> Neighborhood associations, or civic leagues as we refer to them in Norfolk, Virginia, are an "uncharted" part of the democratic governance model. As city manager, I have experienced the good that they can provide in terms of participatory democracy and their evilness, especially if they become a political pawn for elected officials. However, in the situation of development or redevelopment and land use decision making, I have not experienced neighborhood associations being in a position to "extort" developers. If that is the case, I think the local government has failed in the establishment of a system that would permit legitimate citizen/resident involvement, but safeguard against inappropriate behavior. Such a system would provide for impact fees, infrastructure and service level investments from the developer to be paid to the city, not an individual civic league.
>
> However, that said, I do believe there is a broader issue around the potential unethical behavior of individual citizens within such a group and/or the use of such groups by elected officials for political or personal gain. While some would say that is just the relationship of stakeholders and politics, manipulation of true public opinion to garner the appearance of public support for a certain position or stand on an issue is wrong—and that is what I have experienced as the problematic use of neighborhood associations.

Pamela Gibson, Assistant Professor, Department of Urban Studies and Public Administration, Old Dominion University, Virginia:

> There are tremendous financial, political, legal, and ethical issues surrounding these quasi-governmental entities that have received much

(Nevada) to very little (Virginia) public attention. Conflict of interest concerns (a national private organization, Community Association Institute, with legal liaisons advising in the formulation of state laws related to "private powers" of associations); legal liability questions (governments currently treat these associations as businesses and not communities in which dispute resolution is found only in the courts through counterproductive lawsuits); and ultimately questions of fiduciary responsibilities as these neighborhood associations, including the developers and governing boards, have very little, if any, oversight—little transparency in their transition of ownership and operations, no open bidding for service provision contracts, (some have argued) arbitrary increases in assessments and strong-armed tactics for "compliance" with "approved" mailboxes, house colors, and landscaping designs! As these neighborhoods age and membership lacks insurance and reserve funds for upkeep or recovery from natural disasters, they will look for governmental support. As one local housing official told me while I was researching associations, "I don't know where we're to get the money to maintain the roads, swimming pools and entrance signs for these neighborhoods. But, we'll be expected to find it."

Karl Thoennes III, Judicial Circuit Administrator, Unified Judicial System, State of South Dakota:

Is there anything wrong with getting developers to improve one's neighborhood? Certainly not, and requiring developers to mitigate or balance damage is good public policy. However, in the West Tampa scenario we're talking about a payoff in cold hard cash to a constituency group who would otherwise hold its support hostage. Still, I'm not sure why the scenario should cause any great ethical indignation. The private sector buys public support and goodwill with cash all the time, so I don't think the developer should be embarrassed. On the other hand, if the local prosecutor is looking for a statute violation, perhaps the neighborhood association should worry about a prostitution charge. To me, the neighborhood association's behavior is not much different than, say, a vocal opponent of a new Wal-Mart store accepting a briefcase of cash to go home and be quiet.

At least in the present scenario the payoff went from a private developer to an essentially private constituency group. I can ethically swallow that sort of exchange far more easily than when public agencies do the same thing. The government sells development and profit opportunities for cash all the time. The FCC auctions off portions of the broadcast spectrum, for example. The Park Service grants exclusive access to concessionaires in exchange for some cut of the action. I happen to be a trial court administrator, so I'm most familiar with situations like photo red light systems where local government gets a cut of the ticket revenue. Some court systems receive a share of online access fees from the software companies who (re)sell public court records (I know, I know, they're allegedly selling the retrieval convenience, not the records themselves). I could even swallow the frequently offered rationale that this is all creative, innovative public revenue generation if the nontax revenue actually supplanted tax money that would otherwise be raised, but I'm fairly confident that the little research done in this area indicates otherwise. (I know, I know, taxes may not go down, but the alternative revenue allegedly reduces the amount of the tax increase that would have otherwise been necessary.)

Author's Note: Case based on stories in *St. Petersburg Times*, June 23, 2007 and the *Tampa Tribune*, June 23, 2007.

5.12 Outsourcing City Management Ethics

Cases: 5.7

Suppose you are hired as an independent contractor to manage a newly incorporated community of 7,000 residents. The community is zoned almost entirely rural residential and agricultural. The town has a "council-administrator" form of government. With the blessing of elected city officials, you staff the city with personnel from your consulting firm, which includes your daughter as the town clerk and your wife as your assistant. The town's attorney believes that you should not have hired your daughter and that salaries should be made public. After first refusing to make public your $114,000 salary, you change your mind.

In the meantime, the town's attorney suggests that an opinion should be sought from the state ethics commission regarding whether the anti-nepotism law applies to contracted employees. Several months later, the state ethics commission renders an opinion that independent contractors are not public employees and therefore not subject to the state's ethics law.

Happy with this finding, you are even more delighted to discover that one of your employees drafts a four-page press release extolling you and your team as "new age" governmental leaders.

Discussion Questions

1. Are there ethical issues in this case, especially given that you are not subject to the state's ethics laws?
2. If so, what are they?
3. Does this situation illustrate a significant loop hole in the law?

Commentary by Author

Outsourcing is a popular form of privatizing the delivery of public services that can have significant ethics problems. First is the matter of transparency. The fact that an independent contractor is not a government employee means that he can do things that are out of the public's eye. Most city managers are public employees and their salaries are public information. Second, nepotism in this case is blatant. Third is the issue of accountability. Ordinarily in a council-manager government, accountability is in the hands of the city council and it is reasonable to expect this to be so in this case—but it may not be so. This case suggests that the community has a government that is part private and part public. Is it no wonder that there may be little accountability and other practices often thought to be on the ethical fringe?

Author's Note: Based on a real case, see "State Rules Town Official Exempt from Ethics Law," *Miami Herald*, March 9, 2006.

5.13 When the County Knows Best—Or Does It?

Case: 3.8

The West Nile virus, an illness transmitted from wildlife to humans by mosquitoes, has made its second appearance in two years in Phoenix, Arizona, resulting in a number of confirmed fatal cases among birds and a growing number of positive cases in humans, reported by hospitals and doctors to the Maricopa County health department's vector control program. In response, the county has tracked the locations of most intense activity, ramped up its public education program to ask people to be vigilant in draining stagnant water sources where mosquitoes breed, and advised the public to wear repellent, particularly in the evenings and early morning when the insects are most active.

After plotting the outbreaks, the county identified a large "hot zone" of cases and determined that this area—mostly residential neighborhoods—should be fogged with insecticide to reduce the mosquito population. The insecticide is a synthetic pyrethroid called Anvil. According to the EPA "pyrethroids can be used … without posing unreasonable risks to human health when applied according to the label. Pyrethroids are considered to pose slight risks of acute toxicity to humans, but at high doses, pyrethroids can affect the nervous system."

Maricopa County proceeded with a program to fog an area about eight square miles in the early morning hours of a Friday—a time when mosquitoes are active, winds are calm, and most people are in their homes asleep. Maricopa County also made the decision not to notify residents in the affected area in advance that their neighborhood would be fogged.

Many homes, however, use evaporative cooling, a process that draws outdoor air into the home. Consequently, the pesticide fog was drawn into the homes, exposing the residents while they slept. Some symptoms of pyrethroid exposure include rash and breathing difficulties. Persons with lung ailments and small children are susceptible at a lower dosage than the "average" person. Persistent exposure or exposure to large concentrations can cause other health problems. Pyrethroids are a carcinogen.

While it is unknown how many residents of Phoenix were affected by the insecticide, none knew they may have been exposed. Therefore, none knew whether, if they did show symptoms, they should seek medical treatment. I am one who came down with a rash after sleeping with an evaporative cooler running on a night when the county fogged my neighborhood. Evaporative coolers bring in outside air, cooling the air with water. In this case, the water was off, so it was ambient outdoor air being drawn in. I woke up to the smell of it, but had no idea as to the source. I learned a few days later that one of my neighbors saw the trucks on our street at 3:00 a.m. the day I came down with the rash.

Discussion Questions

1. Why did the county health department proceed with this application of pesticides without notifying the residents in the target area that they could be exposed, what the pesticide was, and what actions they should take if they wished to limit their exposure?
2. Is it possible that county officials believed they knew what was in the best interest of the citizens?
3. Was this an act of insensitivity? Incompetence?

Commentary by Author

It is hard to imagine that a modern, professionally managed county like Maricopa County would fog a neighborhood without informing residents in advance. There may be an explanation. Perhaps county officials believed that the problem was so acute that they couldn't take the time to notify residents. Short of an emergency situation, it is difficult to accept an alternative explanation.

5.14 Legal, Wrong … Or Morally Required?

Case: 4.4

Articles have appeared daily in the Richmond, Virginia, press framing an ethics debate—whether to use a "loophole" in federal Medicaid regulations to collect $259 million from the federal government. Through several transactions, the state of Virginia could receive matching funds for money it never actually spends. Both participating localities and the state would net large sums that could be used for health care or for any other public purpose since the money would go into the general fund.

The state official leading the effort to secure this funding has argued adamantly that it is morally required that the state seek and accept the money since not doing so would penalize fiscally stressed health programs and needy Virginia citizens. Many localities and associated nursing homes have refused to participate and are zealous in asserting that it would be morally wrong to accept the money since it would be acquired through gimmickry and subterfuge—even through legal gimmickry and subterfuge! An intermediate position is that it would be OK to accept the money if it is used only for Medicaid-related purposes.

Discussion Questions

1. What is the ethically correct position?
2. Do legality and need trump honesty and forthrightness?
3. Is this really an ethical problem?
4. Or is it a public relations problem created when the press made it visible to the public?

Commentary by Author

Does anything go when it comes to securing federal money? Of course not but state officials fully understand that it is "playing the game" correctly by doing whatever appears to be legal to extract federal funds. This is the moral minimum in the eyes of most public administration ethicists. The Virginia controversy highlights the maneuvering, dodging, and strategizing that can happen when federal funds are at stake.

5.15 Needed: Ethics or Manners for Elected Officials?

Case: 3.6

Could the impolite behavior of an elected official while conducting a meeting be an ethical matter? Or could it be a matter of bad manners? Here are several instances.

Dateline: a small community in Central Florida—After concluding all the official business on the weekly city commission meeting agenda, the mayor, a downtown businessman, issued a personal complaint that some business owners were allowing their employees to park directly in front of their businesses. The mayor ranted for thirty minutes with no one to gavel him down because he held the gavel and in the course of the ranting referred to downtown business people who take up customer parking as "nit wits, idiots, and *#@ kissing cousins."

Two commission members took offense at the mayor's tirade and chastised him, albeit politely. The Chamber of Commerce made the incident a *cause célèbre*, and there was much letter writing referring to the collective embarrassment of the incident. One offended commissioner requested that staff develop a code of conduct for adoption at the next city commission meeting—and he didn't mean Robert's Rules of Order or the state's ethics statutes. Rather, he talked about a code that would speak to an elected official's professional behavior, civility, and common courtesy.

Dateline: Pittsburgh, Pennsylvania—"It's a pack of lies!" shouted the council president at the personnel director. The four hour meeting over how to pay for a study on whether women and minorities working for the city are paid fairly ended badly. The personnel director was incensed by the accusation and walked out of the meeting. A fellow council member bemoaned a "lack of civility."

Information Source: www.post-gazette.com/pg/08227/904179-53.stm (accessed August 15, 2008).

Discussion Questions

1. What would you do if you were the staff person given the assignment to draft a code of conduct for elected officials?
2. Would you turn to a professional code of ethics such as the American Society for Public Administration code or the International City/County Management Association code for help?
3. Do codes address these kinds of issues?
4. Or do we simply have a case of an ill-mannered mayor who needs an injection of common sense and civility?

5. In the Pittsburgh case, would you have walked out of the council meeting? If not, what would you have done?

Commentary by Author

Civility among local elected officials is increasingly diminishing. Why? There are probably numerous reasons. One could be the influence of Sunshine Laws that prevent discourse among officials outside of the officially scheduled meetings. Another could be the growing, perhaps negative, influence of communication technology that encourages people to be more direct and blunt with each other. Impersonalism bred through technology may not bode well for face-to-face events.

5.16 Mayors as Exemplars—Fact or Fiction?

Case: 6.9

Elected officeholders can be, but too often are not, exemplary leaders. Suppose you were the mayor of a city, population 31,580, and ran successfully for office on a platform of bringing ethical governance to your community. You are a genuinely committed mayor and also a devoted father. You find yourself in a situation in which you need to get your daughter to summer camp and at the same time, negotiate an agreement for a local option sales tax. What would you do? Your assistant speaks up: "Oh, I can get your daughter to summer camp. No big deal!" Done deal.

Forty-five minutes later, you realize that you have violated the city's ethics code by allowing your assistant, while on duty, to transport your daughter to camp. Embarrassed by this ethical lapse, you take out your pen and file an ethics complaint against yourself.

Fantasy? Not so. This is a real case of Mayor Steven Brown of Peachtree City, Georgia. After due deliberation, the Ethics Board found that no formal reprimand was necessary but that Mayor Brown should reimburse the city for the employee's time. Mayor Brown readily complied and reimbursed the city $8.94.

Information Source: "Managing Municipal Ethics," November 5, 2002, www.gmanet.com.

Discussion Questions

1. Are most mayors as ethically sensitive as Mayor Brown? Why or why not?
2. Did Mayor Brown do the right thing? Or, is he merely seeking public attention?

Commentary by Author

Mayors and ethics don't always go together so well. Consider Detroit's flamboyant and controversial Mayor Kwame Kilpatrick. He was charged with eight felony counts, including perjury, misconduct in office, and obstruction of justice. The perjury charge is related to false testimony that he gave during a trial of the deputy police chief, who was dismissed. The deputy sued the mayor for wrongful dismissal and during the trial, both he and his chief of staff denied they had an affair and had conspired to fire the deputy, but evidence strongly pointed to the opposite conclusion.

Prison sentences sometimes catch up with a mayor. Sharpe James, Newark's mayor from 1986 to 2006, was sentenced to twenty-seven months in prison on fraud charges stemming from the sale of city properties to a former companion for a fraction of their costs. Upon sentencing, Mr. James exclaimed, "All my life I have simply tried to help the City of Newark. I tried to make Newark, New Jersey, the best city in the world. If I made a mistake it was not malicious or with intent." Alas, good intentions didn't keep him out of jail. Nearly two dozen New Jersey mayors have been charged with corruption since 2000.

> **Information Source:** Alan Feuer and Nate Schweber, "Newark Ex-Mayor Gets 27 Months as U.S. Judge Chastises Prosecution," *New York Times*, July 30, 2008, p. A16 and August 1, 2008.

5.17 (Un)Official Misconduct

> Cases: 3.7, 4.2, 4.7, 4.9, 5.6, 6.7, 6.8, 6.10

Unofficial misconduct? Do you know what that is? Official misconduct? Do you know what that is? Hmmm! Not sure. Consider the case of Detroit Mayor Kwame Kilpatrick. The Detroit city council by a vote of 5-4 asked Governor Granholm to remove Mr. Kilpatrick from office for a secret deal he struck with three Detroit police officers to settle an $8.4 million whistle-blower suit. The quid pro quo called for the officers' attorney to turn over text messages that showed that Mayor Kilpatrick and his former chief of staff had lied under oath at the trial. Mr. Kilpatrick also happens to stand charged with obstruction of justice and conspiracy.

The mayor's reaction to the council vote? Vetoed! "In an 11-page veto message, Kilpatrick said the only grounds to remove an official from office allowed under the city charter are a felony conviction or lack of qualifications." Moreover, said the mayor, none of the violations asserted by the council against him is a removable offense under the charter or constitute an act of official misconduct under state law. Official misconduct is not mentioned in the sections of the city's charter that are cited by the council.

> **Information Source:** http://en.wikipedia.org/wiki/Malfeasance_in_office; *DetroitFreePress,* http://www.freep.com/apps/pbcs.dll/article?AID=/20080528/ NEWS05/805280352/0/news01 (accessed June 3, 2008).

Discussion Questions

1. How would you define "official misconduct"?
2. How would you change the language of the city charter to ensure that a mayor can be removed from office for conduct that is other than "a felony conviction or lack of qualifications"?

Commentary by Author

So once more—do you know what unofficial misconduct is? Most likely "yes" when you see it. How about official misconduct? Could it be the commission of an unlawful act done in an official capacity that affects the performance of one's official duties? Most likely, yes.

The intersection of law and ethics, which this case illustrates, can feel like a twilight zone where fact, fiction, and fantasy are difficult to sort out. And, procedure looms large as the default that defines right and wrong.

5.18 Building a City of Ethics

Case: 5.8

The Georgia Municipal Association (GMA) initiated an innovative, voluntary program in 1999 to encourage Georgia's 485 cities and towns to seek certification as a "City of Ethics." There are nearly 200 cities (as of May 2008) that have received this designation.

What does a city have to do to qualify as a "Certified City of Ethics"? They must (1) adopt a resolution subscribing to specific ethics principles, and (2) adopt an ethics ordinance. The resolution must embrace the following ethics principles:

- Serve others, not ourselves
- Use resources with efficiency and economy
- Treat all people fairly

- Use the power of our position for the well-being of our constituents
- Create an environment of honesty, openness, and integrity

The GMA Board requires that the ethics ordinance "contain definitions, an enumeration of permissible and impermissible activities by elected officials, due process procedures for elected officials charged with a violation of the ordinance and punishment provisions for those elected officials found in violation of the ordinance."

Some Georgia cities have given their ethics boards the power to fine offenders, but there is uncertainty about whether or not such sanctions are beyond the legal authority of the board.

Once a municipality passes an ethics resolution and ordinance, it submits these documents to the GMA for review and approval by the Executive Committee of the GMA City Attorneys Section. When certified as a City of Ethics, a municipality receives "a plaque and a logo which can be incorporated into city stationery, road signs and other materials at the city's discretion."

Information Source: (http://www.gmanet.com/CitiesOfEthics.aspx, accessed December 11, 2008).

Discussion Questions

1. Would you want your city to be listed as a "City of Ethics"?
2. Why? Why not?
3. Is a City of Ethics designation likely to cause citizens to have greater trust in their city government?

Commentary by Author

This innovative program is not without its critics. Once branded a City of Ethics, does this mean that all is well? Or, is this designation merely a veneer that amounts to nothing more than pulling a hood over the public's eye? In other words, this practice may have the opposite result insofar as it fosters skepticism, if not cynicism, in the citizenry. Nonetheless, there may be significant symbolic value in claiming to be a City of Ethics.

5.19 Ethics Reform in Indiana Municipalities

Case: 5.8

Three communities in Northwest Indiana's Lake County have entered into an inter-local agreement (ILA) to establish the Shared Ethics Advisory Commission (SEAC). All three communities also adopted a shared ethics code. The municipalities are Crown Point (23,443), Highland (26,961), and Munster (22,340). Crown Point is the county seat and Highland and Munster are suburban communities. Lake County is just south of Chicago. Its principal cities are Gary, Hammond, and East Chicago.

The ILA calls for the SEAC to be composed of seven members who should be persons of good character. It presently consists of two retired judges, a retired clergyman, a former banker/lawyer who is a prominent community leader, a university business dean, and an ethics professor, with one vacancy. The principal activity of the commission is to conduct ethics training, but it may also provide ethics policy review and ethics code administration.

The key values in the Shared Code of Ethics are:

■ Honesty/Integrity—to make decisions for the public's best interests, even when they may not be popular.
■ Respect/Civility—to work together in a spirit of tolerance and understanding.
■ Accountability/Responsibility—to make full public disclosure of the nature of any conflict of interest and support the public's right to know the truth and encourage diverse and civil public debate in the decision-making process.
■ Fairness/Justice—to promote nondiscrimination in decision making for our respective community and to make decisions based on the merits of the issue at hand.

Information Source: Lloyd Rowe (lrowe@netnitco.net) and http://www. iun.edu/~lga/.

Discussion Questions

1. What defines a "person of good character"?
2. What would motivate communities to enter into an interlocal agreement to promote ethics in their governments?
3. Is this a "one size fits all" solution to strengthening ethics in government?

Commentary by Author

The idea and reality of a local government shared ethics commission is unusual, if not unique, in America. The vast majority of local governments have no ethics commission and ethics rules typically limited to conflicts of interest, nepotism, equipment use, and favoritism in hiring practices. Nor is there much that passes for ethics training other than knowing what the rules are and how to stay out of trouble.

5.20 The U.S. Department of the Interior: A Work-in-Progress?

Cases: 5.7, 6.3

Can the scandal-ridden Department of the Interior become a model of an ethical workplace? Secretary Dick Kempthorne (George W. Bush Administration) put forward a ten-point plan to do just that. The plan comes on the heels of the sentencing of the former second-ranking official J. Steven Griles to ten months in prison for lying to a Senate committee about his ties to convicted lobbyist Jack Abramoff and the resignation of Julie MacDonald after an internal investigation found that she had politically interfered in scientific advice offered on the Endangered Species Act.

What are the key ingredients of the plan to turn Interior into a model ethical workplace? They include:

- Appointing an experienced ethics lawyer to be Interior's Designated Agency Ethics Officer
- Expanding the ethics staff
- Implementing best ethics practices identified by the U.S. Office of Government Ethics
- Creating a Conduct Accountability Board
- Including a measure for effective management of ethics in the performance standards for members of the Senior Executive Service
- Strengthening conduct and discipline procedures and penalties
- Reviewing policies and procedures governing contacts with lobbyists and policy advocates
- Enhancing ethics communication with employees, including printing Interior's core values—stewardship for America with integrity and excellence—on each employee's badge

Alas, no sooner had Secretary Kempthorne released his plan, then the assistant secretary for Water and Science (who was appointed to chair the newly constituted Conduct Accountability Board) announced his departure from Interior for a lucrative lobbying job with a firm that represents local and state water agencies with interests before the department. These developments prompted

U.S. Senator Ron Wyden (D-Oregon) to query Secretary Kempthorne about the department's strategy to turn the agency into a model ethical workplace.

Discussion Questions

1. What are the shortcomings of a compliance-driven approach to strengthening the ethics culture of an organization?
2. What are the advantages of a compliance-driven approach to strengthening the ethics culture of an organization?
3. Do the advantages outweigh the disadvantages? Or is it the other way around?

Commentary by Author

Will the secretary be able to build a strong ethical environment in Interior? Perhaps. But if one believes that the secret of doing so involves more than just compliance-compliance-compliance, and the secretary's plan emphasizes compliance with rules, regulations, and laws, then there is reason to be skeptical.

Sources: New York Times, June 27, July 10, 2007 and http://wyden.senate. gov/media/2007/Print/print_07192007_Kempthorne.htm.

5.21 UN Ethics Office

Cases: 5.8

The United Nations Ethics Office was established on January 1, 2006, and given the charge (1) to foster a culture of ethics, transparency, and accountability; (2) to develop and disseminate standards for appropriate professional conduct; and (3) to provide leadership, management, and oversight of the United Nations ethics infrastructure. A senior ethics officer heads the office and all staff members are expected to possess an impeccable record for integrity and commitment to professional ethical standards.

Additional responsibilities of the Ethics Office include managing the financial disclosure program; implementing a policy to protect staff against retaliation for reporting misconduct; providing confidential advice and guidance, including administering an ethics helpline; and ensuring annual ethics training for staff. The Ethics Office is not an enforcement office. Charges of unethical or misbehavior are handled by the Office of Internal Oversight Services.

A UN integrity survey conducted in 2004 found that staff members were concerned about the ethics climate. Similar concerns were expressed by the reports of the Independent Inquiry Committee on the oil-for-food program.

Questions

1. Is the Ethics Office taking a compliance-only approach?
2. Does it make sense to separate enforcement from advocacy?

Commentary

Howard Whitton, The Ethicos Group, International Consulting Services:

> The really big idea for the UN scheme was that the whistle-blower protection law is not primarily about protecting whistle-blowers—that is just the strategy to achieve the main objective, which is to get the organization's staff to disclose corruption, fraud, and misconduct when they find it. Only by so doing can the UN answer credibly when asked by potential whistle-blowers and their agents, "Why should we trust the UN to protect us?"—and the right answer is, "Because it's in the UN's interests to protect you."
>
> The other big idea was that whistle-blowing in the UN is not (as it is in the United States) the act of a private individual exercising his or her constitutionally protected right of free speech—it is a duty of UN employment to report corruption and wrongdoing. This difference in conception has major implications.

Author's Note: Since the establishment of the UN Ethics Office the UN has been criticized for failing to set up an effective ethics program.
www.daccessdds.un.org/doc/UNDOC/GEN/N05/619/19/PDF/N0561919.pdf?OpenElement
www.globalpolicy.org/reform/topics/general/2006/0117ethics.htm (accessed July 10, 2006).

References

Klosko, G. 1992. *The Principle of Fairness and Political Obligation.* Lanham, MD: Rowman & Littlefield Publishers.

Menzel, D. 2008. "Strengthening Ethical Governance in Local Government." *PMplus* online. http://icma.org/pm/9009/.

Chapter 6

Ethics in the Workplace

> When employees own the culture of their workplace—when they feel responsible for "how things work around here"—they won't permit wrongdoing.
>
> **Institute for Global Ethics,** www.globalethics.org/services-for
> -organizations.php

Working in a government or nonprofit organization can be rewarding and exciting and also filled with many ethics decisions. While public organizations, small and large, typically have a personnel manual that details what is acceptable and unacceptable behavior, there is no assurance that an employee is fully aware of the "dos" and "donts". Moreover, every organization has its own culture and values about "how we do things around here." Sometimes that can mean that how we do things around here is the right way and there are no exceptions. An employee who finds himself in disagreement either has the choice of conforming or finding a new job. And, in a worst-case situation in which the employee cannot walk, he may find himself victimized by the organization. Working in the "shadow of organization," as Robert B. Denhardt (1991) puts it, can eventually challenge the individual's moral autonomy and strip him of his humanity. How many times have you found yourself saying, "the organization made me do it"?

A whistle-blower is generally someone who refuses to accept an organizational imperative to go along to get along. He or she can be defined as a person who reacts to fraud, waste, and the abuse of power by going outside normal reporting channels (the media for example) and exposing the unacceptable act. Few of us are or will be whistle-blowers and most of us will not find ourselves in a work environment where fraud, waste, and the abuse of power are commonplace. Still, we are very likely to find ourselves in a workplace where ethical bright lines are not always clear and we will have to exercise ethical judgment.

The cases in Chapter 6 illustrate the need for ethical judgment when one is confronted with mundane and not so mundane situations. Consider the concluding case. The city manager discovers that his two top staff members are having an intimate relationship in the office. What should he do? What is right and wrong about the situation? Other cases in this chapter focus on soliciting funds from fellow employees, holding auctions, inflating performance evaluations, hiring family members and friends, and falsifying government documents in the name of the public interest.

The cases in Chapter 6 are cross-listed in a matrix with the ethical competencies in Appendix 4. The matrix cells enable the reader to identify specific cases with specific competencies. For example, the competency *"embrace and promote ethical behavior and practices in the workplace"* is highlighted in several cases, including 6.3 "Polish this Draft" and 6.10 "A Late Night Surprise."

6.1 Auctions in the Office

Controversies: 4.15
Key Words: superior-subordinate, chain of command, favoritism
Case Complexity → Low
CD: 3.8 Ethics Test

Suppose you got this message during the Christmas season: "The final tally is in and $3,540 was raised to help Paula Jones, a single mother in our department with no medical insurance, cover the medical costs of her leukemia-stricken daughter. A check will be sent tomorrow. The beautiful, handcrafted oak bookcase went for $1,134."

"Oh, you want to know who won the bookcase? After a heated auction contest between Liz, Joe, and Jane, Liz won the bookcase! Thanks to all who donated items for the auction and thanks to all who participated."

So, what's the ethical dilemma? Liz is supervised by Jane, Jane is supervised by Les, and Les is supervised by Joe. Now, even though Les did not bid on the bookcase, he is included to make clear the chain of command. Joe → Les → Jane → Liz

Discussion Questions

1. Is it appropriate for supervisors to compete with subordinates in this kind of office situation?
2. Should Joe not bid because he is the second line supervisor to Jane and the third line supervisor to Liz?
3. Should Jane have backed out because she is Liz's supervisor?
4. Les decided it was not right for him to participate because he supervised Jane and Liz.
5. Do workplace auctions for charity or other well-intended office situations foster ill will and perhaps unethical behavior when supervisors are pitted against organizational subordinates?

Case Assessment

Debra A. Taylor, Detective, Sarasota County Sheriff's Office, Florida:

> This case creates an ethical dilemma because supervisors and subordinates are competing against each other to win a certain item within the workplace. Resentment may occur if one person wins over the other. Also, favoritism can be suggested if the rules of the auction are not clearly stated and understood by all participants. Also, anytime you allow donations, charity, or fundraisers to be conducted in the workplace many problems may arise. Members are sometimes bullied or feel pressured to give money or buy a certain product that a fellow employee's child may be selling or raising money for a sport team or other organization. Employees who do not donate may feel alienated or believe those members that contribute to the charity have an advantage. Therefore, it is best to keep auctions and other money raising activities out of the workplace to eliminate the potential for ethical wrongdoing.
>
> Here is how I would answer the questions:
>
> It is inappropriate for supervisors and subordinates to compete in any type of workplace auction even if it is for a charity or a good cause.
>
> Putting the command structure aside, auctions may create problems such as favoritism and resentment among employees, which can also lead to low morale within the organization and possible wrongdoing.
>
> Fundraisers and charity donations should not be conducted in the workplace regardless of command structure.
>
> Les decided it was not right for him to participate because he supervised Jane and Liz. Les was trying to limit his involvement in a situation that could have become an ethical dilemma within the workplace.

Do workplace auctions for charity or other well-intended office situations foster ill will and perhaps unethical behavior when supervisors are pitted against organizational subordinates? Yes, they certainly can.

LaVonne Bower, MADD, Manasota, Florida:

There are two ways this could be ethically sticky: (1) If a supervisor is bidding against subordinates and makes it known he wants the item being auctioned, he could pressure the others to stop bidding. This then lowers the amount of money raised, which is not fair and unethical. (2) The second possible situation could be that the subordinates may feel an obligation to bid more than they can afford to please the supervisors. It would be best if the auction were a silent auction or done in some way so that nobody knows how much the other is bidding until the "winner" is revealed.

The other possible ethical problem is that once you do one fundraiser for someone, you open the door to doing them for others. Who then decides who is worthy or not? I suggest that people let other organizations do fundraisers, or make the donation privately. I do know that most banks will open a trust account for these types of situations so that people can make donations and know that the funds are going to that specific person. This keeps people from feeling pressured to make a donation or as to the amount they give.

6.2 Workplace Solicitations

Controversies: 3.11, 4.15
Key Words: email, charity, solicitation
Case Complexity → Low
CD: 5.2 Hillsborough County, Florida, Solicitation Policy

Suppose you received this e-mail on the office server:

Good morning, I have a sample of my 2005 desk "Night-Sky Photography" calendar in my office if anyone would like to see it before purchasing. Please call me first to make sure I am in the office. Price is $15.00. I am taking Christmas orders. Remember, ⅓ of the profit for the calendars goes to Bette (in purchasing) to help out her husband who has recently come down with MS. Thanks, Ron

It is not uncommon to receive e-mail from staff about charitable organizations trying to raise money by selling candy, magazines, or cookies as the Girl Scouts do annually.

Discussion Questions

1. Should you object about such solicitation at work for organizations supporting "good" causes?
2. Does the good of helping Bette, a fellow employee, with the expenses associated with her husband's MS outweigh the personal profit motive?
3. Are the solicitations by a soccer mom to raise funds for her son's team the same thing as this enterprising fellow who is putting part of his profit to help a well-liked and financially troubled employee?
4. Should a public administrator see either one or both as unethical in the workplace?
5. Or is this the kind of situation where we shrug and turn our head the other way?
6. What should I do?
7. Suppose the Human Resources director asked you to draft a policy dealing with workplace solicitations, what would your policy cover? All solicitations? Some? Try your hand at drafting the policy.
8. Critique the solicitation policy in Exhibit 6.1.

EXHIBIT 6.1

Solicitation Policy

Any activity on behalf of profit-making organizations or for private profit is strictly prohibited on county premises. You are permitted to solicit for nonprofit organizations or nonprofit purposes during your free time, such as lunch breaks, in nonwork areas, as long as it does not affect other employees who are working. Abuse of this privilege may be grounds for disciplinary action.

Case Assessment

Mary Mahoney, Management and Budget Department, Hillsborough County, Florida:

> I have been with a large Florida county government for many years and have seen all the situations cited in this case and more.
>
> Our county government has handled e-mail solicitations with a policy that prohibits an employee from soliciting for anything via e-mail. Disciplinary action, including termination, can result. Florida has a strong open records law that county administration takes very seriously and applies to e-mail, incoming and outgoing. This helps reinforce the concept that an employee's e-mail usage is not for personal use, although some incidental personal use is allowed. Certainly, the

gentleman soliciting the sale of his photo calendars would fall into that category.

If the gentleman wished to post a notice on a county bulletin board, he could do so providing he follow another county policy. In fact, there is a classified advertisement section on the county's intranet site where employees are allowed to sell merchandise such as cars, boats, etc., but commercial sales are prohibited.

In our county government, employees may personally solicit on county premises for private nonprofits provided it is done during free time during the work day. A county employee may not at any time during the work day solicit on behalf of profit-making organizations. An employee helping her daughter sell Girl Scout cookies can solicit during her break as long as it doesn't affect other employees. She cannot solicit for her Avon business.

There may be another underlying issue with this case. By mentioning the personal health situation of another person, the husband of an employee, in an organization-wide e-mail, he may be violating the federal Health Insurance Portability and Accountablity Act (HIPAA) and, in Hillsborough County, our HIPAA policy.

Should I personally object about the case's solicitation at work for organizations supporting "good" causes? In my opinion, it is not a public manager's personal duty to judge whether the cause is "good" or not. It is our job to make sure there are policies and procedures and then follow those. If I were a supervisor, I would counsel the employee sending out the e-mails because our county policy prohibits this type of solicitation. I would direct him to stop his sales through the county's e-mail account and advise him not to personally solicit any employees during work hours or his free time during his working hours. Although the cause may seem worthy, the fact is he is personally selling his calendars and making a profit. The organization has no control on whether or not those profits go to the "worthy cause." His "worthy cause" is in fact a person, not a private nonprofit organization. Besides, how would an individual know that his profits go to that person or when he would start pocketing the proceeds?

Does the good of helping the fellow employee outweigh the personal profit motive? To me, that is a philosophical question, and not one for the workplace.

Are solicitations by a soccer mom to raise funds for her son's team the same thing? No, the soccer team is a nonprofit entity (at least I hope it is) and the funds are not going directly to the child, but to the team. Again, the soccer mom would need to follow county policies and procedures.

You raise the issue of a "well-liked and financially troubled employee." Our duty is to all—not just those who are "well-liked." This could lead to perceptions that the organization is biased based on race, ethnicity, religion, or even political affinity. In turn, such perceptions could lead to legal actions on the part of those who see disparate treatment because they are not "well liked." I won't even get into the "financially troubled employee" part of this question.

And when does solicitation for charities cross the line from voluntary to involuntary? That's another question.

Is the solicitation in this case unethical? Well, according to the Hillsborough County Code of Ethics, the calendar sale probably is especially since there are already county policies that prohibit this activity. The Girl Scout cookie sale is another matter. The Girl Scouts are a bona fide nonprofit organization and nondiscriminatory. In fact, it receives funds from the local United Way campaign. The United Way is authorized for payroll deduction. (Ethically I must disclose that I was an active Girl Scout from seven years old until a sophomore in college. I was an assistant troop leader for my daughter's troop for five years. I sold lots of cookies to coworkers, but always followed the county's policies. I still support the organization through personal donations and cookie purchases. I still have four boxes of Thin Mints in the freezer.)

Do we turn our heads and shrug? Well, I can't if I am a supervisor of someone soliciting. Then it is my obligation to enforce county policies and procedures. If I'm not, then it is my obligation to notify the Human Resources Department of my concern about the possible violation. If the person selling the calendar is a coworker, I might personally advise him to stop if I knew him well. Otherwise, I would notify my department director of my concerns. I would not purchase the calendar.

Do any of the Hillsborough County's policies and procedures and codes stop the solicitations? A very large percentage of them are stopped, but some still get out on e-mail or on bulletin boards or through direct transactions. Just this week, there was an e-mail soliciting contributions to pay funeral expenses of a county employee's son. The young man was killed during a robbery he committed the past weekend.

Victoria Reinhardt, Commissioner, Ramsey County, Minnesota:

I believe that it is one of the better parts of human nature to want to help the people we care about. It may be an adult wanting to help a child raise funds for school or recreation, or individuals wanting to ease the pain of a coworker who has to face an unexpected medical or financial challenge. Recently my sister's coworkers chipped in to buy meals for her family while she recovered from surgery and got through chemotherapy. When it came to selling Girl Scout cookies, I envied the girls whose parents worked in an office because they didn't have to go door-to-door, although that experience did pay off years later. Finally, if you are on the receiving end of a card or gift through the sunshine fund, you know how important the little things can be. I believe these are all good things that help improve the quality of life in the workplace.

With all of that said, I also believe there must be clear parameters about solicitations in the workplace, especially about how they are made. No one should feel pressured to buy or give based on who is asking. Therefore, solicitations should not be done person to person. However, use of the employee break area for products, or sign-up sheets for products that will be delivered at a later date, allow an individual to make a decision about whether they want to participate. For helping an individual with health or personal difficulties, a respectful e-mail letting people know the situation and how they can help, if they so choose, or an envelope that is simply passed from staff to staff, can work very well.

6.3 Polish this Draft!

Controversies: 3.12, 5.20
Key Words: performance appraisal, Senior Executive Service, abuse of power
Case Complexity → Low
CD: 4.17 President Obama's Executive Order

Annual performance appraisals typically result in anxious moments for all, especially the person receiving the appraisal. Yet others can be drawn into the anxiety circle that can have ethical or not-so-ethical overtones. Consider yourself an employee who works in a large city agency as a staff member for a senior manager. You are routinely expected to provide "input" for the manager's annual evaluation. Suppose your input goes directly to his secretary and thus to him—is anyone going to say anything but glowing things about what happened under his watch? Probably not.

Now consider an even more uncomfortable situation. Suppose you, as the best writer on the staff, are given the task of polishing the draft of the senior manager's performance evaluation which had been put together using the "input" that everyone had provided. Trying not to violate your own ethical standards, you simply edit it, correcting grammar and rewording so it will read more smoothly. You return it to his secretary who shares it with her boss. Then, the boss sends it back to you and pronounces "it is not good enough" with instructions to "make me look like a god."

Discussion Questions

1. Would you voice your ethical concerns to the boss?
2. Would you report your boss to his boss?
3. Would you request a transfer to another agency?
4. Would you simply turn your head and make your boss "look like a god"?

Case Assessment

Bruce Rodman, U.S. Railroad Retirement Board, Chicago, Illinois:

> This represents a fairly common occurrence in government, as staff members are often expected to provide input and editorial assistance in preparing their supervisor's "self assessment" for appraisal purposes. This is particularly true for senior managers who have broad-based responsibilities. In such an instance, they often have no choice but to rely on staff members to provide needed detail on the unit's overall performance during the year. Ideally of course, the person whose performance is being appraised would be the one to take the information and fashion it into a comprehensive overview of his or her own performance during the year. However, this scenario presents less of an ethical problem with a capital "E"—in that it involves something of questionable legality, a conflict of interest, or unfair advantage—but one with a lowercase "e" dealing with workplace expectations and propriety. It also begs the question of who exactly should be responsible for the senior manager's appraisal—him or his superior? Technically, it is the supervisor, but a self-appraisal is often requested that more or less becomes the final product.
>
> It is one thing to accentuate the positive and another to tell an outright lie, and it is not clear from this case which is in play. The first thing the employee should do is talk directly to the boss in order to obtain a clearer understanding of expectations. It sounds like much communication is through the secretary, so something could have been lost in translation. If that is not the case, the employee should definitely voice any concerns. Perhaps the boss will take greater personal responsibility for the document or give the assignment to someone else. It could also create ongoing tension, in which case the employee may want to investigate other job opportunities. Rather than going to the designated agency ethics official, who typically deals with "capital-E"

problems, other likely sources of guidance and support are the agency's human resources director or perhaps an employee assistance program counselor (who is usually trained in social work with experience in workplace problems). Regardless of whether the employee decides to comply with the assignment to the best of his abilities and principles, he should keep copies of all documentation, including edited drafts and written directions, as evidence of how the situation developed. As a last resort, he could raise his concerns with the supervisor's supervisor—for whom the appraisal document is actually being prepared—although this could heighten everyone's interest in pursuing other opportunities.

Joanne E. Howard, Senior Consultant MCIC (Metro Chicago Information Center), Chicago, Illinois:

> I would not voice my ethical concerns to the boss. First, the boss has obviously risen through the hierarchy or gotten the job because he or she thoroughly understands the system. I would follow the chain of command and edit the report for grammar and appropriate wording. However, once the boss came back to me requesting that I "make him look like a god," I would draw the line. I would indicate I had done the best that I could and that I had no other input in my arsenal. This is a form of "passive" insubordination; however, I would immediately begin to look for another position outside of his chain of command.
>
> 1. Would you report your boss to his boss? If I found another position outside of the organization, I would let my parting shot be a meeting with the big boss to report my experience. I would, however, not initiate this meeting until I was on my way out of the organization.
> 2. Would you request a transfer to another agency? My request for a transfer would depend on how egregious the behavior of the boss had been in the past. Every employee is cast in the role of the dutiful sycophant at some point in their career. My request for a transfer would depend on how many times I had been asked to play this part, my role in the organization, how valued I felt as an employee, my level of responsibility in the pecking order, how many people I had reporting to me, and my age and family situation at the time of the transfer request. It is easy to respond to hypothetical situations when you only have yourself in mind. However, if you are the head of household or your income is needed to support children in

private school or college, you have a sick parent that rely on your income, the situation immediately changes and takes on more poignancy.

3. Would you simply turn your head and make your boss look like a god? In many ways, most of us would respond to this question based on our level of experience, the state of the economy, and our household responsibilities. No one in this economy is going to "cut off their nose to spite their face"—times are just too critical. I do, however, think that most self-respecting employees placed in this position would do the right thing, review their situation (home obligations and work-life balance), and stay in place if they could but leave if they could not stomach it. Remember, no deed goes unpunished, even if the employee is in the right.

6.4 Hiring Your Supervisor's Friend

Controversies: 4.15, 6.11
Key Words: hiring, supervisor, abuse of power
Case Complexity → Low
CD: 4.27 President Obama's Executive Order

As a middle manager in charge of making a recommendation for a job opening in your city organization, you form a search committee and appoint a chair to conduct the search. Shortly after the search gets underway, you receive a call from your supervisor, Anne, informing you that a family friend is one of the candidates. Anne assures you that the call is in no way an attempt to influence the search process. Nonetheless, she reiterates the closeness of her relationship with the candidate and comments about the person's excellent qualifications for the position. The search committee recommends a rank order of three persons. As it turns out, Anne's friend is ranked number two in what is, by the chair's own account, a close and difficult ranking process.

Discussion Questions

1. Should you recommend your supervisor's friend for the job under these circumstances?
2. Would it be morally permissible to do so? Why or why not?
3. Suppose you are the supervisor, Anne, in this case. Have you done anything wrong?

Case Assessment

James Pfiffner, Professor, School of Public Policy, George Mason University:

> If the choice among the top candidates is a close one, Joe should interview them personally and make his own decision about recommending one to his superior. He should make the call on the merits and try to ignore his boss's inappropriate words. If there is a genuine tie between the top two candidates, he can report that to his boss. After all, the boss is doing the hiring, not Joe.

Posted on ETHTALK listserv by D. Gayle Baker:

> You are placed in a precarious situation by your supervisor. If you recommend the supervisor's friend, and the committee selects someone else, the supervisor may behave unfavorably to you. If you do not recommend the friend, the supervisor may ask you why he was not recommended and again may behave unfavorably toward you. If the search committee selects the candidate on his own merit without the recommendation, then it seems the process has worked without prejudice. However, hiring friends or family members in the direct chain of command within the same organization seems incestuous and undesirable.
>
> Has the supervisor done anything wrong? Yes, although she knows that the person has great qualifications and would be an asset to the organization, if the friend were hired and reported through the chain of command to you and the supervisor, then the morale in the office would be affected by the appearance of "favoritism." If, however, the friend could be placed in a different department within the organization, then that would be a preferable way to gain a great employee and not impact existing trust in management.

6.5 To Praise or Not to Praise!

Controversies:
Key Words: policy, personal leave, whistle-blowing
Case Complexity → Low
CD: 4.35 Ethics Management for Public Administrators

It is brought to your attention as manager that someone in your department took a sick day to attend the funeral of an uncle. The bereavement policy in your county agency does not provide paid leave covering this relationship. A coworker discovers that the person is being paid for an unauthorized personal leave day and comes to you as the supervisor.

Discussion Questions

1. What action should you take?
2. Should you use discourage this kind of "reporting"?
3. Is this a case of "whistle-blowing"?
4. Should you praise the behavior?
5. Is this a genuine ethical dilemma? Or is it a management issue? Both?

Case Assessment

Paul Sharon, ICMA Range Rider, Jacksonville, Florida, and (former) City Manager in Clarendon Hills, Illinois, South Haven, Michigan, Lombard, Illinois, North Andover and Ashland, Massachusetts, and Hudson, New Hampshire:

> Is this the hated playground "tattle-tale" of your childhood grown up?
>
> While we might want, instinctively, to "out" this individual to his or her colleagues, to let them know there's a snitch in their midst, that's inappropriate.
>
> A good supervisor should, objectively, assume no ill intent on the part of either the reporter or the employee who put in for bereavement leave. Further assuming that this behavior is not chronic on the part of either party, I do not see this necessarily as an ethical dilemma.
>
> My approach with the "snitch" would be to thank her for bringing it to my attention, and suggest, perhaps, that she had been in a similar situation and had been unable to use bereavement leave—this will or should give the impression that there must have been some personal reason for bringing this specific incident up, and I did not expect that this was, or was going to be, regular behavior on her part.
>
> As for the employee who put in for the bereavement leave, a private, personal conversation is in order, in which the limitations of the bereavement policy are explained. I would suggest to this employee that he may have considered this uncle to be a "favorite uncle," even perhaps the last "next-of-kin," sincerely extend my sympathies, but make it clear to him that such use of bereavement leave was inappropriate, and needed to be accounted for.

Kathy Livernois, Director of Human Resources, St. Charles, Illinois:

> The manager of the department must investigate this issue further. The following questions must be answered:
>
> - Did anyone approve the use of an unauthorized personal leave day, for example, a direct supervisor? If not, is the employee allowed to submit this to payroll directly?
> - If someone, such as a direct supervisor, approved the use of the day, then the manager should meet with the direct supervisor to determine the facts. If the facts are as indicated whereby the supervisor allowed the personal leave day for a relative not covered under the bereavement policy, the question remains as to why.
>   - If the supervisor's reason was because he or she did not want to see the employee suffer further (either because it would have been without pay or use of the employee's vacation time) the answer would be the same; however, the tone in which it is delivered would be different. The tone would be one of appreciating the supervisor's reason, explaining, however, that policies must be followed so as not to allow inconsistencies which could lead to further problems in the future.
>   - If the supervisor's intent was because he or she disagreed with the policy and believed uncles should be covered, then this would be a flagrant violation of the policy and the tone would be stern. The supervisor would receive appropriate discipline based on the flagrant disregard of policy.
>   - Regardless of the tone in which the message is delivered, the direction would be that a correction needs to be made. Uncles are not covered and, therefore, the employee will need to either take the day without pay or use an approved form of paid leave. It would be the supervisor's responsibility to deliver this message to explain his or her error in allowing the personal leave day.
> - If the employee was allowed to submit it to payroll directly, then the following questions must be answered:
>   - Was the employee aware of which family members are covered under the bereavement policy? If the employee did not know, then the manager would inform the employee of the policy. The manager would inform the employee that a correction in type of time away will be made.
>   - If the employee was aware that an uncle is not covered in the bereavement policy, then the manager needs to ask why the employee still used a personal leave day. If the employee blatantly chose to take the unauthorized personal leave day

regardless of the policy, then not only will the correction in the type of day taken be made, but the employee should receive appropriate discipline for the flagrant disregard of policy.

The reporting of this information would not be discouraged. It is important in an organization that policies are followed consistently by all supervisors and employees. The manager may state to the coworker that he or she appreciates the information and will follow up accordingly; however, the coworker should not be praised for the behavior.

This is not a case of whistle-blowing. Whistle-blower complaints focus on conduct prohibited by a specific law that could cause damage to public safety, waste taxpayer dollars, or violate public trust. This reporting was none of the above. Instead, this is a management issue combined with an ethical dilemma. Does the supervisor attempt to help the employee or be forthright in following policy? Or did the supervisor just not agree with the policy and then follow his or her own policy? The supervisor must follow the policy, as written, but needs to provide the employee with an empathetic explanation as to the reason for the policy.

6.6 Ignorance or Insider Trading?

Controversies: 4.15, 4.16
Key Words: ethics orientation, grants, contracts, RFP, information
Case Complexity → Low
CD: 6.2 International City/County Management Association Code of Ethics
CD: 6.4 American Institute of Certified Planners Code of Ethics

You are a young policy analyst in your second month of work for a city's law enforcement agency. You have received no ethics orientation, although an ethics booklet was handed to you on the first day of work. You have not read it. Your basic job is to analyze agency operations to make them more effective and efficient. To do this, it is necessary for you to read the case reports of the agency's field agents. These reports are classified confidential or secret as the case may be. You have been granted an interim secret clearance, pending completion of a background investigation, which will take a year.

As a related duty, you sit on a grant and contract review board that evaluates proposals from outside contractors for studies with the same general purpose. Over the few weeks you have sat on the board, you have become quite disappointed by the low quality of the bids. Few contractors seem to have carefully read the RFPs, and many are at best only nominally qualified to do the work.

One day, an acquaintance of yours who is affiliated with a very prestigious think tank calls and explains that the think tank is thinking about filing a proposal. Your friend says that he has several questions about what the agency is really looking for. You eagerly fill him in. "Finally," you think, "we'll get a good proposal, and the county will get some solid research for all the dollars they're granting."

A few days later, you come across the ethics manual in your desk drawer, and, it being a slow day, decide to read it. You are both surprised and a little apprehensive to learn that no one but the contact person named in the RFP is to reveal any information about a Request for Proposals. Upon reflection, you realize that what you have done could be considered a form of "insider trading," that is, providing information that could be advantageous to only a few persons.

Discussion Questions

1. What should you do?
2. Should you discuss the situation with a veteran colleague?
3. Should you tell your boss?

You decide to discuss the problem with your office-mate, a 30-year veteran government employee who has been in this agency over ten years. He advises that "if you tell Max (the division chief) you divulged confidential material, you'll never see another confidential file."

This is very plausible. Max cut his teeth as a security investigator protecting nuclear weapons secrets at the height of the Cold War.

What should you do?

Case Assessment

Gerald Caiden, Professor of Public Administration, School of Policy, Planning and Development, University of Southern California, Los Angeles:

> A mistake is a mistake whether made intentionally or inadvertently. Everyone makes mistakes; we are only human. Most mistakes are harmless and of little consequence unless one is a perfectionist. Most people just keep quiet and await the outcome. Usually, nothing much occurs at all and the mistake is soon forgotten by all. When the mistake is discovered, it may be too late for a correction to be made and again it is best forgotten. In a democracy, the courts will not accept self-incrimination and one is judged innocent until proven guilty. My advice is: "Do not deliberately draw attention to oneself, especially not a beginner and try to keep matters quiet and confined."
>
> But some mistakes may well have serious consequences that need to be rectified or corrected. To avoid this harmful situation, it is best

to warn one's supervisor (Max) and come clean. It is then up to the supervisor to decide what has to be done. The supervisor may take a dim view of the perpetrator and hold it against him. Or the supervisor may demonstrate and use the case as a learning experience for the perpetrator, an experience expected to be taken to heart and avoided in the future.

If the mistake is so grave that the supervisor has to take responsibility, he may have to find an appropriate response. In this case, the confidential information was given in error. Max and the perpetrator must await a submitted RFP at which point it may have to be returned, with an explanation about how the mistake occurred and that it was a breach of the law or established practices. Max should then cancel the RFP and re-advertise so that the rejected applicant can reapply. Is there any obligation to take any applicant at all? Is there really an overwhelming reason why the RFP should not be withdrawn and revised? Is the law being broken? Is there any conflict of interest involved? Is anything underhanded taking place or perceived to be taking place?

What, in this case, is judged to be the appropriate disciplinary action should the mistake be that serious? Should the policy analyst feel guilty or suspect that victimization is occurring as a consequence of the mistake, the analyst should look for alternative employment. The agency will lose credibility for its failure to recognize an honest mistake, a person of integrity and conscience who has taken the experience too much to heart and needs counseling. Max would similarly lose and should the response be seen as a cop out, a gutless supervisor for not taking the blame and just another cowardly bureaucrat following orders instead of using judgment, plain common sense, and compassion. Max would then make a good totalitarian tool devoid of democratic understanding. Unfortunately, there are far too many like Max in supervisory positions in all regimes.

This response is by MPA students in the Ethics in Public Service course supervised by Professor Rod Erakovich at the School of Urban and Public Affairs at the University of Texas at Arlington:

It can be asserted that the analyst is guilty both of insider trading and ignorance; however, the latter is the cause of the former. Moreover, it is our belief that the young analyst did not intentionally act unethically when divulging the information. The analyst realized his mistake only after he familiarized himself with the formal ethics booklet provided in training. The organization abdicated the responsibility of creating a collectively accepted values system. Although the agency provided the analyst with the ethics booklet, the culture of the organization was not conducive to employees collectively embracing ethical standards. Without clearly understanding the organizational values, the analyst is forced to rely on his own individual values to resolve the dilemma.

The analyst is faced with two basic approaches to resolving this dilemma. He may accept the role of whistle-blower and admit his error while also drawing attention to the failure of the organization to ensure employees are aware of all ethical responsibilities. Or, in the interest of self-preservation, he may admit to nothing and accept the ethical culture of the organization. As noted by Montgomery Van Wart in his book, *Changing Public Service Values*, the analyst is faced with the dilemma of sacrificing his individual values of honesty, consistency, coherence, and reciprocity in order to preserve his position of employment. Conversely, the analyst may choose to uphold his own civic integrity and risk the loss of his employment.

The personal ethical choice for the analyst is whether to approach the division chief in an honest and forthright manner. The analyst should explain the circumstances of the incident and illustrate his lack of knowledge. Although unlikely within this organization, it is possible the division chief may accept the analyst's error and take steps to improve the culture of the organization. However, from the analyst's perspective as a new employee, it is more likely that he will conceal his mistake and subsequently accept the current values put forth within the organization in order to sustain employment.

Another issue surfaces when evaluating the leadership roles within this organization. The division chief for the analyst does not communicate standards or expectations to his team members. Based on the information provided, it appears this leader operates by using a culture of fear among his employees, and he approaches problem issues reactively. His leadership style is not indicative of an open and transparent culture within the organization. By not developing transparency in the culture, the division chief has effectively encouraged a climate of secrecy with employees to keep mistakes quiet. In order to change this behavior within the division and organization, he must develop an environment conducive to open exchange and transparency.

The shortcomings in this dilemma are not solely that of the analyst or the division chief. This agency failed to effectively communicate its expectations to employees because of a poorly developed values system that was sparingly embraced in a reactive environment. A large part of the organizational failing can be attributed to the absence of a strong code of ethics, leadership, and employee ownership of the organizational values. The analyst was given an interim secret clearance for a position on a grant and contract review board after only two months of employment. A federal agency should not delegate such clearance without enumerating the conduct expected of employees within high-security positions.

To prevent a similar recurrence of this dilemma, the agency must develop clearly stated and collectively accepted values. Furthermore, the agency must allow employees to participate in the development of values and ethical standards in order to encourage individual and ultimately collective ownership. Employee ownership of organizational values encourages operation under an agreed framework of ethical standards. By involving employees in the values formulation process and eagerly transmitting the organizational values to new employees, the agency will develop strong ownership of values and personal action to uphold them.

It is also imperative that employees be empowered with the necessary tools to conduct themselves in the most professional and ethical manner within any given organization. The internal structure of the agency should echo underlying cultural values embraced by leadership and employees alike. In this ethical dilemma, no clear organizational values are evident. The agency seems to have a reactive approach to ethical standards and dilemmas in the workplace. This is evidenced by the analyst's behavior and the reaction of his coworker.

Ultimately, the agency must also accept a proactive role. Deep structural and organizational reforms must be made in order to develop a culture of transparency in which values are operational. If the agency had recognized the importance of transcending organizational values, it is possible the analyst would have embraced the values and maintained lawful and ethical behavior.

6.7 When the Boss Marries a Subordinate

Controversies: 5.17, 6.11, 6.16
Key Words: leadership, city, police, responsibility, rumor mongering, discipline
Case Complexity → Moderate
CD: 4.35 Ethics Management for Public Administrators

As the city's (population 25,000) public safety director, you are charged with over-seeing the police and fire departments—frequently not an easy job. Nonetheless, you take your job seriously and are constantly concerned about working conditions and equity among the city's fifty police officers and thirty firefighters. Alas, you meet and fall in love with one of your female police officers, let's call her Irene, and in time, enter marital bliss. Your wife does not report directly to you but you do have responsibility for signing off on her annual evaluation.

Although you do not believe you are treating your officer-wife any differently than other patrol officers in the police department, not everyone agrees. In fact, one of her male colleagues, let's call him Officer Stone, complained via e-mail several times to her supervisor, Lt. Jones, that your officer-wife, Irene, was receiving preferential treatment. Lt. Jones listened carefully to Officer Stone and eventually brought his complaint to your attention. Somewhat dismayed and convinced that you have done nothing wrong, you feel that Officer Stone is merely stirring up trouble and spreading malicious rumors. Consequently, you reprimand him for unprofessional behavior.

Frustrated, Officer Stone shares his concerns and discontent with his wife, Karen, who decides to take things into her own hands. "I can't take it any more," she exclaims, "I am going to write an anonymous letter to the press and community groups about the mismanagement and low morale of the department that the public safety director has caused." In the letter, Karen also charges that your marriage to Officer Irene is illegal as she had unlawfully divorced her husband from a previous marriage.

The letter prompts you to investigate the situation—who wrote it? Officer Stone? Someone else? You bring the matter to the county prosecutor. He tells you that no law has been violated and he therefore will not investigate. Nonetheless, you want to get to the bottom of this and order the police chief to conduct an internal investigation. The investigation proceeds. The chief reports to you that Officer Stone did not write the letter but that he knew his wife had sent the letter.

The city's personnel policies do not prohibit fraternization among employees, although relatives of the city manager and city council are prohibited from working for the city.

Discussion Questions

1. What would you do next?
    a. Would you reprimand Officer Stone once more?
    b. Would you fire him for not being forthcoming about his wife's letter writing?
    c. Would you send him to counseling?
    d. Would you demand a public apology from Officer Stone's wife?
    e. Is doing nothing an option?

2. Who would you consult?
3. If you decide to fire him, is there an ethical issue? How would you rationalize the decision?
4. What would you expect ex-officer Stone to do?

Case Assessment

Sam Halter, (former) City Administrator, Tampa, Florida and ICMA Range Rider:

> The actions of public officials are always subject to review by their subordinate staff and the public. Even if an official's actions are technically correct, if these actions are perceived to be inappropriate by the public or subordinates they can become indefensible.
>
> In this case, the public safety director has taken actions (the reprimand of Officer Stone and ordering additional investigation of the matter) which will likely be perceived by his staff and ultimately the public as inappropriate. Even though there has been no documentation of preferential treatment given to his wife, the director's actions convey the impression he is using his position to cover up acts of favoritism.
>
> It is never a good practice for a public official to have a relative in a subordinate position. Despite efforts to avoid perceived acts of favoritism, sooner or later the official will find himself being accused of an inappropriate action. To prevent this from happening, the director needs to stop trying to discredit Officer Stone and take steps to get his wife employed by another agency.

Fred Meine, Professor, Troy University, Florida:

> This case presents a common and perplexing problem for organizations, particularly hierarchical ones such as police departments and military organizations. While such organizations often have antifraternization policies, once people get married such policies often break down, leading to problems like the ones in this scenario. This city does not have a fraternization prohibition, but a questionable personal relationship (fraternization) is clearly the root of the problem that developed. The matter is usually dealt with by ensuring there is no official superior-subordinate relationship between the parties involved—something difficult to do in this case.
>
> This situation is all about the perception of favoritism. The perception may or may not be true whether the public safety director (PSD)

intended it or not, since Irene may be treated differently by her supervisors just because of her relationship. Doing nothing is not a viable option since situations like this only fester and become more problematic. So, the question is what to do.

While it may have been appropriate to reprimand Officer Stone if his initial complaining to his supervisor was unprofessional in nature, unless it is clear that Stone supported his wife's letter writing it may be difficult to hold him accountable for the media issue. This may very well be a case where trying to diffuse a negative situation through direct contact is the best approach. The PSD could meet with Officer Stone and his wife in an effort to defuse the situation, and only if that does not help the situation find other ways to deal with Officer Stone more officially. Caution is dictated in the area of official action, because adverse action against Officer Stone carries with it ethical implications or at least will likely contribute to even greater problems relating to perceptions of getting back at Stone. After all, perception is reality, and working to change perceptions could address the problem. The PSD might also totally divorce himself from the personnel evaluation process for Irene because of their relationship—again as a way to address perception.

Last but not least, the PSD should put to rest the question of the legality of his marriage to avoid future accusations.

6.8 Stacking the Deck

Controversies: 4.10, 5.17
Key Words: county, law, contractors, fairness
Case Complexity → Moderate

As the assistant to the director of a county department responsible for managing capital construction projects, your responsibilities are defined through an ordinance that requires that contractors be qualified each year, through a fair and consistent process, to bid on large construction projects. The process requires the submission of a nineteen-page form on the basis of which the contractor would be placed on a list that is distributed to county agencies.

Your office is under pressure to make the bidding process more open, particularly to minority-owned companies. As a result, the office is inundated with dozens of forms each week. It is your job to process these forms and maintain an accurate, up-to-date list and then distribute the list.

Your office is also responsible for assessing the county's "controlled mainte-nance" needs, which include everything from toilets that won't flush to unsafe elevators. The available funding for these projects is estimated at about 10 percent of what is needed each year. Accordingly, one of the director's responsibilities is to increase funding by working with the capital development committee. This is primarily a technical responsibility insofar as the maintenance needs can be docu-mented and prioritized according to their importance in the operation of county agencies. But there is also politics involved. The importance of the office, not to mention its funding, depends on the level of its responsibilities.

You receive a call from the director, who has been making his rounds on the road visiting facilities in the county. He informs you that a contractor has sent us the qualification form and hopes to bid on a rather large capital construction proj-ect. He also informs you that the president of this particular company was a good friend of a county commissioner who happens to be on the capital development committee. His instructions to you are simple: "Put the form on the top of the stack as soon as it arrives and get them on the list so that they can submit a bid."

Discussion Questions

1. Should you put the form on the top of the stack?
2. Should you confront the director and ask for an explanation?
3. Should you resign?

Case Assessment

Paul Lachapelle, Assistant Professor, Extension Community, Development Specia-list, Department of Political Science, Montana State University:

> The issue of "stacking the deck" is a recurrent ethics dilemma, but it is also a dilemma that is avoidable and can be readily addressed. In fact, in the interest of applying good governance principles—transparency, accountability, and equity—the matter should be addressed promptly and resolved.
>
> Your responsibilities, as the assistant to the director of a county department, are clearly defined in statute. You are the administra-tor who makes certain that the process is fair and consistent. What this means is that you are responsible for ensuring that all parties have an equal opportunity to bid on any capital construction proj-ect. Your responsibilities, however, do not stop there. You are also obliged to address the unscrupulous request of your director. For this reason, you should confront the director immediately and verbally "remind" the individual that the request violates county ordinance

and would be illegal. This would give the supervisor the opportunity to withdraw the request, avoid a public embarrassment, and end the situation.

If the director persists, then you should document in writing the details of the situation and the specific request to "move the form" and provide copies to the local government's legal counsel, elected public body, and ethics board (if one exists). "Stacking the deck" is neither ethical nor sensible; it "trumps" principles of good governance and the "gamble" is far too risky.

6.9 The Chief-of-Staff's Daughter

Controversies: 3.15, 5.16
Key Words: mayor, nepotism, merit
Case Complexity → Moderate
CD: 4.17 President Obama's Executive Order

The mayor of Edisonville, a midwestern community of 50,000, was reelected on a campaign pledge to make the city more responsive to its citizens. During the campaign, one irate citizen described how difficult it was to obtain city budget data. "I just found the city bureaucracy to be a labyrinth, a maze, to work through." As a member of council, you agree—"a lot of people don't know who to call. I think it just shows we're not as user-friendly as we might be."

"What should we do?" you ask. A colleague pipes up: "Why not appoint an ombudsman—a person who can troubleshoot citizen problems and perhaps get things done faster and more effectively." The idea is brought to the mayor, who thinks it is terrific. "Let's do it! There's money in the current year's budget to cover the position; all that we need to do is to write the job description."

A few weeks later the job description is posted in the city's personnel job directory. Seven finalists are interviewed; all are well qualified. Among the finalists is the mayor's chief-of-staff's daughter, June. Her work experience includes nearly three years as a constituent services representative for Governor Hur. The mayor reviews the list of finalists and appoints his chief-of-staff's daughter.

Discussion Questions

1. Is this an act of cronyism?
2. Is it an act of nepotism? June does not report directly to her dad, the chief-of-staff, but reports to the director of the Citizen Information Center. The

mayor did have to sign a waiver of Municipal Code Section 6.78.432 which bars the city from employing a supervisor's immediate family members in the supervisor's department.

3. Should you speak to the mayor about this decision? Make an issue out of it at the next council meeting?

Case Assessment

Posted on the ETHTALK listserv by Tom Babcock:

> I would pose the case study question another way: Should a well-qualified candidate for a city position be passed over solely because her father was the mayor's chief-of-staff? Isn't there inherent unfairness in denying employment solely because of parentage? This type of classism may have been common in Europe in the sixteenth through nineteenth centuries—and imported to the United States along with English colonists—but I've always believed under American forms of governance it was individual accomplishment, qualification, and ability that count, not lineage. Also, what is the loss to the city? Do we stand to lose some of the best and brightest because they have some connection to the political power structure?
>
> Case in point: A few years ago I found myself in several MPA classes with the daughter of a member of our city council. She was an outstanding student, a true valuable resource for any city. Through the proper personnel process she became an intern for the city, then moved to a permanent position. Although ours is a charter mayor/council form of governance with a strong manager, the informal influence of council members cannot be ignored, and is a fact of life. Under the strictest interpretation of ethics guidelines, a member of the council has, collectively with other members, a supervisory role over the city manager and his subordinates. Thus, every department is under their control. Should that have prevented a council member's daughter from receiving an internship; from staff employment?
>
> Fortunately, in this case, it did not. Although this employee's mother has since left the council, she remains a valuable asset to the city. She continues to be an asset. She has moved up in the bureaucracy entirely on her own merit.

Mark Monson, Deputy Director for Administration, Department of Health Professions, State of Virginia:

> The sole purpose of the new position is to help make the bureaucracy of city government more responsive to the citizens. In order to be successful, the new ombudsman has to have the full support and ready ear

of the mayor—and everyone has to know that he or she has them both. For this to work, the mayor has to hire someone with whom he is completely comfortable. In this case, it is the daughter of the chief-of-staff.

But the bottom line will always be results. If the daughter doesn't get the job done, the fact that she's his chief-of-staff's daughter will put added pressure on the mayor to replace her. Plus, the fact that she's the daughter of the mayor's chief-of-staff will increase the pressure on her to succeed.

Let's remember that we're not talking about a building inspector or a police officer. This position is a highly charged political position. The rules and requirements for such a position can legitimately be very different.

6.10 A Late Night Surprise!

Controversies: 3.20, 4.10, 5.17, 6.11
Key Words: city manager, code of ethics, city policy, morality
Case Complexity → High
CD: 4.12 Ethics Management in Cities and Counties
CD: 6.1 American Society for Public Administration Code of Ethics
Ethical reasoning questions are included with this case.

Assume you are the city manager of a financially strapped municipality and find yourself working uncharacteristically late one night in your office. The offices are empty and quiet and as you are leaving, you notice a sliver of light coming from the door of the new budget director, Susan. You decide to stop in and praise her for her excellent report in which she discovered errors that will save the city millions of dollars, projecting for the first time in many years a budget surplus. As you approach her office, you can see through the few inches the door is open that Susan is in a passionate embrace with Gary, the assistant city manager. City employment policy strictly forbids dating between employees, threatening dismissal to those who do.

Your code of ethics requires you to enforce this policy, yet at the same time you do not want to lose either or both of these valuable employees. It would be difficult, if not impossible, to bring in someone else with their experience and credentials for the amount of money the city is able to pay.

Discussion Questions

1. What should you do?
2. Should you report Susan and Gary in accordance with policy?

3. Should you overlook the situation believing the city will be best served in the long run?
4. Should you speak to each of them and threaten to tell if they don't end the relationship?

Ethical Reasoning Questions

1. Is there an ethical issue facing the city manager? Susan? Gary?
2. What is the ethical issue?
3. What might be done to resolve the situation?
4. Does the preferred course of action satisfy the needs/preferences of the primary stakeholders?
5. Is the preferred course of action ethical?

Case Assessment

Posted on the ETALK listserv by Dan Dunmire:

> The city manager should look outside of the current policy box and analyze all of his alternatives. If legislating morality worked, there would be no need for vice squads. In my opinion, you should not come between two people who are in love or are falling in love even if they happen to be public officials. Instead, if he feels he needs to do something about Susan and Gary, he should work to change the policy prohibiting dating between employees. Is an embrace in a public office after hours in the bowels of a government building considered dating or is dating seen as an open affair in public? Either way, who cares? The ethical thing to do is to have the guts to eliminate a staid and outdated policy. Ethics is a matter of judgment of doing the right thing and then having the guts to take responsibility for your actions and standing behind your decision.

Ed Daley, City Manager, Hopewell, Virginia and former President, International City-County Management Association:

> The assistant city manager and finance director are key members of the city's executive management team. They and the city council set the tone for city employees and the public's perception of what behavior standards are acceptable for the organization.
> The city manager must, at a minimum, notify the assistant and the finance director in writing that the behavior will cease immediately and result in termination if it occurs again. The notice and counseling should focus on the employees' excellent work records and value to the

city. But, their responsibility for setting behavior standards takes priority over their administrative competencies.

It is too easy for the city manager to overlook behavior by the executive team that not be tolerated for line employees. Being "valuable" to the organization should not be a license to deviate from behavior standards. If anything, they should be held to a higher level since they set the standard for other employees and send a message to the employees about what is acceptable. The manager needs to think about what type of message he wants to send down the line!

The manager's alternative in this case is to officially authorize everyone to play "Bob and Carol, Ted and Alice."

Results

OK, now we get to the bottom line—what did the city manager do? The city manager did not speak to them directly. He used the next staff meeting (with Susan and Gary in attendance) as an opportunity to discuss the policy and introduced a hypothetical situation for discussion that closely mirrored the one he was in. After discussion about alternative approaches to handling the situation, the staff agreed that they would tell if in the same position. Business went on as usual and he never encountered Susan and Gary in a romantic embrace again. He doesn't know if they understood the veiled warning he was trying to give them or they simply ended the relationship. He's generally happy about the outcome, though discussion at the staff meeting led to another couple (both supervisor-level city workers) being "outed." He's struggling with this now.

Controversies

6.11 Romance and Housing in City Government

Cases: 3.6, 4.6, 6.4, 6.7, 6.10

Should managers be forbidden from having romantic relationships with employees they supervise? In Tampa, the city housing chief had a romantic relationship with his top aide, who moved mysteriously and rapidly through city ranks. Moreover, the housing chief and his aide are building a 4,200-square-foot home for the bargain basement price of $105,000. And, surprise, the builder received more than $1 million in housing contracts through the city's housing department.

Sizing up the situation, one city council member says that "our 4,500 employees need to know that the promotional process is based on merit." Moreover, he believes that there should be a disclosure policy aimed at city employees who award large contracts to people with whom they do personal business. "City employees should have to disclose such potential conflicts to the public," he contends.

Discussion Questions

1. Do you think there should be a city policy that forbids managers from having affairs with employees they supervise?
2. Should city employees who award large contracts to people with whom they do personal business be required to disclose this information?
3. Would such policies prevent unethical, if not illegal, practices?

Information Source: *Tampa Tribune*, August 31, 2001.

Commentary by Author

The city housing chief and several others were indicted on fraud and corruption charges that eventually landed the romantic pair in court in 2004. The builder confessed to bribing the city housing chief and the couple (now married) were tried and found guilty of more than twenty-five counts of conspiracy, wire fraud, and accepting bribes and gratuities. The housing chief was sentenced to five years in a federal penitentiary and his new bride received a sentence of three years and five months. The developer was handed a five-year probationary sentence.

6.12 Trusting Employees—Should You or Shouldn't You?

Cases: 3.3, 4.2, 5.2, 5.9

In 2002, small businesses lost an average of $127,000 to fraud and embezzlement by employees, with a total impact estimated at hundreds of billions of dollars a year. And the problem, according to the Association of Certified Fraud Examiners, is getting worse. Why? What's happening in the small business world? Are there a million little Enrons out there? One answer is straightforward—small businesses must place their trust in employees (often only one employee handles the financial books) far more heavily than big businesses. A small business owner simply must pay more attention to the work at the grass roots level and growing the business into a profitable enterprise.

Consider the case of a small businessman in Kansas who saw no reason to doubt the integrity of his bookkeeper of twelve years. While the bookkeeper was on vacation, the owner received a bill from the medical insurer saying that a $3,000 monthly premium was overdue. A check of the records indicated the bill had been paid. Further investigation of the company's books showed that other checks had been used to pay $10,000 in credit card charges—the company owned no credit cards.

The bottom line—the FBI determined that the bookkeeper had stolen more than $248,000. The bookkeeper was sentenced to eighteen months in prison and ordered to make a complete restitution of the funds. The owner says that he has received $1,000 but doesn't expect to receive more. In the meantime, the business is in a financially precarious position, with the owner having to lay off three workers and delaying his retirement by seven to ten years.

Discussion Questions

1. What would you do to strike the balance between trusting and not trusting your employees?
2. Is this something we should be concerned about in small public or nonprofit agencies?

Information Source: Based on a story reported in the *New York Times*, May 6, 2004, C-6.

Commentary by Author

The message here is that trust and opportunity, especially the opportunity to take advantage of the trust bestowed upon one in small organizations, can result in personal and organizational trauma. Daniel T. Satterberg, King County prosecuting attorney in the state of Washington, asserts that "employees steal an estimated $30 billion to $100 billion per year from their employers. The U.S. Chamber of Commerce estimates that more than 30% of business failures are caused by employee theft. Employee theft can devastate businesses and fellow employees." Furthermore, he claims that "the most common employee theft is the one trusted person in a small business that takes high or extra paychecks, or writes checks to him or her self, to 'cash,' to personal creditors, to an accomplice, or to a bogus company creditor that is actually the trusted person."

Information Source: http://www.metrokc.gov/proatty/Fraud/employee.htm (accessed August 12, 2008).

6.13 Toilet Paper Ethics

Case: 4.9

Have you ever wondered about what you can and cannot take home from the office? Many city or county employees use employer-supplied pens and pencils at home and elsewhere and don't get particularly upset about the ethics of doing so. But what should you do when the office toilet paper starts disappearing? Is this an ethics crisis? A management crisis? Both of the above? As a city manager once advised, when employees start taking toilet paper home, you've got a serious problem!

As it turns out, while toilet paper may not be a prime commodity for employees to take home in most organizations, there are many other commodities that seem to walk out the door regularly. A recent article in the *New York Times,* (July 12, 2000) points out that employee theft is a growing enterprise. A KPMG survey of 5,000 business firms found that the average loss per company between 1994 and 1998 due to the filing of false expense claims, cash advances, fraudulent checks, bad credit card charges, and medical insurance claims had jumped considerably. Theft and misuse of company credit cards by employees, for example, tripled to an average loss of more than $1.1 million per firm.

Discussion Questions

1. What would you do if you discovered that an employee in your city agency was using his credit card to purchase gasoline for his private vehicle?
2. Would it matter if he did this only once rather than repeatedly?
3. What can you do as a manager to prevent the theft and misuse of city credit cards?

Commentary by Author

Dateline Chicago, Illinois—FBI agents arrested the elected president of the Harvey Park District, Harvey, Illinois, and its two top administrators for allegedly spending $144,000 in park funds for nonpublic purposes by using district credit cards to pay for personal expenses. The defendants were also charged with illegally obtaining personal services and cash payments from park district vendors.

Information Source: U.S. Department of Justice, *United States Attorney Northern District of Illinois,* www.usdoj.gov/usao/iln (accessed August 12, 2008).

6.14 Ethics in Business and Government

Case: 5.3

Ethics is about day-in, day-out living and working with others. The respect and dignity with which you treat your boss, subordinates, coworkers, friends, and even strangers who you may never encounter again in your lifetime matter if you aspire to be an ethical person. Moreover, it doesn't matter if you are gay or straight, Republican or Democrat, female or male, or employed in the public or private sectors. Consider the 2007 National Business Ethics Survey conducted by the Ethics Resource Center. The survey canvassed, by telephone, more than 3,400 U.S. employees (1,929 responded) to learn about the ethical practices in the organizations for which they work. (The report can be accessed at http://www.ethics.org/research/nbes.asp.)

On the positive side, the survey findings indicate that (1) the number of formal ethics and compliance programs in corporate America are increasing and (2) companies are moving beyond a singular focus on complying with laws and regulations and adopting a more comprehensive integrity approach to reduce misconduct.

On the negative side, ethical misconduct remains very high, with more than half of employees reporting that they witnessed misconduct of some kind; many employees do not report misconduct, with one in eight fearful of retaliation; and only 9 percent of companies have strong ethical cultures.

The report is available online at http://www.ethics.org/research/NBESOffers. asp.

Discussion Questions

1. Are ethics practices and behaviors in the business world different than those found in public service? If so, why?
2. Are ethical standards in business organizations higher or lower than those in public service organizations?
3. Is there more unethical behavior in government than in business?

Commentary by Author

A report published in 2008 by Integrity Interactive on European corporate integrity found that most businesses are well advanced in developing formal codes of conduct, although less advanced in terms of implementing policies and practices to support their codes. The survey also found that nine out of ten companies provide training in the company's code of conduct with many mandating training, and one out of five links some of their employees' salary or bonus to ethical behavior.

KPMG, a global firm with more than 120,000 employees specializing in auditing, taxing, and advisory services, advocates a culture of integrity and claims a robust ethics program that includes a values-based compliance code of conduct. The KPMG web site states that "every year, all members of our firm are required to affirm an agreement to comply with the Code of Conduct. Additionally, all partners and employees complete mandatory training that reinforces the principles of the Code and further builds understanding of the firm's expectations".

> **Information Source:** www.integrity-interactive.com. http://www.us.kpmg.com/about/conduct.asp, accessed August 15, 2008.

6.15 Assessing Ethical Judgment of a Potential Employee

> Cases: 4.8, 5.8

I'm working on updating interview questions for individuals seeking employment with my agency. I'd like to add an ethics question. Specifically, I'd like a question without a clear-cut "correct" answer. I don't want the applicants to think we want a specific answer. Many ethics situations often don't have clear-cut answers for public administration professionals, but for an applicant, getting the question from an interviewer, they might appear to. I'm interested in how a potential employee reaches a decision, more so than the decision itself. What might be an appropriate question?

Discussion Questions

1. Can the ethical judgment of a potential employee be determined in an interview?
2. Won't an employee look for the "correct" answer when asked how he would deal with a hypothetical ethical situation?

Commentary

Larry Cobb, Professor Emeritus, Public Administration, Slippery Rock University, and Executive Director of EthicsWorks:

> I would suggest that the interviewer say: "Talk about how you would approach a situation where your supervisor asks you to do something that to your mind is legal, but unethical."

Terry Rhodes, Vice President for Quality, Curriculum, and Assessment, Association of American Colleges and Universities:

> I would suggest that the interviewer ask the candidate to react to the following: "If you were a manager and you had received a verbal acceptance for a position and then the person wished to withdraw for a better offer elsewhere, what would you do?" I believe that this provides an opportunity for the person to indicate how he or she thinks about things, that is, what they would take into consideration and so forth.

Ann Hess, Staff Director, Boston City Council:

> I ask a specific question during the interview process by posing a hypothetical situation. When I interview staff for the city council (one staff, fourteen bosses), I try to gauge an applicant's understanding of the need to be confidential while respecting divergent interests across bosses.
>
> The hypothetical situation goes like this: You, as a central staff member, are asked to compile some research for one councilor. Another councilor comes to you with a request for information on the same issue, but the councilor has a different position on the issue. Part I: How do you comply with each person's request? Part II: The first councilor comes back to you and asks who else is working on the issue and what else have you produced for them. What do you say?
>
> I usually give the applicant five minutes to draft some informal comments and responses and then we talk about it. I look for how they come to the decision—while there is no specific right answer, better candidates will discuss wanting to know level of confidentiality in advance, providing both sides of the story to both councilors with focus on the particular position they are advocating, the inability to disclose who else they are doing research for, and how they present that fact to the requesting councilor with respect and understanding. It covers a lot of ground.

Sam Halter, (former) City Administrator, Tampa, Florida and ICMA Range Rider:

> Public administrators are frequently confronted with tough ethical issues. One approach is to ask: "Please describe an ethical issue you have had to address in your career and the way you handled it. If confronted with the same issue today, would you handle it in the same way?"

Mary Jane Kuffner Hirt, Professor of Political Science, Indiana University of Pennsylvania:

> You are the assistant manager in a community and have just been informed by a council member that council intended to fire the town manager at the next public meeting. The council member asked whether you are interested in being considered for the manager's position. What is your response to the council member? Do you warn the manager that he or she is about to be fired?

Jody L. Harris, Director of Program Services, State Planning Office, Executive Department, State of Maine:

> A technique called competency-based interviewing or behavioral event interviewing helps assess professional qualities important to job success. A competency is something that goes beyond technical job skill or education. It focuses on a behavior, attitude, or leadership skill, such as vision or creativity, problem solving, or judgment. It focuses on the actual behavior of a candidate rather than on a hypothetical situation. It requires more time. You might, for example, spend fifteen to twenty minutes on a single question.
>
> The questions ask the candidate to describe what they actually did that demonstrates the competency or behavior for which you are looking. For example, to assess integrity or ethical judgment, you might ask, "Tell me about a time when a policy decision was made that conflicted with your personal beliefs and ethics. How did you resolve it?"
>
> The questions should be broad so as to give the candidate room to find a situation in their experience where they demonstrated the competency. It is important that the candidate select their own incident or story (no leading by the interviewer). Key is to get the person to describe what they actually did, said, thought, and felt. If they say, "We did something …" ask them, "What did you do specifically?" There are lots of resources on the technique.
>
> Competency-based interviewing requires skill and practice and, of course, the competencies or behaviors you interview for must be related

to the job to be performed. But the research says you get better candidates and the candidates who are not selected are more satisfied that the process was fair.

6.16 Evaluations and Promotions Can Get Sticky

Cases: 4.5, 4.8, 6.7

As a middle manager in a county social services agency, you are responsible for conducting the annual evaluations of a half-dozen supervisors.

Promotions within your agency depend heavily on a person's annual rating and these are often inflated or "overwritten" by evaluating managers. Promotions are typically awarded only to employees who are rated outstanding on nearly every measure. You feel that your supervisors are dedicated, hardworking employees who perform at a "fair" to "better than average" level. But you know that if you rate them as less than outstanding they will not get promoted. You want your supervisors to get promoted.

Discussion Questions

1. What should you do?
2. Is evaluation inflation a real problem?
3. What can be done to encourage evaluators to be honest in their evaluations of subordinates?

Commentary

Posted on the ETHTALK listserv by Thad Juszczak, Director, Global Public Sector, Grant Thornton LLP:

Some issues that can help a manager in this situation would be:

1. Are some of the other people in other offices who are rated outstanding actually performing at a better level than your people? If so, and you rate your people outstanding, how is anyone supposed to differentiate?
2. As managers, we all want our people to get promoted, but why would you want to promote people who are actually performing at a fair or better than average level instead of people performing at an outstanding level?

3. As a manager, what are you doing to improve the actual performance level of your people to outstanding? If they don't have the potential ever to perform outstandingly, why do you want to promote them?
4. What has the manager done in terms of discussing this situation with the next level of management?

Maybe you can't change the world, but perhaps you can change your division.

6.17 Product Endorsements: Are They Ethical or Unethical?

Cases: 3.10, 5.3

High-ranking city officials, in and out of uniform, are often asked to endorse commercial products or professional services. Most cities and professional codes of conduct either prohibit or discourage such endorsements, but not everywhere. The former chief of police in Tampa, Florida, routinely endorsed products from a vendor who sold the city $2.37 million worth of surveillance equipment. The same firm donated $50,000 to the National Organization of Black Law Enforcement Executives when the chief ask for a donation. The former chief is now a consultant to the vendor.

An investigation by city council concluded that the chief had not violated any legal or ethical policies. Why? The Tampa Police Department policy then in effect allowed endorsements with the prior approval of the chief of police. The new police chief rejects this policy. As he puts it, "We're not going to be in the business of selling other people's products with our uniforms. I believe in keeping the vendors at arm's length."

Information Source: *Tampa Tribune*, November 7, 2003, Metro 1.

Discussion Questions

1. Most cities place commercial advertisements on city-owned buses and some cities put advertisements on the city's web site. How does this commercialization of a product differ from an endorsement by a city official?

2. Book authors, including academics, often seek favorable comments from a public official that are placed on the cover of the book or posted on the publisher's web site. Is this kind of endorsement different than a police chief endorsing, say, a stun gun manufactured by a firm?

Commentary by Author

Endorsements of commercial products by public officials whose city, county, state, or federal agency does business with the government can easily result in an unethical situation. Product endorsements can motivate both parties to share financial gain through bribes, kickbacks, or postemployment opportunities for government officials. The phrase "pay to play" (payola) has often found expression in the private sector in marketing and selling songs for radio and television in the past. There is every reason to believe that similar results could happen if public officials endorse commercial products.

6.18 To Keep Quiet?

Cases: 3.7, 4.5, 5.9

Bob heard from his manager that their staff will be downsized. It could be as little as 5 percent or as much as 30 percent. However, the supervisor told Bob that "we're all under strict orders to keep it quiet" so that the agency's best employees will not seek other jobs. Ron, one of the finest professionals in Bob's unit, upon hearing the downsizing rumors, told Bob that he was sure that he could get another job at a new business if a reduction in force occurred. However, their openings will close soon. Ron asks Bob, "Will there be layoffs?" and "Should I get another job now?"

Discussion Questions

1. What advice should Bob offer to Ron?
2. Should Bob be quiet? After all, shouldn't he respect and protect confidential information?
3. If Bob tells Ron, "Yes, there will be layoffs," will Bob's integrity be compromised?
4. Is intentionally placing employees at risk by not sharing information acceptable?
5. Is the bottom line unambiguous truth telling?

Source: James B. Bowman and Russell L. Williams, "Ethics in Government: From a Winter of Despair to a Spring of Hope," *Public Administration Review* 57, no. 6 (Nov.–Dec., 1997): 517–526.

Commentary by Author

This situation is very challenging for both Bob and Ron. Perhaps the culprit is Bob's supervisor for telling him that there will be layoffs and he should not tell anyone. Or, perhaps the culprit is the top management that is less than forthcoming. Of course, someone, maybe many persons, will have to run the numbers to be sure what the downsizing will actually be. In the meantime, it might be prudent for the organizational leaders to inform employees that the fiscal situation is bleak and force reduction may be necessary.

6.19 A Culture of Ethical Failure

Cases: 3.1, 3.2, 3.4, 4.9, 5.5

Did you ever wonder what a public agency looks like that is awash in unethical practices and behavior? Consider the following:

- More than a dozen employees in a fifty-member organization received meals, ski trips, sports tickets, paint ball, and golf outings from industry representatives.
- Employees engaged in substance abuse and promiscuity. Social outings included alcohol, cocaine, and marijuana filled parties.
- Many employees didn't think ethics rules applied to them because they needed to socialize with industry representatives.
- A high-ranking manager arranged a million-dollar deal for two retired employees.
- Key qualification criteria upon which bidders would vie for lucrative contracts were shared with a contractor before bid proposals for the first contract were due.
- The director of the agency netted more than $30,000 from improper outside work and hid information about the true nature of his outside employment.
- The director engaged in sexual relations with subordinates and some members engaged in brief sexual relationships with industry contacts.
- The director received annual ethics training.

This is not fiction. It is a description of the Royalty-in-Kind Program in the Minerals Management Service of the Minerals Revenue Management in the U.S. Department of the Interior (DOI). The Office of Inspector General (OIG) released a blistering report describing the "culture of ethical failure." The investigation "revealed that a relatively small group of individuals wholly lacking in acceptance of or adherence to government ethical standards; management that through passive neglect, at best, or purposeful ignorance, at worst, was blind to easily discernable misconduct; and a program that had aggressive goals and admirable ideals, but was launched without the necessary internal controls in place to ensure conformity with one of its most important principles: Maintain the highest ethical and professional standards."

The report took two years to complete and cost $5.3 million. The OIG turned over its findings to the Justice Department for possible criminal action against the director, who retired before the report was released. The Justice Department, without explanation, declined to prosecute.

Discussion Questions

1. Why didn't employees in the agency who were not unethical speak up?
2. Is this an example of the failure of ethics training?
3. If so, why did it fail?
4. Is this an example of the ethical pitfalls of privatization?
5. What would you do to turn this organization around?

Commentary by Author

A culture of ethical failure does not occur overnight. In this case, the prime culprit was the director, who turned an innovative program for collecting royalties from the oil and gas industry into a "sweetheart" arrangement that infected others in the organization. Can you imagine working in an organization like this? Would you be able to resist the temptation to "go along to get along" and maybe worse? This worst case situation is a total betrayal of assuming a "public office is a public trust."

Sources: Derek Kravitz and Mary Pat Flaherty, "Report Says Oil Agency Ran Amok," washingtonpost.com, September 11, 2008; and Earl E. Devaney, Inspector General, U.S. DOI, Office of the Inspector General, "OIG Investigations of MMS Employees," September 9, 2008.

Reference

Denhardt, R. 1991. *In the Shadow of Organizations*. Lawrence, Kansas: University Press of Kansas.

LESSONS LEARNED ALONG THE JOURNEY

Chapter 7

The Complete Ethical Manager

As we practice resolving dilemmas we find ethics to be less a goal than a pathway, less a destination than a trip, less an inoculation than a process.

Ethicist Rushworth Kidder

If you have immersed yourself in the cases and controversies in this book and listened carefully to the "sounds" of the assessments by practitioners and others, you know that becoming an ethical government manager is not an easy task. Indeed, some might say it is impossible given human frailties and the complexities of modern day organizations. Yet, if you think of this effort as a journey and not a destination, becoming an ethical manager is a very rewarding journey. Effective government management is too significant an enterprise to warrant less than a full, sustained commitment to ethical governance.

What central lessons can we draw from the cases in this book that would be useful to those about to begin the journey to become an ethically competent manager? And, how might we describe the journey itself? These two questions are addressed in this concluding chapter.

Lessons Learned

The cases and controversies offer many lessons. The first lesson is that a public manager is first and foremost a moral agent who is responsible for his behavior. Laws, rules, codes of ethics, professional associations, and one's organization can certainly guide behavior, but the manager whose ethics are entirely determined by them has reduced his moral self to a wafer-thin ethical life. There is no question but that these "external" influences are important. Still, as the whistle-blower in Case 5.4 "What's a Whistle-Blower to Do?" found, much discomfort can arise when one's commitment and loyalty to the organization is demanded above all else, right or wrong. And, as the village employee in Case 5.6 "To Obey or Not to Obey?" discovered, taking things into one's own hands because she disagrees with existing village policies and her boss does not always produce the right ethical choice. Indeed, it can lead to rationalizing wrong behavior as right behavior.

Another lesson learned is that doing things right from a legal or personal perspective is not necessarily interpreted that way by others. The county administrator, county attorney, county commission, and property appraiser in Case 4.9 "Mired in an Ethics Swamp" all believed that they had done nothing illegal. So, too, did the grand jury that investigated them. Still, public perception of wrongdoing became so widespread that nothing short of mea culpas and resignations were the order of the day. The ethical illiteracy of county leaders overrode the legality of their actions. Similar convulsions seized a professionally managed city when it was revealed that the leading candidate for the city manager's job had been investigated for abusing his terminally ill wife (Case 3.10 "Withholding Information: When Is it Ethical or Unethical?"). The would-be city manager, who had proclaimed himself to be a highly ethical leader, was suddenly confronted with the public perception that he had deceived the city commission by withholding information about these accusations. He rationalized that they were unsubstantiated and therefore not relevant.

These two cases illustrate that the appearances of unethical behavior can be as damaging as the reality of unethical behavior. Appearances also snagged the long-time county administrator in Case 4.7 "Appearances Matter ... Investing in Real Estate." His loan to his daughter to finance the purchase of investment property and subsequent entanglement brought conflict of interest accusations and led to an investigation to determine if they were true and if the manager had lied to cover up. Although absolved of wrongdoing, the county manager's integrity and ability to lead were damaged.

A third important lesson is that ethical awareness and sensitivity are essential qualities that are sometimes obscured by self-delusion. This lesson was learned in the school of hard knocks by the long-time, successful city manager in Case 5.8 "City of Progress I." This case, as the reader may recall, involved a well-regarded professional manager who decided to seek a sex change or gender reassignment from male to female. It is an axiom of first order for city managers to "do no harm" to their communities. In this case, the "outing" of the city manager produced a community firestorm that engulfed him and others. Years of stellar service, friendships, and loyalty did not protect the manager when "push came to shove." He had, in his own view, self-deluded himself into believing that he could change his gender without changing communities. Ethical awareness and sensitivity to community, elected superiors, and coworkers matter.

Another lesson is that exemplary leadership is critical to encouraging ethical behavior in government organizations. Leaders who "walk the talk" are likely to motivate followers to do the same. In Case 4.1 "Should You or Shouldn't You Accept a Pay Raise?" the city manager understood that for him to accept a pay raise higher than city workers was surely unfair and likely to be demoralizing to the city workforce. It would be the wrong thing to do. A similar outlook characterized the city manager in Case 5.7 "Escape from an Ethics Swamp" who persuaded his management team and supervisors that their behavior and calls for doing the right thing would ripple through the workforce and turn around a culture that had become ethically challenged. He was absolutely right.

Exit, voice, loyalty—as noted earlier, ethics means engagement, action; it is a contact sport. If your boss asks you to fudge the truth or lie outright as in Case 5.5 "When the Chief Asks You to Lie" or Case 4.5 "Going Along to Get Along?" do you speak up, stay loyal to the organization, or do you quit? What is the right thing to do? The lesson here is that failing to speak up can corrode one's own sense of integrity and, if this occurs on a wider scale, can infuse the organization with an unhealthy culture. Still, exercising one's voice is not an easy thing to do. Indeed, it can be very difficult. Moral muteness often envelops many who are faced with these choices.

The sixth lesson is that striking a balance between duty and right behavior is not as straightforward as it might seem. Sometimes the balance turns on selecting from two right decisions. Consider Case 6.10 "A Late Night Surprise." The city manager happens late at night upon two high-level subordinates engaged in intimate behavior in the workplace. City policy forbids such behavior and even threatens dismissal. The manager is torn between the duty to follow city policy and fire the employees or counsel them in some manner. Both are the right thing to do.

There are other times when duty, law, and morality collide. In Case 3.8 "When Duty and Morality Clash" the director of a county agency resists lowering the county flag to half-mast in honor of a deceased county official who is perceived to have been a racist and hate monger. The director is ordered to follow the county ordinance recognizing the deceased official. In another Case 3.9 "Follow the Law or Conscience?" a county clerk must choose between carrying out civil marriage ceremonies to same sex partners as the law calls for or not doing so as her conscience calls for. Striking a balance between duty, law, and conscience is not so simple. Is it?

These six lessons are by no means all that might be found in the cases and controversies in this book, but they are very, very important. While these lessons are valuable, they only acquire real meaning if acted upon. There is no substitute for working through the cases in this book as the pathway toward becoming more ethical. One must immerse oneself in order to integrate the material into one's ethical compass. The lessons merely point to what is right or wrong behavior, how one might promote that, and what pitfalls to avoid, but these lessons and conclusions are no substitute for actually being ethical and putting in the hard work of immersion to gain the wisdom that underlies the much needed judgment. There are no shortcuts.

We turn next to a description of the journey to become an ethically competent manager. Is there a "best" route of travel? Or are there many roads to a destination that seems so elusive?

The Journey

The journey is one of discovery with, always, the prospect of a wrong turn or a blind alley. There are no guarantees or warranties from experience or educational achievement. Of course, if you don't know where you want to go, any road will get you there. That's why it is so important that you know your ethical destination even if it seems that there is yet another mile to go. So, the very first step on this journey is to know your destination. The ethical competencies identified in Chapter 2, Exhibit 2.2, are the road marks to the destination and definition of the ethically competent government manager: **C**ommitment → **K**nowledge → **R**easoning → **A**ction → **P**romotion.

Let's take a close look at the road marks and ask ourselves, what road should we travel?

- *Be knowledgeable of ethical principles*—everyone has an ethical worldview and while there can be significant differences within and across cultures, there are fundamental ethical principles that we learn early in life. They include fairness, justice, human dignity, benevolence, compassion, equity, and more. Absent these guiding principles, one might well agree with the advice offered by the villains in the musical *Annie*: "It doesn't matter how you treat people on the way up if you're not planning on coming down." Alas, this is hardly a guiding philosophy that the ethically competent government manager would embrace. (The codes of ethics on the CD are packed with ethical principles.)
- *Be aware and informed of relevant professional codes of ethics*—as a government manager, the road here takes one through the labyrinth of local-state codes of ethics, occupational codes, and practices embraced by professional associations such as the International City/County Management Association, and aspirational codes that raise the level of ethical discourse such as the code of the American Society for Public Administration.
- *Recognize and promote constitutional principles of equality, fairness, representativeness*—public service in a democracy demands that those who serve others keep these principles uppermost in mind. The day-in and day-out hum of the government workplace can distract one from these principles but it does not minimize their importance. The road traveled here requires a continuous awareness of what serving the public in a democracy is all about.

■ *Recognize and support the public's right to know the public's business*—state sunshine laws and the Freedom of Information Act signed into law by President Lyndon Johnson in 1966 are designed to keep government open and accessible to citizens, the media, and organized interests. Openness and transparency are critical safeguards that keep our democracy alive and well. The administrative side of governance is especially difficult to observe and access for ordinary citizens. Government managers are duty bound to practice transparency, although at times it slows the wheels of governance. The road to acquiring this competency is knowledge of sunshine laws and a commitment to the true spirit of supporting the public's right to know.

■ *Respect the law*—means just that. Public managers play a key role in energizing laws and ordinances. Of course, it is not always clear what lawmakers or city commissioners intended, but it is incumbent on administrators to make every effort to carry out the law with as much clarity of intent as possible. Due diligence is the watchword that every government manager must subscribe to, no exceptions. How does one acquire due diligence? The answer is experience and learning from others in similar situations.

■ *Serve the public interest*—government managers are on the frontline of democracy. They are the foot soldiers who ensure the public interest, however difficult that may be to define in any given situation, is not sacrificed on the alter of special interests. There is no legitimate alternative. The challenge is to be skillful and astute enough to ferret through competing interests to advance the public interest. The road to this competency lies in the manager's ability to tolerate differences and be resilient in the face of conflicting interests. At times, as Kenneth Ashworth (2001) wryly notes, you get caught between the dog and the fireplug.

■ *Engage in ethical reasoning*—this competency can be more easily acquired than others as it centers on being ethically sensitive and being able to define a problem and assess, in a systematic manner, alternative courses of action that can lead to ethically acceptable outcomes. Educational programs sponsored by universities, institutes, and professional associations offer many roads to acquiring this competency. Some statewide professional associations assist as well. For example, the Florida City-County Management Association has an innovative online program that government managers can take to build their reasoning skills. Also, some governments have effective ethics training resources and programs that do the same.

■ *Recognize and differentiate between ethical and management issues*—while perhaps not of the same order as other competencies, it is important for the manager to be able to discriminate and act on differences in issues. The myriad of cases in this book provide the reader with plenty of practice in acquiring this competency. Still, the cases are not a substitute for direct experience.

At the same time, experience alone may be a false teacher and is almost always an unforgiving teacher.

■ *Respect and protect privileged information*—in this time of lightening fast communication technology and powerful tools for seeking information, managers are challenged more than ever to guard against disclosing privileged information. Whether the information comes in the form of bids for government contracts or sensitive personal data, the ethically competent manager must be diligent and faithful in respecting and protecting information. The road to this competency is filled with troublesome potholes. Nonetheless, sensitivity, knowledge, and due diligence are must-have qualities of the manager.

■ *Embrace and promote ethical behavior and practices in the workplace*—to paraphrase Kenneth Ashworth (2001, 166), "conduct yourself so that your behavior may serve as the pattern for the behavior of your colleagues, superiors, and subordinates." Little more needs to be said about the road to travel to acquire this competency.

■ *Refuse to do something unethical*—has anyone ever asked you to do something unethical? Ordered you to do something unethical? Chances are this has not happened to you or others with any regularity. Still, one instance in a lifetime may be enough to cause you to take a deep breath and ponder what you should do. Learning how to say "no" is easy to do in the abstract, but sometimes it gets down to how you say "no." This is a skill that can be learned through experience and study in professional educational programs and even on your own if you are sufficiently motivated.

■ *Maintain truthfulness and honesty*—a competency that will no doubt serve you well in your quest to become an ethically competent manager. Yet, it is a challenging competency to acquire. It is not that most people are dishonest; rather, it is that learning how to practice honesty day-in and day-out is not easy. Perhaps the admonishments of Aristotle are valuable in this regard. As an advocate for virtue, he advised that one can only acquire a virtue through practice. Honesty and truthfulness have to be practiced and balanced with delicate diplomacy on some occasions. President Harry Truman was often challenged to "give 'em hell," to which he retorted, "I never did give anybody hell. I just told the truth and they thought it was hell."

■ *Guard against conflict of interest or its appearance*—this competency is reflected in every government code of conduct that exists. Yet, it is frequently unfulfilled and indeed all too often causes good managers to stumble and crash on the pavement of unethical behavior. While this competency requires one to know what a conflict of interest is in her jurisdiction and act to avoid it, the ethically competent manager must be able to size up a situation so that neither the reality nor the appearance of wrongdoing raises its ugly head. In other words, the manager must have nearly a sixth sense about her.

But ethical awareness is not just a sixth sense, it can be learned through study and experience as cases in this book illustrate.

■ *Be responsible for one's behavior*—this is the many hands problem in government. That is, it is rarely the case that a single administrator is responsible for the actions taken in her agency that have real consequences for others. It is usually the case that there are many people involved, thus many hands. So when things either don't turn out so well or could have turned out better, it is easy to find that no one is at fault. This reality, however so, also enables individuals to duck responsibility. Taking responsibility doesn't mean putting a mask over reality, but it does mean stepping forward when circumstances demand that responsibility be assigned. The road to this competency is especially challenging and must be traveled with sincerity and humility.

Journey's End ...

It is my fondest hope that you have begun your journey, and the cases in this book have helped you along the way. As you surely are aware at this moment, your quest to become an ethically competent manager has put you on a journey without end. It is an admirable journey that will span your entire professional life and career. Make the best of it!

Reference

Ashworth, Kenneth. 2001. Caught Between the Dog and the Fireplug. Washington, D.C.: Georgetown University Press.

Bibliography

Adman, A. M. and D. Rachman-Moore. 2004. "The Methods Used to Implement an Ethical Code of Conduct and Employee Attitudes." *Journal of Business Ethics* 54:225–244.

Andersson, S. 2008. "Studying the Risk of Corruption in the Least Corrupt Countries." *Public Integrity* (Summer) 10:193–214.

Anechiarico, F. and J. B. Jacobs. 1996. *The Pursuit of Absolute Integrity: How Corruption Control Makes Government Ineffective.* Chicago: University of Chicago Press.

Barnard, C. 1938. *The Functions of the Executive.* Cambridge, MA: Harvard University Press.

Barnes, L. B., C. R. Christensen, and A. J. Hansen. 1994. *Teaching and the Case Method,* 34th ed. Boston: Harvard Business School Press.

Bellah, R. N., R. Madsen, W.M. Sullivan, A. Swidler, and S. M. Tipton. 1991. *The Good Society.* New York: Random House.

Bellomo, T. 2005. "The Making of an Ethical Executive." *New York Times,* February 14. http://query. nytimes.com/gst/fullpage.html?res=9A07E1DB153AF937A25751C0A9639C8B63 &n=Top%2FReference%2FTimes%20Topics%2FSubjects%2FB%2FBusiness%20 Schools&scp=1&sq=ethical%20executive&st=cse.

Bennett, C. G. 1960. "Mayor Inducts Board of Ethics." *New York Times,* January 8, 14.

Berman, E. M. 1996. "Restoring the Bridges of Trust: Attitudes of Community Leaders toward Local Government." *Public Integrity Annual,* 31–49.

Berman, E. M. and J. P. West. 1997. "Managing Ethics to Improve Performance and Build Trust." *Public Integrity Annual,* 23–31.

———. 2003. "Solutions to the Problem of Managerial Mediocrity." *Public Performance & Management Review.* 27 (December): 30–52.

Berman, E., J. West, and A. Cava, 1994. "Ethics Management in Municipal Governments and Large Firms: Exploring Similarities and Differences." *Administration & Society,* 26 (August): 185–203.

Better Government Association. 2002. "The BGA Integrity Index." Chicago.

Blakely, E. J. 2008. "Ethics in Times of Crisis. *Public Integrity* (Fall) 10:355–363.

Bok, D. 1978. "The President's Report, 1977–78." Cambridge, MA: Harvard University.

Bok, D. 1990. *Universities and the Future of America.* Durham, NC: Duke University Press.

Bonczek, S. J. 1998. "Creating an Ethical Work Environment: Enhancing Ethics Awareness in Local Government." In *The Ethics Edge,* edited by E.M. Berman, J.P. West, and S.J. Bonczek, 72–79. Washington, D.C.: International City/County Management Association.

Bossaert, D. and C. Demmke. 2005. *Main Challenges in the Field of Ethics and Integrity in the EU Member States.* Maastricht, The Netherlands: European Institute of Public Administration.

233

Bowman, J. S. 1977. "Ethics in the Federal Service: A Post-Watergate View." *Midwest Review of Public Administration* 11 (March): 3–20.

———. 1981. "Ethical Issues for the Public Manager." In *A Handbook of Organization Management,* edited by William B. Eddy. New York: Marcel Dekker.

———. 1990. "Ethics in Government: A National Survey of Public Administrators." *Public Administration Review* 50 (May/June): 345–353.

Bowman, J. S. and R. L. Williams. 1997. "Ethics in Government: From a Winter of Despair to a Spring of Hope." *Public Administration Review* 57:517–526.

Brewer, G. A. and S. Coleman Selden. 1998. "Whistle Blowers in the Federal Civil Service: New Evidence of the Public Service Ethic." *Journal of Public Administration Research and Theory* 8 (July): 413–439.

Brown, S. 2005. "Managing Municipal Ethics." http://www.gmanet.com/event_detail/default.a sp?eventid=6445&menuid=GeorgiaCitiesNewspaperID (accessed December 29, 2005).

Bruce, W. 1994. "Ethical People Are Productive People." *Public Productivity and Management Review.* 17 (Spring): 241–252.

Brumback, G. B. 1998. "Institutionalizing Ethics in Government." In *The Ethics Edge,* edited by E. M. Berman, J. P. West, and S. J. Bonczek, 61–71. Washington, D.C.: International City/County Management Association.

Burke, J. P. 1986. *Bureaucratic Responsibility.* Baltimore: Johns Hopkins University Press.

Burke, F. and A. Black. 1990. "Improving Organizational Productivity: Add Ethics." *Public Productivity and Management Review* 14 (Winter): 121–133.

Chan, S. 2005. "Transit Leader to Pay Fine in Ethics Case." *New York Times,* August 27. http://www.nytimes.com/2005/08/27/nyregion/27mta.html?_r=1&scp=1&sq=transit%20leader%20pay%20fine%20in%20ethics%20case&st=cse.

Chicago Board of Ethics. *2003–04 Annual Report.*

COGEL. 2004. *Ethics Update.* Jacksonville, FL: Council of Governmental Ethics Laws.

Cohen, S. and W. Eimicke. 1999. "Is Public Entrepreneurship Ethical?" *Public Integrity* 1 (Winter): 54–74.

Committee on Standards in Public Life. 2004. Tenth Report. *Getting the Balance Right—Implementing Standards of Conduct in Public Life.* London: Her Majesty's Stationery Office.

Connolly, C. 2005. "Director of NIH Agrees to Loosen Ethics Rules." *Washingtonpost.com,* August 26.

Cooper, T. L. 1982. *The Responsible Administrator: An Approach to Ethics for the Administrative Role.* Port Washington, NY: Kennikat Press.

———. 1984. "Citizenship and Professionalism in Public Administration." *Public Administration Review* 44 (March): 143–149.

———. 1986. *The Responsible Administrator: An Approach to Ethics for the Administrator Role,* 2nd ed. Milwood, NY: Associated Faculty Press.

———. 1987. "Hierarchy, Virtue, and the Practice of Public Administration: A Perspective for Normative Ethics." *Public Administration Review* 47 (July/August): 320–328.

———. 1998. *The Responsible Administrator,* 4th ed. San Francisco: Jossey-Bass.

———. 2006. *The Responsible Administrator.* 5th ed. San Francisco: Jossey-Bass.

Cooper, T. L., ed. 2001. *Handbook of Administrative Ethics,* 2nd ed. New York: Marcel Dekker.

Cooper, T. L. and D. E. Yoder. 2002. "Public Management Ethics Standards in a Transnational World." *Public Integrity* 4 (Fall): 333–352.

Council for Excellence in Government. 1992–1993. "Ethical Principles for Public Servants." *The Public Manager* 21:37–39.

Cox, R.W. III Ed. 2009. *Ethics and Integrity in Public Adminstration.* Armonk, New York: M.E. Sharpe.

Dao, J. 2005. "Governor of Ohio Is Charged With Breaking Ethics Law." *New York Times,* August 18. http://www.nytimes.com/2005/08/18/national/18taft html?scp=3&sq=governor%20of%20ohio%20ethics%20law&st=cse.

Davis, M. 1999. In R. W. Smith, "Local Government Ethics Boards: A Panel Discussion on the New York Experience." *Public Integrity* 1 (Fall): 397–416.

deLeon, L. 1996. "Ethics and Entrepreneurship." *Policy Studies Journal* 24 (Autumn): 496–514.

Denhardt, K. G. 1988. *The Ethics of Public Administration: Resolving Moral Dilemmas in Public Organizations.* New York: Greenwood.

_____. 1989. "The Management of Ideals: A Political Perspective on Ethics." *Public Administration Review* 49 (March/April): 187–192.

Denhardt, R. B. 1981. *In the Shadow of Organization.* Lawrence, Kansas: The Regents Press of Kansas.

Dobel, J. P. 1993. "The Realpolitik of Ethics Codes: An Implementation Approach to Public Ethics." In *Ethics and Public Administration,* edited by H. G. Frederickson. Armonk, NY: M.E. Sharpe.

Dobel, J. P. 1999. Public Integrity. Baltimore: The Johns Hopkins Press.

Ellet, W. 2007. *The Case Study Handbook.* Boston: Harvard Business School Press.

Ellsberg, D. 2004. "Truths Worth Telling." *New York Times,* September 28. http://query.nytimes.com/gst/fullpage.html?res=9F04E4DD1738F93BA1575AC0A9629C8B63.

Fawcett, G. and M. Wardman. 2005. "Ethical Governance in Local Government in England: A Regulator's View." Paper presented at the Ethics and Integrity of Governance: The First Transatlantic Dialogue, Leuven, Belgium, 2–5 June.

Ferrieux-Patterson, M. N. 2003. "Conflict of Interest—Vanuatu's Experience." Paper presented at the 4th Regional Anti-Corruption Conference of the ADB/OECD Anti-Corruption Initiative for Asia and the Pacific, Kuala Lumpur, Malaysia, 3–5 December.

Finn, R. 2005. "Albany's Ethics Policeman Would Like More Muscle." *New York Times,* March 25. http://www.nytimes.com/2005/03/25/nyregion/25lives.html?scp=1&sq=albany%27s%20ethics%20policeman&st=cse.

Florida Commission on Ethics. 2004. *Annual Report to the Florida Legislature for Calendar Year 2004.*

Florida Office of Inspector General. 2005. *Contract Management of Private Correctional Facilities,* Internal Audit Report Number 2005-61, June 30.

Folks, S. R. 2000. "A Potential Whistle-Blower." *Public Integrity* 2 (Winter): 61–74.

Follet, M. K. 1924. *Creative Experience.* New York: Longmans, Green.

Frederickson, H. G. 1997. *The Spirit of Public Administration.* San Francisco: Jossey-Bass.

Frederickson, H. G., ed. 2003. *Ethics and Public Administration.* Armonk, NY: M.E. Sharpe.

Frederickson, H. G. and D. K. Hart. 1985. "The Public Service and the Patriotism of Benevolence." *Public Administration Review* 45:547–553.

Frederickson, H. G. and M. A. Newman. 2001. "The Patriotism of Exit and Voice: The Case of Gloria Flora." *Public Integrity* 3 (Fall): 347–362.

Garvey, G. 1995. *Facing the Bureaucracy: Living and Dying in a Public Agency.* San Francisco: Jossey-Bass.

Gawthrop, L. G. 1984. *Public Sector Management, Systems, and Ethics.* Bloomington: Indiana University Press.

_____. 1998. *Public Service and Democracy: Ethical Imperatives for the 21st Century.* Chappaqua, NY: Chatham House Publishers.

_____. 1999. "Public Entrepreneurship in the Lands of Oz and Uz." *Public Integrity* 1 (Winter): 75–86.

Georgia Municipal Association. 2005. *Ethics in Government: Charting the Right Course,* Atlanta, Georgia.

Geuras, D. and C. Garofalo. 2005. *Practical Ethics in Public Administration.* 2nd ed. Vienna, VA: Management Concepts.

Ghere, R. K. 1996. "Aligning the Ethics of Public-Private Partnership: The Issue of Local Economic Development." *Journal of Public Administration Research and Theory* 6 (October): 599–621.

Gibson, P. A. 2009. "Examining the Moral Reasoning of the Ethics Adviser and Counselor." *Public Integrity* (Spring) 11:105–120.

Gilman, S. C. 1995a. http://www.oecd.org/dataoecd/30/22/2731902.htm (accessed January 2, 2006).

_____. 1995b. "Presidential Ethics and the Ethics of the Presidency." *Ethics in American Public Service: The Annals of the American Academy of Political and Social Science* 537:58–75.

_____. 2005. "Ethics Codes and Codes of Conduct as Tools for Promoting an Ethical and Professional Public Service: Comparative Successes and Lessons." Paper prepared for the Poverty Reduction and Economic Management, the World Bank, Washington, D.C.

Gilman, S. C. and C. W. Lewis. 1996. "Public Service Ethics: A Global Dialogue." *Public Administration Review* 56 (November/December): 517–524.

Glazer, M. P. and P. M. Glazer. 1989. *The Whistleblowers: Exposing Corruption in Government and Industry.* New York: Basic Books.

Goldsmith, S. and W. D. Eggers. 2004. *Governing by Network: The New Shape of the Public Sector.* Washington, D.C.: Brookings Institution Press.

Gong, T. 2000. "Whistleblowing: What Does It Mean in China?" *International Journal of Public Administration.* 23 (11): 1899–1923.

Graham, K. 2005. "Parks Worker Accused of Taking Bribe." *St. Petersburg Times,* February 24:1B.

Groeneweg, S. 2001. *Three Whistleblower Protection Models: A Comparative Analysis of Whistleblower Legislation in Australia, the United States and the United Kingdom.* Public Service Commission of Canada. http://www.psc-cfp.gc.ca/research/merit/whistleblowing_e.htm (accessed January 3, 2006).

Grosenick, L. 1995. "Federal Training Programs: Help or Hindrance?" *The 'Public' Manager* 24 (4): 43.

Harling, K. and J. Akridge. 1998. "Using the Case Method of Teaching." *Agribusiness* 14 (1): 1–14.

Harris, G. 2005. "Report Details FDA Rejection of Next-Day Pill." *New York Times* November 15. http://www.nytimes.com/2005/11/15/politics/15pill.html?scp=1&sq=fda%20rejection%20of%20next%20day%20pill&st=cse.

Hart, D. K. 1984. "The Virtuous Citizen, the Honorable Bureaucrat, and 'Public' Administration." *Public Administration Review* 44:111–120.

Hejka-Elkins, A. 2001. "Ethics in In-Service Training." In *Handbook of Administrative Ethics,* 2nd ed., edited by T. L. Cooper, 79–103. New York: Marcel Dekker.

Henry, N. 1995. *Public Administration and Public Affairs,* 6th ed. Englewood Cliffs, NJ: Prentice Hall.

Herrmann, F. M. 1997. "Bricks without Straw: The Plight of Government Ethics Agencies in the United States." *Public Integrity Annual*, 13–22.

Hess, A. 2003. "Assessing the Ethical Judgment of a Potential Employee-II." *Public Administration Times*, September.

Hirt, M. J. 2003. "Assessing the Ethical Judgment of a Potential Employee." *Public Administration Times*, July.

Hodge, W. 2005. "Citing Abuse of Authority, U.N. Dismisses Elections Chief." *New York Times*, December 7. http://query.nytimes.com/gst/fullpage.html?res=9B06E0 D61331F934A35751C1A9639C8B63&scp=1&sq=Citing%20Abuse%20of%20 Authority,%20U.N.%20Dismisses%20Electons%20Chief&st=cse.

Hoekstra, A., A. Belling, and E. Van Der Heide. 2005. "Beyond Compliance—A Practitioners' View." Paper presented at the Ethics and Integrity of Governance: The First Transatlantic Dialogue, Leuven, Belgium, 2–5 June.

Huberts, L. W. J. C., J. Maesschalck, and C. L. Jurkiewicz. Eds. 2008. *Ethics and Integrity of Governance: Perspectives Across Frontiers.* Cheltenham, UK: Edward Elgar.

Hunt, M. 2005. "Ethics and British Local Government: The Relevance of Compliance Strategies." Paper presented at the Ethics and Integrity of Governance: The First Transatlantic Dialogue, Leuven, Belgium, 2–5 June.

Jenkins, C. 2005. "Penalty for Judge Is Seen Two Ways." *St. Petersburg Times*, November 19:1.

Jennings, B., J. L. Nelson, and E. Parens. 1994. *Values on Campus: A Report.* Braircliff, NY: Hastings Center.

Jensen, D. P. 2004. "County Ethics Reform Stalled." *The Salt Lake Tribune*, December 6: C1.

Johnson, R. 2003. *Whistleblowing: When It Works—and Why.* Boulder, CO: Lynne Rienner Publishers.

———. 2005. "Comparative Whistleblowing: Administrative, Cultural, and Ethical Issues." *Proceedings of 2005 International Conference on Public Administration*, October 21–22, Chengdu, P.R. China.

Jos, P. H. 1989. "In Praise of Difficult People: A Portrait of the Committed Whistleblower." *Public Administration Review* 49:552–561.

Keller, E. K., ed. 1988. *Ethical Insight Ethical Action: Perspectives for the Local Government Manager.* Washington, D.C.: International City/County Management Association.

Kernaghan, K. 2003. "Integrating Values into Public Service: The Values Statement as Centerpiece." *Public Administration Review* 63 (November/December): 711–719.

Kudo, H. and J. Maesschalck. 2005. "The Ethics Law and Ethics Code in Japanese Public Administration: Background, Contents and Impact." Paper presented at the Ethics and Integrity of Governance: The First Transatlantic Dialogue, Leuven, Belgium, 2–5 June.

Lambert, B. 2005. "Audit Describes 8 Years of Looting by School Officials." *New York Times*, March 3. http://www.nytimes.com/2005/03/03/nyregion/03roslyn.html?scp=1&sq= audit%20describes%208%20years%20looting&st=cse.

Lasthuizen, K. 2008. *Leading to Integrity: Empirical Research into the Effects of Leadership on Ethics and Integrity.* Amsterdam, The Netherlands: VU University, Dissertation.

Lawrence, P. 1953. "The Preparation of Case Material." In *The Case Method of Teaching Human Relations and Administration*, edited by K. R. Andrews. Cambridge, MA: Harvard University Press.

Lewis, C. W. 1991. *The Ethics Challenge in Public Service: A Problem Solving Guide.* San Francisco: Jossey-Bass.

Lewis, C. W. and S. C. Gilman. 2005. *The Ethics Challenge in Public Service: A Problem Solving Guide,* 2nd ed. San Francisco: Jossey-Bass.

Light, P. C. 1999. *The New Public Service.* Washington, D.C.: The Brookings Institution.

Lovell, A. 2003. "The Enduring Phenomenon of Moral Muteness: Suppressed Whistle-blowing." *Public Integrity* 5 (Summer): 187–204.

Lui, T. T. 1988. "Changing Civil Servants' Values." In *The Hong Kong Civil Service and Its Future,* edited by I. Scott and J. P. Burns. Hong Kong: Oxford University Press.

Lui, T. T. and I. Scott. 2001. "Administrative Ethics in a Chinese Society: The Case of Hong Kong." In *Handbook of Administrative Ethics,* edited by T. L. Cooper. New York: Marcel Dekker.

Mackenzie, G. C. 2002. *Scandal Proof: Do Ethics Laws Make Government Ethical?* Washington, D.C.: Brookings Institution.

Manske, M. W. and H. G. Frederickson. 2004. "Building a Strong Local Government Ethics Program." *Public Management* 86 (June): 18–22.

Markus, M. L. 1994. "Finding a Happy Medium: Explaining the Negative Effects of Electronic Communication on Social Life at Work." *ACM Transactions on Information Systems* 12 (April): 119–149.

Martirossian, J. 2004. "Russia and Her Ghosts of the Past." In *The Struggle Against Corruption: A Comparative Study,* edited by R. A. Johnson. New York: Palgrave Macmillian.

Mayer, J. P., ed. 1966. *Democracy in America.* New York: Harper & Row.

McAuliffe, D. 2002. "Social Work Ethics Audits: A New Tool for Ethical Practice." Paper presented at the International Institute of Public Ethics/Australian Association for Professional and Applied Ethics Conference, Brisbane.

McFadden, R. D. 2005. "Stanley Kreutzer, 98, Author of New York City Ethics Code." *New York Times,* February 22. http://www.nytimes.com/2005/02/22/obituaries/22kreutzer.html?scp=1&sq=stanley%20kreutzer&st=cse

Menzel, D. C. 1992. "Ethics Attitudes and Behaviors in Local Governments: An Empirical Analysis." *State and Local Government Review* 24 (Fall): 94–102.

_____. 1993. "The Ethics Factor in Local Government: An Empirical Analysis." In *Ethics and Public Administration,* edited by H. G. Frederickson, 191–204. Armonk, NY: M.E. Sharpe.

_____. 1995. "The Ethical Environment of Local Government Managers." *American Review of Public Administration* 25 (September): 247–262.

_____. 1996a. "Ethics Complaint Making and Trustworthy Government." *Public Integrity Annual,* 73–82.

_____. 1996b. "Ethics Stress in Public Organizations." *Public Productivity & Management Review* 20:70–83.

_____. 1997. "Teaching Ethics and Values in Public Administration: Are We Making a Difference?" *Public Administration Review* 57 (May/June): 224–230.

_____. 2001a. "Ethics and Public Management." In *Handbook of Public Management and Practice,* edited by K. T. Liou. New York: Marcel Dekker.

_____. 2001b. "Ethics Management in Public Organizations." In *Handbook of Administrative Ethics,* 2nd ed., edited by T. L. Cooper. New York: Marcel Dekker.

_____. 2005a. "Research on Ethics and Integrity in Governance: A Review and Assessment." *Public Integrity* 7 (Spring): 147–168.

_____. 2005b. "Building Public Organizations of Integrity." *Proceedings of 2005 International Conference on Public Administration,* October 21–22, Chengdu, P.R. China.

_____. 2006. "Ethics Management in Cities and Counties." *Public Management* 88 (January/February): 20–25.

_____. 2007. *Ethics Management for Public Administrators.* Armonk, NY: M.E. Sharpe.

Menzel, D. C. and K. Carson. 1999. "A Review and Assessment of Empirical Research on Public Administration Ethics: Implications for Scholars and Managers." *Public Integrity* 1 (Summer): 239–264.

Miceli, M. and J. P. Near. 1985. "Characteristics of Organizational Climate and Perceived Wrongdoing Associated with Whistle-Blowing Decisions." *Personnel Psychology* 38:525–544.

Morin, R. and D. Balz. 2005. "Bush's Popularity Reaches New Low." *Washingtonpost.com*, November 4.

Nelson, M. 1999. www.transparency.org/iacc/9th_iacc/papers/day4/ws3/d4ws3_mnelson.html.

New York State Ethics Commission. 2004. *The Ethics Report,* September.

O'Leary, R. 2006. *The Ethics of Dissent: Managing Guerrilla Government.* Washington, D.C.: CQ Press.

Osborne, D. and T. Gaebler. 1992. *Reinventing Government: How the Entrepreneurial Spirit Is Transforming the Public Sector.* Reading, MA: Addison-Wesley.

Ouchi, W. C. 1981. *Theory Z: How American Business Can Meet the Japanese Challenge.* Reading, MA: Addison-Wesley.

Palidauskaite, J. 2006. "Codes of Ethics in Transitional Democracies: A Comparative Perspective." *Public Integrity* 8:35–48.

Perry, J. L. 1993. "Whistleblowing, Organizational Performance, and Organizational Control." In *Ethics and Public Administration,* edited by H. G. Frederickson, 79–99. Armonk, NY: M.E. Sharpe.

Peters, T. J. and R. H. Waterman. 1982. *In Search of Excellence.* New York: Harper & Row.

Phillips, F. and G. Vaidyanathan. 2004. "Should Case Materials Precede or Follow Lectures?" *Issues in Accounting Education* 19 (3): 305–31 9.

Pope, J. 2005. "Observations Concerning Comparative Administrative Ethics in Europe and the U.S." Paper presented at the Ethics and Integrity of Governance: The First Transatlantic Dialogue, Leuven, Belgium, 2–5 June.

Reamer, F. G. 2000. "The Social Work Ethics Audit: A Risk-Management Strategy." *Social Work* 45 (July): 355–366.

Report of the National Performance Review. 1993. *Creating a Government that Works Better & Costs Less.* Washington, D.C.: U.S. Government Printing Office.

Richter, W. L. and F. Burke, eds. 2007. *Combating Corruption/Encouraging Ethics.* Lanham, MD: Rowman & Littlefield.

Rivenbark, W. C. 2007. "Using Cases to Teach Financial Management Skills in MPA Programs." *Journal of Public Affairs Education* 13 (2): 451–460.

Roberts, R. N. 1988. *White House Ethics: The History of the Politics of Conflict of Interest Regulation.* New York: Greenwood Press.

Rohr, J. A. 1978. *Ethics for Bureaucrats: An Essay on Law and Values.* New York: Marcel Dekker.

_____. 1986. *To Run a Constitution: The Legitimacy of the Administrative State.* Lawerence, Kansas: University Press of Kansas.

_____. 1989. *Ethics for Bureaucrats: An Essay on Law and Values,* 2nd ed. New York: Marcel Dekker.

Ronstadt, R. 1994. *The Art of Case Analysis,* 3rd ed. Dana Point, CA: Lord Publishing.

Rosen, B. A. 2005. *The Shadowlands of Conduct: Ethics and State Politics.* Washington, D.C.: Georgetown University Press.

Rosenbloom, D. H. 1995. "The Use of Case Studies in Public Administrative Education in the USA." *Journal of Management History* 1:33.

Schneider, B., ed. 1990. *Organizational Climate and Culture.* San Francisco: Jossey-Bass.

Scott, W. G. and D. K. Hart. 1979. *Organizational America.* Boston: Houghton Mifflin.

———. 1989. *Organizational Values in America.* New Brunswick, NJ: Transaction Publishers.

Shared Inquiry Handbook. 2007. Chicago: The Great Books Foundation.

Simmons, C. W., H. Roland, and J. Kelly-DeWitt. 1998. *Local Government Ethics Ordinances in California.* California Research Bureau, California State Library.

Slackman, M. 2005. "Albany Ethics Case That Died Points to Loophole, Not a Crime." *New York Times,* February 25. http://query.nytimes.com/gst/fullpage.html?res=9C07 E3D7173DF936A15751C0A9639C8B63&sec=&spon=&&scp=1&sq=albany%20 ethics%20case&st=cse

Smith, M. K. 2001. "Peter Senge and the Learning Organization." www.weleadinlearning. org/msapro03.htm (accessed December 6, 2005).

Smith, R. W. 2003. "Enforcement or Ethical Capacity: Considering the Role of State Ethics Commissions at the Millennium." *Public Administration Review* 63 (3): 283–295.

———. 2004. "A Comparison of the Ethics Infrastructure in China and the United States." *Public Integrity* 6 (Fall): 299–318.

Smothers, R. 2005. "11 New Jersey Officials, Including 3 Mayors, Face Charges of Corruption." *New York Times,* February 23. http://www.nytimes.com/2005/02/23/ nyregion/23jersey.html?scp=2&sq=11%20New%20Jersey%20Officials%20 including%20three%20mayors&st=cse

St. Petersburg Times. 2005. Editorial. "Ethical Questions." March 20:2P.

Svara, J. H. 2007. *The Ethics Primer for Public Administrators in Government and Nonprofit Organizations.* Boston: Jones and Bartlett Publishers.

Tenebaum, J. S. 2002. "Lobbying Disclosure Act of 1995: A Summary and Overview for Associations." www.centeronlilne.org/knowledge/whitepaper.cfm?ID=1796 (accessed January 2, 2006).

Terry, L. 1995. *Leadership of Public Bureaucracies.* Thousand Oaks, CA: Sage Publications.

———. 1998. "Administrative Leadership, Neo-Managerialism, and the Public Management Movement." *Public Administration Review* 58 (May/June): 194–200.

Testerman, J. 2005. "LaBrakes Get More than 8 Years." *St. Petersburg Times,* February 26:1A.

Thompson, D. F. 1985. "The Possibility of Administrative Ethics." *Public Administration Review* 45:555–561.

———. 1992. "Paradoxes of Government Ethics." *Public Administration Review* 52 (May/ June): 254–259.

Treaster, J. B. and J. Desantis. 2005. "Storm and Crisis: The Police." *New York Times,* September 6. http://query.nytimes.com/gst/fullpage.html?res=9C0CEED91531F 935A3575AC0A9639C8B63&sec=&spon=&&scp=8&sq=STORM%20and%20 crisis%20police&st=cse

Troxler, C. 2005. "In Politics, What's Unethical Today Is Legal Tomorrow." *St. Petersburg Times,* October 20:1B.

Truelson, J. A. 1991. "New Strategies for Institutional Controls." In *Ethical Frontiers in Public Management,* edited by J. S. Bowman, 225–242. San Francisco: Jossey-Bass.

United Nations. 1999. *Public Service in Transition: Enhancing Its Role, Professionalism Ethical Values and Standards*. New York: UN Division for Public Economics and Public Administration.

———. 2004. *Organizational Integrity Survey*. www.un.org/News/ossg/sg/integritysurvey. pdf (accessed December 29, 2005).

U.S. Senate, Joint Hearings before the Senate Select Committee on Secret Military Assistance to Iran and the Nicaraguan Opposition and the House Select Committee to Investigate Covert Arms Transactions with Iran, One Hundredth Congress First Session 100-7 Part I, July 7, 8, 9, and 10, 1987.

U.S. Office of Government Ethics. 2005. OGE, DT-05-003, February 23.

Valentine, S. and G. Fleischman. 2004. "Ethics Training and Businesspersons' Perceptions of Organizational Ethics." *Journal of Business Ethics* 52:381–390.

Valmores, D. J. 2005. Commissioner, Civil Service Commission. "Presentation on Fighting and Preventing Corruption" ASEAN+3 Senior Officials Consultative Meeting on Creative Management for Government, 30 September–1 October 2005, Bangkok, Thailand.

Van Blijswijk, J. A. M., R. C. J. van Breukelen, A. L Franklin, J. C. N. Raadschelders, and P. Slump. 2004. "Beyond Ethical Codes: The Management of Integrity in the Netherlands Tax and Customs Administration." *Public Administration Review* 64 (November/December): 718–727.

Van Wart, M. 1998. Changing Public Service Values. New York: Garland Publishing.

Varian, B. 2005. "E-mails Get Tampa Workers in Trouble." *St. Petersburg Times,* April 19:1B

Victor, B. and J. B. Cullen. 1988. "The Organizational Bases of Ethical Work Climates." *Administrative Science Quarterly* 33:101–125.

Walker, D. M. 2005. "Ethics and Integrity in Government." *Public Integrity* 7 (Fall): 345–352.

Wang, D. 2004. "Striving for Excellence in Civil Service Training." In *Windows on China,* edited by M. T. Gordon. Amsterdam: IOS Press.

Waring, C. G. 2004. "Measuring Ethical Climate Risk." *Internal Auditor* 61 (December): 71–75.

West, J. P. and E. M. Berman, eds. 2006. *The Ethics Edge*. Washington, D.C.: ICMA Press.

———. 2004. "Ethics Training in U.S. Cities: Content, Pedagogy, and Impact." *Public Integrity* 6 (Summer): 189–206.

White, T. I. 2007 (February 12). "Data, Dollars and the Unintentional Subversion of Human Rights in the IT Industry." Center for Business Ethics, Bentley College, Waltham, MA.

Whitton, H. 2009. "Developing the Ethical Competency of Public Officials: A Capacity-Building Approach." In Cox, R. W. III Ed. 2009. *Ethics and Integrity in Public Administration*. Armonk, New York: M.E. Sharpe, 236–256.

Wiley, C. 1995. "The ABC's of business ethics: Definitions, Philosophies and Implementation." *Industrial Management* 37 (1): 22–27.

Wilgoren, J. 2005. "Chicago Mayor Questioned in Federal Corruption Inquiry." *New York Times,* August 27. http://www.nytimes.com/2005/08/27/national/27daley. html?scp=1&sq=chicago%20mayor%20questioned&st=cse

Williams, R. L. 1996. "Controlling Ethical Practices Through Laws and Rules: Evaluating the Florida Commission on Ethics." *Public Integrity Annual*, 65–72.

Wilson, J. Q. 1993. *The Moral Sense*. New York: The Free Press.

Wilson, W. 1887. "The Study of Administration." Reprinted in *Political Science Quarterly* 56 (December 1941).

Winston, K. 2000. "Teaching Ethics by the Case Method." *Journal of Policy Analysis and Management* 19, no. 1 (Winter): 153–160.

Witmer, D. P. 2005. "Developing a Behavioral Model for Ethical Decision Making in Organizations: Conceptual and Empirical Research." In *Ethics in Public Management*, edited by H. G. Frederickson and R. K. Ghere. Armonk, NY: M.E. Sharpe.

Witt, E. 1992. "Is Government Full of Crooks or Are We Just Better at Finding Them?" In *Essentials of Government Ethics*, edited by P. Madsen and J. M. Shafritz. New York: Meridian/Penguin.

Wye, C. 1994. "A Framework for Enlarging the Reform Agenda." *The Public Manager* 23:43–46.

Xu, L. and Z. Peng. 2004. "China's Public Administration Education." In *Windows on China*, edited by M. T. Gordon. Amsterdam: IOS Press.

Zajac, G. and L. K. Comfort, 1997. "The Spirit of Watchfulness: Public Ethics as Organizational Learning." *Journal of Public Administration Research and Theory* 7 (October): 541–569.

Zauderer, D. G. 1994. "Winning with Integrity." *The Public Manager* 23:43–46.

Zhu, Q. 2000. "The Process of Professionalization and the Rebuilding of Administrative Ethics in Post-Mao China." *International Journal of Public Administration* 23 (11): 1943–1965.

Appendix 1

Chapter 3 Case Competency Matrix

Competencies	Chapter 3				Cases					Chapter 3
	3.1	3.2	3.3	3.4	3.5	3.6	3.7	3.8	3.9	3.1
Be knowledgeable of ethical principles	XX	XX	XX	XX				XX	XX	XX
Be aware and informed of relevant professional codes of ethics		XX	XX		XX	XX				XX
Recognize and promote constitutional principles of equality, fairness, representativeness						XX			XX	
Recognize and support the public's right to know the public's business										
Respect the law								XX	XX	
Serve the public interest	XX		XX	XX		XX			XX	
Engage in ethical reasoning							XX			XX
Recognize and differentiate between ethical and management issues		XX	XX	XX	XX					

Respect and protect privileged information						
Embrace and promote ethical behavior and practices in the workplace						
Refuse to do something unethical						
Maintain truthfulness and honesty			XX			XX
Guard against conflict of interest or its appearance	XX					
Be responsible for one's behavior		XX				XX

Appendix 2

Chapter 4 Case Competency Matrix

Competencies	Chapter 4				Cases				Chapter 4	Encouraging Ethical Behavior
	4.1	4.2	4.3	4.4	4.5	4.6	4.7	4.80	4.9	
Be knowledgeable of ethical principles	XX								XX	
Be aware and informed of relevant professional codes of ethics			XX						XX	
Recognize and promote constitutional principles of equality, fairness, representativeness				XX					XX	
Recognize and support the public's right to know the public's business			XX				XX		XX	
Respect the law			XX						XX	
Serve the public interest		XX	XX		XX			XX	XX	
Engage in ethical reasoning					XX		XX		XX	
Recognize and differentiate between ethical and management issues	XX	XX	XX	XX	XX	XX		XX	XX	

Respect and protect privileged information						XX	
Embrace and promote ethical behavior and practices in the workplace			XX			XX	
Refuse to do something unethical		XX					
Maintain truthfulness and honesty							XX
Guard against conflict of interest or its appearance				XX			XX
Be responsible for one's behavior	XX			XX			XX

Appendix 3

Chapter 5 Case Competency Matrix

Competencies	Chapter 5 5.10	Cases 5.2	5.3	5.4	5.5	5.6	5.7	5.8	5.9	Chapter 5 5.1
Be knowledgeable of ethical principles				XX	XX		XX	XX	XX	
Be aware and informed of relevant professional codes of ethics					XX			XX	XX	
Recognize and promote constitutional principles of equality, fairness, representativeness					XX		XX		XX	
Recognize and support the public's right to know the public's business				XX			XX			
Respect the law					XX	XX	XX			
Serve the public interest		XX	XX	XX	XX	XX		XX	XX	
Engage in ethical reasoning		XX			XX	XX			XX	
Recognize and differentiate between ethical and management issues	XX	XX	XX			XX	XX	XX	XX	XX
Respect and protect privileged information							XX			
Embrace and promote ethical behavior and practices in the workplace	XX							XX		XX
Refuse to do something unethical				XX	XX					
Maintain truthfulness and honesty			XX	XX		XX			XX	XX
Guard against conflict of interest or its appearance										
Be responsible for one's behavior	XX				XX	XX			XX	XX

Appendix 4

Chapter 6 Case Competency Matrix

Competencies	Chapter 6			Cases						Chapter 6
	6.1	6.2	6.3	6.4	6.5	6.6	6.7	6.8	6.9	6.10
Be knowledgeable of ethical principles						XX				
Be aware and informed of relevant professional codes of ethics			XX					XX		
Recognize and promote constitutional principles of equality, fairness, representativeness								XX		
Recognize and support the public's right to know the public's business									XX	
Respect the law						XX		XX		XX
Serve the public interest			XX						XX	XX
Engage in ethical reasoning										XX
Recognize and differentiate between ethical and management issues				XX	XX		XX	XX		XX
Respect and protect privileged information						XX		XX		
Embrace and promote ethical behavior and practices in the workplace	XX	XX	XX	XX	XX		XX		XX	XX
Refuse to do something unethical				XX				XX		
Maintain truthfulness and honesty		XX	XX		XX	XX	XX		XX	XX
Guard against conflict of interest or its appearance	XX	XX							XX	
Be responsible for one's behavior		XX		XX	XX		XX			

Index

D

Daley, Ed, 64, 209–210
deception
  good *vs.* bad, 65–66
  withholding background information, 13,
    60–65, 226
Deicke, Randy, 147–148
Delano, Mary, 136
Denhardt, Robert D., 183
Devaney, Earl E., 8
discipline, 201–204
Dobel, Patrick, 64
documents, falsifying
  county Sheriff's position, 135–137
  for greater good, 75–76
Drumm, Jim, 138
Dubnik, Melvin J., 53–54
Duggan, Kevin, 158–159
Duncan, Ronnie E., 114
Dunmire, Dan, 209
duty and morality flag issue, 52–56

E

elected officials
  ethics *vs.* manners, 174–175
  officials as exemplars, 10–11, 175–176
  political *vs.* administrative public service,
    47–49
  vs. appointed officials, 74–75
email solicitations, 186–190
employees, *see also* Intimate office
    relationships; Workplace
  abusing trust, 211–212
  assessing ethical judgment, 215–218
  ethics test for local government, 128–130
  lying for superior, 146–148
  personal expenses, 213
endorsements for products, 219–220
entrepreneuralism on Internet, 41–43
EPA, restoring integrity, 154–159
equality, road marks, 228
equity
  lying, good intent for community, 148–151,
    226
  pay raises, 80–83, 227
  religious expression in the workplace,
    90–93
Erakovich, Rod, 199
ethical competence
  assessment measures, 24–26

cases, 22–23, 26–28
codes of ethics, 28
compact disk (CD) resources, 24–26,
    28–30
cross-indexing, 25
Ethical Competency Matrices, *20,* 25, 28,
    243–254
fundamentals, 17–21
government articles and papers, 29
instructor's guide, 30
learning from cases, 22–23
online resources, 30
organization of cases, 26–28
rating scales, 29–30
reasoning and awareness, 21–22
road marks, 228–231
slide presentations, 29
syllabi for teaching, 30
tests, 29–30
training materials, 26–28
workplace policies, 29
workshops, 29
Ethical Competency Matrices
  building organizations of integrity,
    251–252
  encouraging ethical behavior, 247–249
  ethics in the workplace, 253–254
  fundamentals, *20,* 25, 28
  professionalism and ethics, 243–245
Ethical Decision Making in Local
    Government, 24, 29
Ethical Environment of Local Government
    Managers, 24, 47–49
ethical illiteracy as obstacle, 4
Ethical Illiteracy in Local Government, 25,
    106–119
ethical reasoning
  ethical competence, 21–22
  gender reassignment, 162
  insider land deal, 117
  intimate office relationships, 209
  as road mark, 228
  road marks, 229
  withholding information, 63
ethic audits, 12
ethics
  in action, 10–12
  defined, 8–10
  importance, 12–13
  learning ethics online, 130–131
  orientation, 197–201
  reform, 178–179

Mahoney, Mary, 187–189
managers, *see also* City managers
 managerial ethics and politics, 69–70
 politics and managerial ethics, 69–70
 public managers/private consultants,
  36–38
 recognizing ethics *vs.* management issues,
  20, 28, 229–230
managers, ethical
 fundamentals, 28, 225
 lessons learned, 225–228
 road marks, 228–231
manners *vs.* ethics, 174–175
Marcy, Henry, 46–47
marriage, *see also* Intimate office relationships
 between boss and subordinate, 201–204
 same sex, 56–60, 227
matrices
 building organizations of integrity,
  251–252
 encouraging ethical behavior, 247–249
 ethics in the workplace, 253–254
 fundamentals, *20,* 25, 28
 professionalism and ethics, 243–245
Matt (character), 97
Matthews, Douglas E., 86–87
Max (character), 198
mayors, credentials of hiring candidates,
  206–208
meetings
 ethics *vs.* manners, 174–175
 Sunshine Law violation, 151–153
Meine, Fred, 203–204
membership violations, codes of ethics,
  121–124
Menzel studies, 134
merit, *see also* Performance appraisals
 credentials of hiring candidates, 206–208
 promotions based on, 210–211
Miaoke, Lin, 66
Michaelsen, Mark G., 145
misconduct
 unawareness as obstacle, 4
 (un)official misconduct, 176–177
moderate case complexity
 appearances (real estate investment),
  99–102
 credentials of hiring candidates, 206–208
 duty and morality flag issue, 52–56
 falsifying documents, 135–137
 gender reassignment, 165–167
 going along to get along, 93–96

information *vs.* advocacy, 85–90
lying, 146–151
marriage between boss and subordinate,
  201–204
moral management, 96–99
political *vs.* administrative public service,
  47–49
privacy violation, 50–51
religious expression in the workplace,
  90–93
stacking the deck, 204–206
verbal acceptance of job, 45–47
whistle-blowers, 142–146
money, *see also* Commercialization; Finance
 accepting bonuses, 71–72
 accepting pay raises, 80–83, 227
 advertising space on Website, 139–142
 courage against criminal acts, 124–125
 grants and future funding, 43–45
 information *vs.* advocacy, 85–90
 legal *vs.* moral, 173
 misuse, 43–45, 142–146, 226
 personal expenses, 213
Monson, Mark
 associations and codes of ethics violations,
  123
 credentials of hiring candidates, 207–208
 falsifying documents, 136–137
 privacy invasion, 51
 public managers as private consultants,
  37–38
Moral Development and Reasoning, 25
morality
 and duty flag issue, 52–56
 gender reassignment, 160–165, 226
 intimate office relationships, 208–210,
  227
 legal *vs.* moral, 173
 moral management, 96–99
Muslims, 90–93

N

neighborhood improvements, 167–170
nepotism
 credentials of hiring candidates, 206–208
 outsourcing, 170–171
news media
 findings from study, 40
 gender reassignment, 160–165
 information *vs.* advocacy, 88
 insider land deal, 106–119